Architectural Guide
Verona and Lake Garda

Architectural Guide
Verona and Lake Garda

Sergey Nikitin-Rimsky

DOM
publishers

Contents

Arco dei Gavi

Palazzo della Gran Guardia

Piazza Bra

Arena

Palazzo della Gran Guardia

Castelvecchio

Palazzo Canossa

Duomo

Palazzo della Ragione

San Fermo

Banca Nazionale del Lavoro

Banco Popolare di Verona

Saiko3p (dreamstime)

Saiko3p (dreamstime)

Ghetto nuovo •

Piazza delle Erbe •

Porta Borsari •

Ponte della
Vittoria •

Palazzo Maffei

Loggia del Consiglio

Torre dei Lamberti

Palazzo
Domus No

Basilica di Sant'Anastasia

Istituto Maffei

Portoni della Bra

Duomo

» There be few cities in the fair Italy which excel Verona
in goodliness of situation, as well for so noble a river as the Adige,
which divideth it well-nigh in half with its most limpid waters
and casueth it to abound in the wares which Germany sendeth,
as also for the pleasant and fruitful hills and the delightsome
valleys and sunny fields which encompass it, not to speak of
the many fountains, rich in cool and limpid waters,
which serve the commodity of the city, the four most boble bridges
over the said river and the thousand venerable antiquities
to be seen in place. «

Matteo Bandello, Giulietta and Romeo

Ancient legacies and hidden gems:
Verona and its surroundings

View of Verona and its meandering Adige River

David Zean (dreamstime)

Located along a turbulent mountain river, surrounded by hills, and decorated with belfries, cypresses, and picturesque fortresses, Verona amazes its visitors with a rich variety of heritage, spanning more than 20 centuries, not to mention its regional cuisine and wines. Unlike bigger Italian cities, Verona is quiet and clean. Not surprisingly, it is one of the leaders of tourism in Italy. Still, it maintains its small provincial nature given that, outside of the typical tourist attractions, many of its virtues are overlooked – even by residents themselves. Fyodor Dostoevsky complained that the residents of St. Petersburg were so busy with their own lives that they hardly had time to look around and notice the beauty in the monuments and buildings of the city. I feel the same way about the people of Verona.

When I first arrived in Verona, I had been writing a dissertation that delved into the history of Soviet culture during the 1920s and 1930s. The architectural legacies of Ettore Fagiuoli, Italo Mutinelli, and Francesco Banterle that I stumbled upon in Verona reminded me greatly of the buildings designed by Russian architects Ilya Golosov, Alexey Schusev,

and the Vesnin brothers. Verona's yellow-white military structures were originally built by the Austrian Empire and are still occupied by troops today. Even the alleys, littered with chestnuts, felt like many corners of Moscow and St. Petersburg.

My new friends in Italy introduced me to the masterpieces of the Medieval City: the imperial grandeur of the Basilica of San Zeno, the ornate carvings of the Scaliger Tombs, and the magnificent wooden ceiling of San Fermo church. Teaching at University of Verona gave me the opportunity to explore it, meet its scholars. In 2017, I designed and led Velonotte Romeo, an educational bike ride that aimed to show Medieval Verona with historians from Cambridge and Florence.

Yet, I still felt like something was missing. I wanted to know more about the buildings in Verona, and not just the more famous ones. I wanted to learn about each of their histories, about the architects who built them, and the restorations they had undergone. There are many publications dedicated to special periods of history, sometimes out of print for years, sometimes impossible to find.

Verona's history at a glance

Verona's geographical position has allowed it to flourish as a crossroads town. First, the ancient Roman road Via Postumia, which stretched from Genoa to Aquileia, met with the Via Gallica, connecting the city to Brescia, Bergamo, and Milan. More significantly, two more roads met: the Via Claudia Augusta, which spanned from Verona to present-day Augsburg, and the Via Imperii, which connected Verona to Innsbruck. Bordering Northern Europe, Verona's economy has been historically influenced by travellers, though the city has also supported itself through stone mining and textile production.

As a city that has existed for over 2,000 years, one can see the convergence of many different architectural styles in Verona. Ancient Roman architecture evolved into Romanesque and Gothic styles. From the fourteenth to the fifteenth century, Lombard and Venetian architecture was widely popular. In the sixteenth century, Michele Sanmicheli returned to Verona from Rome and brought neoclassical style with him. The neoclassical style became so popular in Verona that other European styles, like baroque and rococo, were almost entirely ignored. Later, at the beginning of the nineteenth century, the French occupation urbanised Verona. Afterwards, during the period of Austrian rule, this traditional merchant town was reconceived as a city fortress, adding to its architectural variety once again. Since 1866, the city has been part of the Kingdom of Italy, maintaining its military function until the late twentieth century and developing into the Veneto region's economic centre.

Lake Garda, the Valpolicella wine valleys, and the area surrounding the Mincio River are all very important to the Veronese. For almost four centuries, Verona and Garda towns have shared rulers. They both belonged to the Republic of Venice, Napoleon's Cisalpine Republic, the Kingdom of Italy, and the Austrian Empire until finally being annexed by Italy in the 1860s. Due to Garda's shared history with Verona, I've also included buildings and monuments from this region. In architecture, as in love, two people are needed. In the pages that follow, you will find an overview of the leading architects and their patrons during Verona's different historical periods and a discussion of their works in relation to the city.

Verona in the Roman Empire

The city of Verona began on the hill of San Pietro, now known for its famous observation deck. Thanks to Caesar and his Gallic Wars, the city became a Roman municipium in 49 BCE. This change led the Veronese to expand their town down the hill to the bend of the Adige River, where the Romans had built their military base. There is still a Roman city with a grid of streets at the heart of modern Verona. At the intersection of the ancient Cardo Maximus (now Via Cappello and Via Sant'Egidio) and Decumanus Maximus (present day Corso Cavour, Porta Borsari, and Sant'Anastasia), the Roman forum rustled with the Capitoline Temple. Today it is the delightful Piazza delle Erbe. The centrepiece of Roman architecture in Verona is the magnificent amphitheatre, built in the first century CE. The Porta Leoni and Porta Borsari, city gates from the first century BCE to the first century CE, still stand tall. The archaeological site of Corte Sgarzarie displays uncovered ruins from ancient Rome. Outside of Verona, at the end of the Sirmione peninsula on Lake Garda, one can see the impressive remains of the Grottoes of Catullus, once an enormous Roman villa.

The Middle Ages

Streets and alleys in the city are adorned by a dozen beautiful medieval temples in the Romanesque and Gothic styles. Most of the churches of medieval Verona are from the twelfth century, built on the foundations of previous structures after a terrible earthquake in 1117. At the turn of the thirteenth century, medieval walls were erected, large parts of which can still be seen along with the Via Pallone. The walls were reinforced in the thirteenth century by Italian feudal lord Ezzelino III da Romano and again in the fourteenth century by Gian Galeazzo Visconti, ruler of the late-medieval city. Though I will cover early Middle Age architecture in this guide, it would be impossible to include every place. The churches of Sant'Eufemia, Santo Stefano, San Tomaso Becket, Santi Apostoli, as well as the adjacent Chapel of Saints Teuteria and Tosca, are all worth visiting. Outside the city, the Basilica of Sant'Andrea in Toscolano-Maderno in Garda is sure to impress, as are the unforgettable stone reliefs in the abbey of San Pietro in the Verona suburb of San Bonifacio.

San Zeno and the Emperors at the gates of town

Paradoxically, the most renowned Veronese landmark – in terms of architecture and political significance – was actually built outside of the city walls. Pepin the Short, who was King of the Franks and the son of Charlemagne, expelled the Lombards, damaging the Basilica of San Zeno. San Zeno had been the temple of the patron of the city, so Pepin personally built a magnificent temple in its place and gave the new abbey numerous privileges. The king designated it an outpost of imperial power: from now on, the emperors would stay there. This brick tower, decorated with swallowtail merlons, served as their refuge. Not only within San Zeno, but all of Verona was openly Ghibelline, meaning they pledged allegiance to the emperor, until it became a part of the republic. This explains the swallowtail merlons that adorn its fortifications.

The cathedral was later rebuilt in the more luxurious style that we observe today. Only under the Della Scala family, better known as the Scaligers, did the San Zeno abbey lose its independent role in the life of the city. Inside its tower, a fresco depicts the end of the thirteenth century: Europeans taking the oath of allegiance to the emperor. Most researchers believe the emperor shown is Frederick II, who was once the King of Sicily, the King of Germany, the King of Italy and Holy Roman Emperor, and the King of Jerusalem. Supposedly, the fresco was commissioned for Ezzelino III da Romano's daughter's wedding. Ezzelino III da Romano had been a feudal lord who ruled Verona for almost two decades.

Pause for just a moment and picture the towered silhouette of the town of San Gimignano in Tuscany. In the Middle Ages, rich Veronese lived in similar tower houses. Ezzelino III da Romano demanded they be disassembled, leaving only one, Lamberti, that functioned as city hall's bell tower. Verona's success in the thirteenth century was consolidated by the fact that they had a mint and coined money.

Scagliers in the city (1262–1387)

A new control centre is formed around the Piazza Dei Signori next to the old city hall building, now known as Palazzo della Ragione. The Palaces of the Scala family were located there and will eventually

Gianni Ainardi, 2001

Verona during Roman times: a well-protected city in a scenic landscape

Verona in 1590: the city as part of the Venetian Republic

be turned into public administration buildings. Next to them, the Scala family built a monumental cemetery as a symbol of self-glorification: the phenomenal Arche Scaligere, or Scaliger Tombs. Lombard stonecutters from Lake Como helped construct this incredible Gothic structure. Under the Scaligers' rule, brick Gothic bloomed — incredible churches of San Fermo and Sant'Anastasia rose. But these works would not be finished for another century. Sant'Anastasia shaped the magnificent cathedral of the city of Salò, located along Lake Garda.

In 1354, Cangrande II built the Castelvecchio, a castle with a private bridge so that in case of revolt he could always escape to Tyrol and his friends in Germany, just as the Scaligers did. The walls of the Scaligers stretch along the hills above the Veronetta area, from Castel San Pietro to Porta Vescovo, offering fantastic views. You'll also come across the old temples of Santa Maria di Nazareth (Piazzetta Nazareth) and San Zeno in Monte (Via S. Zeno in Monte, 23). The Scaliger castles are strewn along the shores of Lake Garda, from Malcesine to Sirmione, as well as the countryside, like in Valeggio.

Verona Viscontea (1387–1402)

The Duke of Milan, Gian Galeazzo Visconti, dreamed of uniting all of northern Italy under his rule. He ruled over Verona for only five years, but it was enough to erect grandiose defensive structures, including the Castello di San Pietro, Cittadella, and Castello di San Felice above Veronetta. Sadly, Castello di San Pietro and Cittadella no longer exist.

Via Nuova, now Via Mazzini, was built in 1393, linking the Arena to Piazza delle Erbe. The most impressive work of the Visconti era is the Bridge-Dam in Borghetto on the Mincio River, which Visconti intended to use as both a bridge and a military object.

Venetian Verona (1405–1796)

Verona swore allegiance to Venice in 1405, and since then – with a short break – has been a proud part of the Republic, successfully developing into an agricultural centre along the Adige.

The first sign of Renaissance architecture in the city was the graceful Loggia del Consiglio on the Piazza Dei Signori

Verona and its outskirts connections. Paolo Santini, 1777

and opposite the Scaligeri palaces. The stonecutters were from Lombardy, which is why local art historians call this style *lombardesco*. Later on, the Lombards also laid the marble for the Porta Vescovo and Porta San Giorgio.

It was not immediate for the Veronese to fall in love with the Renaissance style of architecture because it was associated with Papal Rome and Florence. The cities of Northern Italy, including Verona, were regularly in a state of competition and sometimes even outright confrontation with their southern counterparts. When Holy Roman emperor Charles V sacked Rome on 6 May 1527, the artists dispersed. It was a chance for Venice and Verona to discover the freshness of the classic order. Two great architects working for the Pope escaped to the Republic: Michele Sanmicheli and Jacopo Sansovino. Sansovino became the main architect of Venice; he completed the ensemble of the Piazzetta San Marco and the main staircase of the Doge's Palace. His taste shaped the Renaissance school in Veneto.

That same year, 1527, Sanmicheli returned to his native Verona after twenty years in Orvieto and Rome. Sanmicheli

(also spelled Sanmichele) was born in Verona when it was part of the Venice Republic. He came from a family of stonecutters – his father, uncle, and brothers were all involved in building. After losing his parents, he made a bold decision to sell the family property and move to Rome. There, he worked with Antonio da Sangallo the Younger and spent time around Donato Bramante. A few years later, he received an order from Orvieto to complete the magnificent Gothic façade of the Duomo. This Orvieto period lasted for almost twenty years.

In the first months of 1526, he supervised the fortifications of the northern borders of the Papal States at the behest of Clement VII. It seems that this small commission won him the role of the expert in military architecture, a distinction that he held for the rest of his long life.

He finally returned to his hometown of Verona in 1527. Legend has it that he was stopped by Venetian officers while inspecting the city's fortifications. After being cleared by the officers, he was invited to work for the Republic. Sanmicheli's main job was to perform government orders related to fortifications and gates in Verona, Peschiera del Garda, and other Venetian naval bases along the Mediterranean, such as Zadar, Famagusta in Cyprus, Crete, and Corfu.

Architectural success with private customers sparked the construction of the Pellegrini chapel in the convent of San Bernardino. A marble gem in the spirit of Tempietto of Bramante, its construction went slowly, and Sanmicheli was suspended from work. Other customers, however, respected his business and invited him to build palaces. His Palazzos Canossa and Bevilacqua defined the style for the new elegant street of Verona, present-day Corso Cavour. This avenue begins and ends with two Roman buildings: the Arch of Gavi and the gates of Borsari.

Sadly, Sanmicheli did not have time to complete most of his projects. The magnificent Porta Palio is one of his best-preserved works since the gate went unused for many centuries.

His final work, the Shrine Santa Maria Della Pace in the Veronese village of San Michele Extra, consists of an unexpectedly vast rotunda outside the city walls. Sadly, it was built with numerous alterations from the original. Francesco Banterle restored it in the twentieth century. Having built the Porta Nuova gate, Sanmicheli laid the new axis of the city, and the modern main street of Corso Porta Nuova would be further developed in the twentieth century.

Thanks to Sanmicheli, the classical order became the language of the city. Verona's streets and alleys are packed with neoclassical palaces of the sixteenth to nineteenth centuries. The foundations of these palaces sometimes have medieval origins. I recommend walking along the central streets of Via Oberdan, Stradone San Fermo, Via Cappello, and Corso Porta Borsari to take in some of these structures.

The style of Sanmicheli was carried out by later architects, including his talented grandchildren, Domenico Curtoni and Bernardino Brugnoli, who are credited with the design of many palaces and churches in the city. Curtoni led the construction of the most significant building in Venetian Verona: the Gran Guardia in Piazza Bra, which wasn't completed until

the end of the nineteenth century. This is because a plague broke out in 1630, killing half of the city's population. It took more than a century for Verona to regain its population and strength.

The architecture of suburban villas began developing in the sixteenth century. Strong patrons ruled the suburbs, though the architects of the estates are mostly unknown. Villa Della Torre is undoubtedly the main treasure of Valpolicella, raised by three generations of the Della Torre family, who were once the religious leaders of the city. After decades of desolation, it has been restored and can be visited for wine tastings and even overnight stays. The only work started by Andrea Palladio in Valpolicella, the Villa Santa Sofia, was built with numerous deviations from the original plan. Palladio's only commission in Verona was Palazzo Dalla Torre.

Verona's Philharmonic Society commissioned its theatre to Antonio Galli da Bibbiena. The theatre has since been rebuilt twice. In its courtyard, the city's first museum emerged to celebrate its ancient past: the Museo Lapidario Maffeiano. Bibbiena presumably designed the stunning interiors of Palazzo Verità-Poeta (Vicolo San Silvestro 6) as well.

In the second half of the eighteenth century, Ignazio Pellegrini and Adriano Cristofali dominated the architectural scene. Part of Cristofali's legacy is the neoclassical Palazzo Erbisti, with its charming, frescoed interiors that now host the Academy of Agriculture Sciences and Letters. He also built Villa Vecelli Cavriani in Mozzecane and the Villa Mosconi Bertani in Novare ad Arbizzano. Cristofali also began working on the magnificent Villa Bettoni di Bogliaco on Lake Garda, but commissioners later replaced him with another master. An architect, aristocrat and member of the military circles, Ignazio Pellegrini (1715–1790) is credited with the completion of the Palazzo Pitti's left wing with royal apartments in Florence. He designed the graceful Giuliari and Forti Emilei palaces in his native Verona. Pellegrini also built the monumental Villa Marioni Pullè, which has sadly laid in ruins for the past 50 years. However, a glimmer of hope emerged in 2019 that German patrons would change its fortune. Another damaged villa had recently been renovated into the Villa Byblos Art Hotel in Valpolicella.

Alessandro Pompei, another nobleman with a passion for architecture, resided in Palazzo Pompei, which was built by Sanmicheli. Pompei wrote the treatise 'Five Orders of the Civic Architecture of Michele Sanmicheli' and created the lovely Doric peristyle of the San Fermo columns – Verona's last public building under Serenissima, which is now visible only through the lock hole. Luigi Trezza, the pioneer of the restoration of the Arena, was engaged in excavations and built magnificent church façades and bell towers in the Sanmicheli style in the Verona region. His works can be found in Avesa, San Massimo, as well as Bovolone.

French Verona (1796–1814)

The Napoleon occupation brought fresh ideas from the town's intellectuals and architects. In less than 20 years' time, the Veronese people built and opened the Maffei Lyceum – the first classical lyceum in Italy. They also dreamed about creating a new main street, Via Napoleonica, which is now known as Corso Porta Nuova. In this period, the Veronese also began to think about the all-class cemetery, which they would begin building in 1838.

In those same years, the French ordered the demolition of the Visconti citadel and Castel San Pietro, also known as Teodorico. The ancient Roman Arch of Gavi was disassembled, but fortunately the blocks were numbered for reconstruction later on. These losses led the city's architects – Luigi Trezza, Giuseppe Barbieri, and Bartolomeo Giuliari – to consider the need to preserve monuments.

From 1801 to 1804, the city was divided into two parts along the Adige River: the Austrians occupied the Eastern part, while the French controlled the Western portion. It was during that time that the name Veronetta, meaning 'little Verona', emerged to describe the eastern shore of Adige in relation to the central city.

Austrian Period (1814–1866)

Extensive development occurred in the city during the Austrian era. After the defeat of Napoleon, Verona was handed over to Austria along with the Venetian lands and Lombardy, thereby forming the Kingdom of Lombard. Verona functioned as an important military base for the Habsburg Empire. The city's geographical significance became even more clear after the first nationalist uprisings of 1848 in Milan and Venice. The Austrians contributed numerous buildings within and around the city, most of which were for military use:

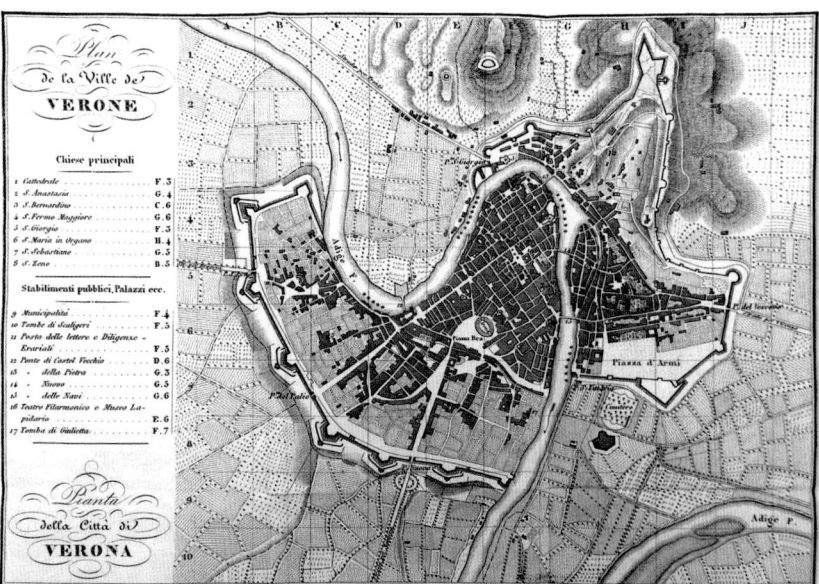

Verona in 1842: still a small town within the walls

barracks, hospitals, forts, and fortresses. Verona became the principal city of the fortified area of Quadrilatero, which included Peschiera, Mantova, and Legnago. The railway connecting Milan with Venice, completed in 1857, was also built with the same military intentions.

I recommend visiting the station in Desenzano, which has preserved its original appearance. Verona's protagonist of the nineteenth century was Giuseppe Barbieri. A student of Trezza, he built the Palazzo Gran Guardia Nuova for the military. It now hosts the mayor's office and has been renamed the Palazzo Barbieri. He also built the Doric Monumental Cemetery on the site of the ancient Roman Field of Mars.

Austrian commissioners initially preferred the neoclassical style, such as the massive hospital at the gates of Porta Palio. Soon their taste was replaced by Rundbogenstil – the Neo-Romanesque style that came into fashion in the German part of Europe. This style complemented Verona's lingering brick Gothic legacy. Castel San Pietro on the hill and Arsenal Franz Joseph I on the riverbank are built in this style. The army moved out of these buildings a couple of decades ago. The castle is expected to become a hotel and the Arsenal to become a shopping centre for tourists, which may seriously damage the lovely atmosphere of the existing shopping streets.

One of the few public buildings from the Austrian period is the Teatro Nuovo, designed by architect Enrico Storari and inaugurated on the night of 12 September 1846 to the sound of Verdi's *Attila*. In those days, Verdi's name equated to Risorgimento, meaning Italian unification for patriots. The phrase 'Viva Verdi' was an acronym for Vittorio Emanuele Re d'Italia, referring to Victor Emmanuel II, who tended to unite the nation under his rule. The theatre grew immediately into a meeting place for local patriots and was therefore repeatedly closed by the authorities in 1849 and 1858. In 1866, Verona, along with Venice, Friuli, and the Duchy of Mantua, was annexed into the Italian Kingdom led by Victor Emanuel II. The year before in Piazza dei Signori – the heart of the city – a monument to Dante was solemnly inaugurated by local sculptor Ugo Zannoni. Like Verdi, the name Dante was synonymous with Risorgimento, but for the poet's 600th birthday, the Austrian authorities could not refuse to put up the statue. The location for the statues was right: the famous poet was housed in the Palazzo Podestà for some time.

Verona becomes Italian

Despite these many changes, Verona was still considered a small town. In 1901, there were less than one hundred thousand people living there, amounting to just three filled Arenas. The first significant projects under a united Italy were

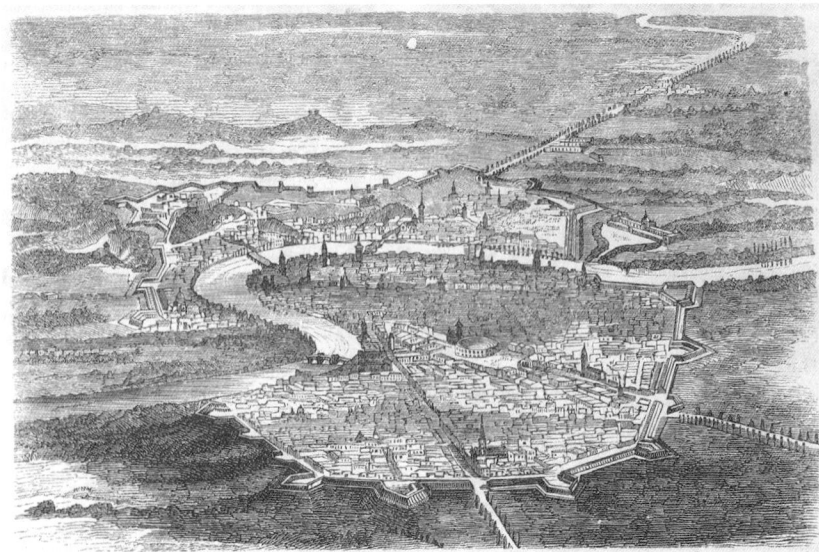

The City-fortress of Austrian Empire: Verona in the 1860's

related to the restoration of the city centre, primarily the Gothic palaces and their grand temples on the Piazza Dei Signore. Camillo Boito, the leader of the Italian restorers, personally oversaw the cleaning of the medieval Palazzo Della Ragione and Loggia Dei Mercanti at Piazza Delle Erbe, sadly damaging original elements. The symbol of San Marco – a winged lion holding open a book – was restored on the palaces and in the squares as a sign of appreciation for Venice.

At the end of the century, the city funnelled its resources into reconstruction after a catastrophic flood. On 17 September 1882, over two-thirds of Verona was submerged by water from the Adige River, which flowed at a speed of 20 kilometres per hour that day. Verona lost two bridges in the flood: the Ponte Nuovo and the Ponte Aleardi. The Ponte Navi was damaged and closed as a result of the flooding. Eleven people were killed, and 40 houses were smashed in the flood, while hundreds more required serious repairs. The flood shattered 20 mills out of the 50 that existed at that time. Before 1882, residential buildings rose directly from the water, as in Venice. After the flood, the city's leadership decided to build modern embankments. Additionally, the canal system in Veronetta was put into a pipe and the Interrato dell'Acqua Morta was constructed over it.

Verona between two wars (1918–1939)

From 1918 to the end of the 1940s, Ettore Fagiuoli had been building across Verona: in urban villas in Borgo Trento, public buildings, and the cemetery. He didn't have any competitors. Fagiuoli studied at the Brera Academy in Milan and the University of Padua and completed his studies at Polytechnic in Milan. His vast education allowed him to achieve success in entirely different styles over many years. There are a few buildings by Fagiuoli in particular that embody the architectural style in Verona. The first are the Fiat garage and Borgo Trento Villas in the style of Art Nouveau that Italians call 'Liberty.' There's also the Vittoria bridge, the neoclassic apartment block on Piazzale Cadorna, and the Cesare Battisti

memorial. Fagiuoli built the New Post and Telegraph Palace in the 1920s, which was recently rebuilt to house 20 exclusive apartments. He also built the world's first kinetic house, Villa Girasole, in the art deco style with and for his friend Angelo Invernizzi. Hopefully, the villa will be restored and open soon for visitors.

Fagiuoli's contemporary and main competitor was Francesco Banterle. After studying architecture at the Royal Higher Institute of Fine Arts in Bologna, Banterle was considered the Veronese clergy and bourgeoisie's favourite professional. One of his first and most impressive buildings was the beautiful one-nave Santa Maria Immacolata church (Via S. Marco, 57) in the spirit of the Liberty style. He designed many villas and buildings in the villages, from Trento to Venezia to Milan. His most striking work remains the vast complex for the Don Calabria Institute, recognised as 'Buoni Fanciulli,' which features an illuminated cross that dominates the Veronetta skyline. Banterle's Palazzo of the Invalids of the War is another remarkable building of the epoch and it is wonderfully preserved inside.

Around this time, engineer and architect Italo Mutinelli developed the trendy art deco-style Villa Rossi in Borgo Venezia. He also designed a remarkable Neo-Renaissance mansion for the same family in Borgo Trento.

To fully immerse yourself in 1930s Verona, walk along the Lungadige Cangrande and Lungadige Campagnola. Close to these embankments you can enjoy two valuable pieces that mark the beginning of Via Generale Gaetano Giardino. The housing for state employees is distinguished by arches in the art deco aesthetic. Beside it is an apartment block designed by an unknown architect, however, the balconies are reminiscent of works of Russian constructivism and German rationalism.

The city's imperial spirit is best captured by the scale and layout of the grand Corso Porta Nuova and the building that houses the Istituto Nazionale Assicurazioni (INA). If you consider travelling around Valpolicella's villas and wineries, take a look at the Aqueduct of the Biffis canal, whose construction finished in 1942.

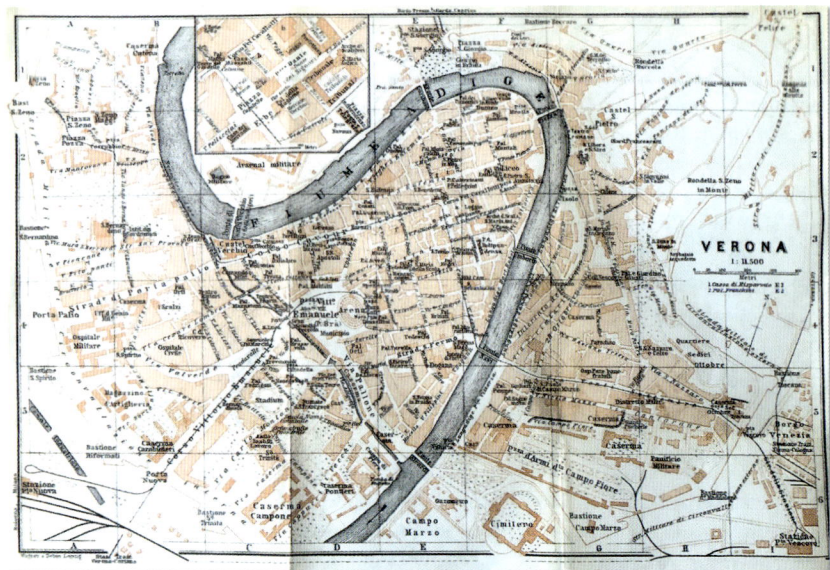

Verona in 1928, just before water used to produce energy brought the city into modernity.

Industrial Verona

Verona was and remains a centre of agricultural production, marble mining, and small manufacturing. After the unification of Italy in 1866, city leaders sought to industrialise the economy according to the model of European megacities.

But there was one problem: Verona lacked coal and therefore a driving force for modern steam engines. Canale Camuzzoni brought water energy to the southern industrial zone of Basso Acquar, which neighbours the Porta Nuova Station hub. However, by the time it was fully constructed, manufacturing in that area had already failed and the canal was not used for another 30 years. It wasn't until the 1920s that the power of water started to work, at which time new plants began to appear in the south, including Cartiere Fedrigoni, il Cotonificio Veneziano, and Mulini Consolaro.

Only a small amount of impressive architecture remains from this brief industrial interlude. For a more comprehensive insight into this industrial legacy, I recommend the photo album *Lo stato dei luoghi* by Enzo and Raffaello Bassotto, who managed to capture this genre of architecture in the 1980s and 1990s.

Magazzini Generali, a vast warehouse complex near Porta Nuova station, remains the most stunning relic of this era. After the warehouse ceased to operate in the 1990s, it became underground Verona's main venue; raves and concerts of every kind brought the space to life. I was lucky enough to experience the unique use of this space at that time. Eventually, the city handed the building over to a private foundation, UniCredit. For 20 years, various renovations have been carried out there, without any clear strategy. Regrettably, this space is underutilised for its potential.

Montorio, a small town about 1 kilometre from Verona, is graced with a lasting industrial legacy from the sixteenth to nineteenth centuries, including mills and hydraulic structures. I wasn't able to include the elegant Paper Mill in San Giovanni Lupatoto in this guidebook, as only an electric booth was preserved from its demolition. However, a magnificent power station in Riva del Garda and a small neoclassical plant in the Verona suburb of Bussolengo still operate. You can visit both through tours, such as Dolomiti Hydrotours. To explore the evolution of papermaking in Italy, be sure to visit the Museum of Paper in Toscolano Maderno, located along Lake Garda. On the eastern or Brescia side of Garda, you will be awed by the limonaie – the greenhouses for the lemon trees; consider visiting one to discover the rich history of lemon growing in this region.

Verona grew rapidly during the economic boom period from 1951 to 1971. The city's population rose from 178,000 to 266,000, a 50 per cent increase. Residents from neighbouring villages and other parts of Italy were attracted to the city at that time, but the population has been slowly declining since then.

Local industries had become largely uncompetitive by the end of the 1980s, and many industrial buildings have since been abandoned or demolished. A spectacular porch decorates the abandoned Mondadori publishing house. The largest industry of national importance in Verona, the confectionery company Bauli, built a curious headquarters.

Verona and restoration of the monuments: Avena, Gazzola, Magagnato

Museologists and preservationists played a central role in the architectural life of Verona in the twentieth century. The first director of the Castelvecchio Museum was Antonio Avena. For 30 years, he headed this institution, restructuring it in the Gothic style with the help of architect Ettore Fagiuoli. Despite protests for the monument's protection, Avena succeeded in radically reconstructing this and other tourist sites. Avena's vision was to create a spectacular, cinematic Verona. He also oversaw the restoration of the Gavi Arch – again with the architectural expertise of Fagiuoli – and of the Prefecture's Palace on Piazza Dei Signori.

In 1958, Verona began what would become a long romance with Venetian architect Carlo Scarpa. He was invited to the city by Licisco Magagnato, the new director of the Castelvecchio, to redesign the Castelvecchio Museum. Scarpa's approach embraced an attitude of informality, featuring quiet backgrounds, empty rooms, and contemplative interpretations of colour, light, and surfaces. This approach became an event in the exhibition design of the 1960s through the 1980s.

Magagnato was one of the co-founders of the Ministry of Cultural Heritage. Though reconstruction lasted more than ten years, both he and the museum became an intellectual epicentre within the city. Magagnato was also the president of La Consulta, a Veronese club for the Italian Association for the freedom of culture (AILC). The group organised lectures by international scholars and economists and is still recalled today as a window to the world.

The slow, meditative Scarpa didn't attract many projects in Verona, except for the Banco Popolare di Verona. The bank was controlled by Giorgio Zanotto, the protagonist of the post-war city. Zanotto had been mayor from 1956 to 1964 and also the head of Cattolica Assicurazioni for some time. An active member of the Christian Democratic Party, the Democristiani, Zanotto also backed the founding of the University of Verona. Architecture stars like Luigi Caccia Dominioni and Pier Luigi Nervi also worked in town during his era. Although he had only two works to show for in town, Scarpa's paradoxical manner and deliberate asymmetry ultimately influenced the architects of Verona and the province until the end of the 1990s.

Walking the streets, one would never be able to tell, but post-war Verona was built by graduates of the Venice Institute of Architecture (IUAV), one of the most avant-garde schools in Europe. Giuseppe Samonà directed the institute from 1945 to 1972 and opened it to international influence. This increasing international influence can be seen with its CIAM summer schools in the late 1950s. The leading minds of Italian architecture could be found teaching there, including Ernesto Rogers, Ignazio Gardella, Carlo Scarpa, and Giancarlo De Carlo, not to mention influential critics such as Manfredo Tafuri and Bruno Zevi. After such a brilliant, open, and intellectual education, it was not easy for the artists to find an equally open-minded patron in the Veneto and Verona, which tended to be more conservative agricultural areas.

The creations of Rinaldo Olivieri, namely the Christmas Star at the Arena (visible from December to the end of January) and the sculpturesque slabs of the church of San Benedetto in Valdonega (Via Marsala 56A), leave strong impressions on their observers. Outside of Verona, Olivieri carried out the construction of an institute in San Bonifacio and the city hall building in Trevenzuolo.

While rapid economic growth between the 1960s and 1980s didn't bring much vibrant modern architecture to the city, high-quality restoration projects and readaptations abounded. In those days, Verona and Venice became centres for the theory and practice of restoration. Piero Gazzola was the editor of the Venice Charter, which set guidelines for preservation and restoration practices around the world.

Fiera Verona headquarters

Fabrizio Mauro

The reconstruction of the half-bombed Palazzo Mosconi became the most remarkable achievement of Libero Cecchini. Cecchini was the author of 600 projects. For the first 20 years of his professional career, he was an employee of Soprintendenza dei Beni Culturali of Verona, a state agency responsible for cultural monuments and led by Piero Gazzola. Cecchini had studied with Piero Gazzola in the Politecnico di Milano, so Gazzola gave him his first commission: the reconstruction of the Roman bridge Ponte Pietra that had been destroyed in the Second World War.

The Era of Basilica Democristiana and University

The Christian Democrats shaped politics and urbanism in Italy immensely in the 1950s and 1960s. The Italian government allocated money for the construction of Catholic churches in new residential areas. How else would one fight for traditional values against the communist threat? The spectacular concrete temples appeared everywhere – we might call them *basiliche democristiane*: the Gesù Divino Lavoratore, the San Matteo temple in popular Borgo Roma, the main Borgo Trento temple peppered with some rationalist elements, and the torn pediment of Sagra Santi Angeli Custodi. And these are only some of the most memorable examples.

An area between Piazza Renato Simoni and Largo Caldera is particularly rich in history

from this period. In 1959, young graduates of IUAV, Cenna, and Calcagni built the Don Carlo Steeb nursing home in the very centre of the city, 500 metres from the Arena. They were inspired by the brick modernism of Alvar Aalto and James Stirling. Cenna and Calcagni designed two campuses of the University of Verona. The campus in Veronetta, with its beautiful garden, is perhaps the most influential post-war public space in the city, along with the Bentegodi Stadium. The stadium's influence is actually not because of its architecture, but because of football's crucial role in Italian society.

Experiments with prefabricated, or modular, housing can be found in Santa Lucia. In the east of the city, the Complesso INA Casa – a social housing complex on Via Montorio – exhibits many of these ideas from the 1950s and 1960s. Roman architects Nello Ena, Candeloro Corbo, and Franco Minissi took part in its creation. The Torre Telecom television tower, located near Montorio and no longer in operation, is an example of the design that wealthy and carefree Italians embraced in the 1980s.

Present day

At the turn of the twenty-first century, the main focus of Veronese architecture has once again become reconstruction. The pool near the Arsenal was turned into a pleasant public space by

Claudio Esposito/Vector Foiltec GmbH

The new entrance to the Fiera Verona by Maffeeis Engineering and Pichler Projects (2020)

David Chipperfield Architects. The Santa Marta Military Flour Mill has become the university's new building. Libero Cecchini curated a restoration of medieval courtyards at Corso Porta Borsari. For almost twenty years, the centre of the city's cultural life has been the Scavi Scaligeri exposition site, which features dungeons and remains of Roman roads under Piazza Dei Signori. Unfortunately, the exposition is closed at this time. In the current difficult economic situation, the city does not have an active development strategy. Moreover, the right-wing city administration has recently closed some of the city's ambitious cultural initiatives like jazz and cinema festivals. Even its famous concert venue, Arena, is in the perennial crisis of ideas, direction, and money.

Borghi di Verona / Verona's Villages

As a result of industrial development, several distinctive areas have arisen around the historical city centre.

Veronetta

This is the birthplace of Verona: the hill of San Pietro. When Romans resettled the city at the loop of the Adige, they built a theatre and a temple on the hill, which was later replaced by a fortress. The Ostrogoth Emperor Theodoric, known in German legends as Dietrich von Bern, built his palace next to the theatre.

Some of Verona's top attractions, like the Giusti Palace and Garden and the Santa Maria in Organo, are located here. Compared to the bustling, polished city centre, Veronetta is a quiet, unassuming area with folk taverns, villas, gardens, monasteries, and small, multicultural communities. Locals often admit it is their favourite district. Veronetta's curving streets – some of which were once canals – are surrounded by houses from the Venetian and Austrian eras. After the flood of 1882, the channels were put into a pipe, giving the embankments a modern look. In the 1980s, Veronetta began transforming once more, when the first university campus was built. It's hard not to be taken with the hills and gardens of Veronetta. Torricelle is a fantastic place for a long and leisurely walk.

Borgo Roma

Another university campus was built in the Borgo Roma proletarian district in the 1980s. This vast area has been developed around the industrial zones in the south of the city, from the Porta Nuova station to the Fiera di Verona district. Only a few sites are included in the book but cycling along the Via Scuderlando may be quite rewarding for lovers of urbanism. A new park was recently laid out next to the former psychiatric hospital of San Giacomo. The grandiose brutalist Church of Christ the Divine Worker is nearby. The hospital is supposed to be transformed into a

Panoramic view of Veronetta, 2008

brain museum. The neighbourhood of Santa Lucia is not far away. It is home to social housing architecture from the 1950s
and 1960s.

Borgo Trento

In the early 1910s, the wealthy bourgeoisie decided to build on the other side
of the Adige – the lands between the former
Austrian Arsenal Franz Joseph and the new
clinical hospital. Along Via Bixio, there are
villas in different exotic variations of Liberty style, the Italian version of art nouveau,
and some pieces of the northern version of
rationalism. After the Second World War, in
the era of the economic boom, condominiums for the middle class were built along
Via IV Novembre and intersecting streets.

Via Tonale, in particular, features houses
by the engineer Bari.

Borgo Venezia

First developed in the 1900s, Venice
Borgo stretches from the monumental
Porta Vescovo gate from the sixteenth
century along the road to Venice. One of
its most interesting cross-streets is Via
Montorio, which leads to the charming
suburb of Montorio. Another highlight is
Villa Rossi. There are plenty more examples of pleasant residential constructions
in addition to cosy cafes along Via Cesare
Betteloni. At the corner of Via Girolamo
Dai Libri 17, for instance, there is a mansion that was built in 1934 and credited
to the engineer Luigi Franceschetti.

Borgo Trento in 1910

Borgo Roma, first half of the 20th century

Borgo Trento in 1960

Borgo Venezia in 1920

Andrea Bertozzi

Google Earth/gmp architekten

gmp architekten

Design proposal for a roof for the Verona Arena by gmp architekten, 2017

Verona City
Route 1

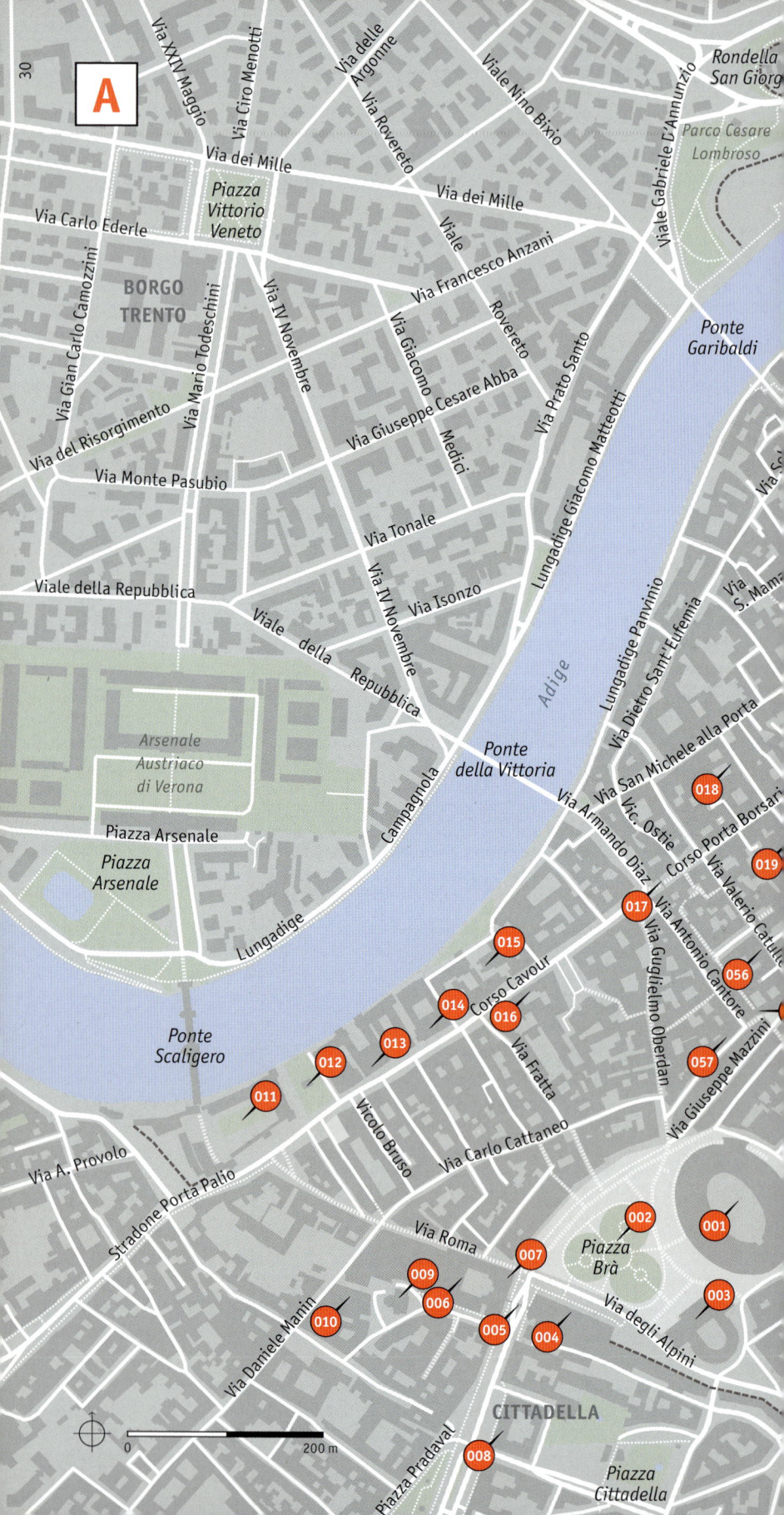

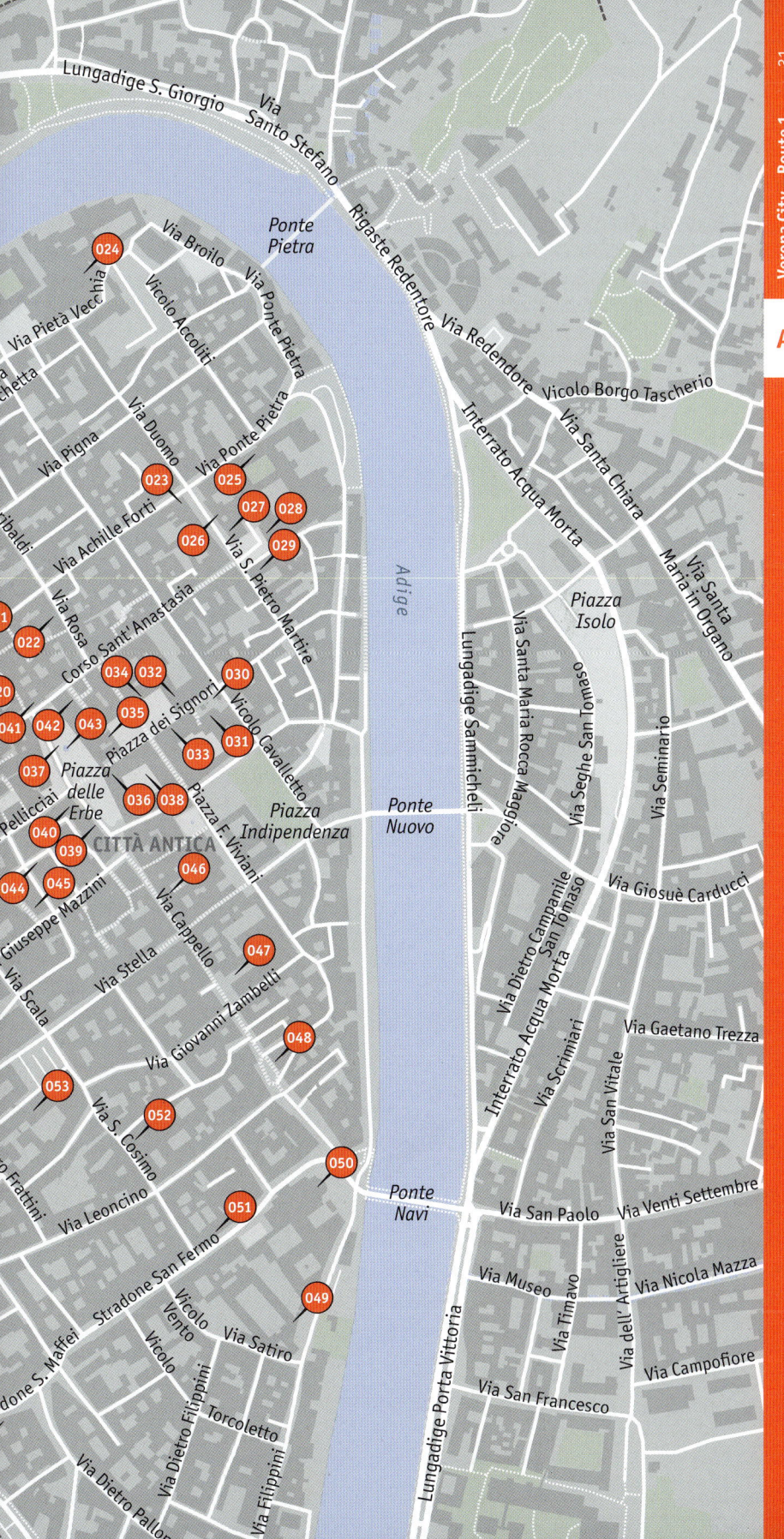

Verona Arena

Piazza Bra 1, Verona
1st century CE

001 A

The Arena viewed from Palazzo Barbieri

Sergey Nikitin–Rimsky

Bread and circuses, they say. The Arena is still the most famous building in the city, just as it was two millennia ago. While all major Roman towns had amphitheatres, few of them survived the Middle Ages. People today come here to feel stones shaped by two thousand years of visitors, to experience the Piranesian grandiosity of its vaults, and to breathe the wet and ancient air emanating from its depths. The Arena was built just beyond Verona's city walls in around 50 CE. The façade was initially composed of three tiers of Tuscan arcades in white and pink limestone from Valpolicella. These are now testified only by the one remaining section next to Via Mazzini, as the rest collapsed after an earthquake in 1117 and the materials were reused to rebuild the houses. Originally measuring 76 by 44 metres and with an overall height of 31 metres, the Arena's capacity was nearly 30,000 in those days. It can now host up to 22,000. Surprisingly, this ancient structure has never stopped functioning as a place of entertainment. For some time, it could be used as a fortress, or as source of stone, but it was the place for entertainment first and foremost – be it for the marriage of a princess, a duel, or the burning of 200 Patarian heretics in 1278. According to the medieval decree, prostitutes could only dwell in the Arena. It was not until the Quattrocento period of the Renaissance that the Veronese seem to have realised the historical value of the site – that this place is quintessential Roman history. The building's now-famous opera tradition began in 1856. They started the annual Arena lyric seasons in 1913 with *Aida*. Since then, it is one of the primary reasons to visit Verona, even though it has been in a constant artistic crisis for some time.

saiko3p (iStock)

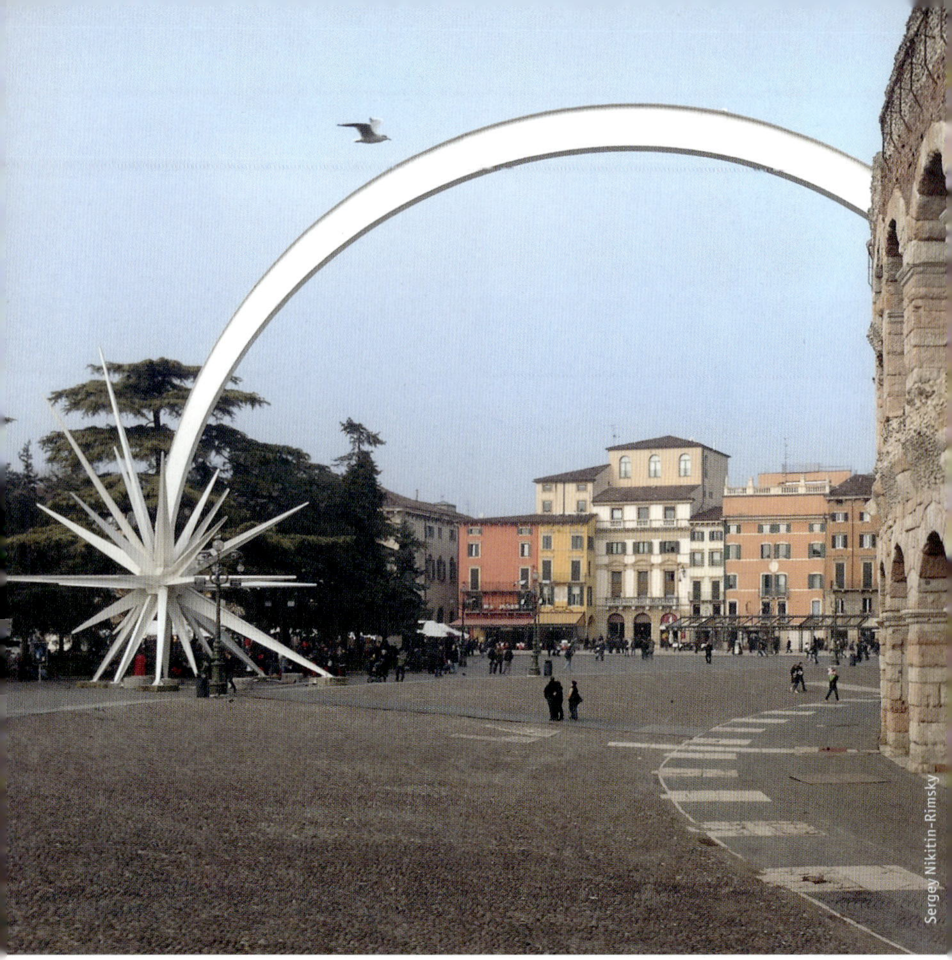

Sergey Nikitin-Rimsky

Christmas Star

Piazza Bra, Verona
Rinaldo Olivieri
1984 and annually since

002 **A**

This steel sculpture can only be seen in December and January, but the star, like the Arena on which it is perched, has become a major landmark of the city of Verona. Fewer people, however, recall the star's religious significance in memory of the Star of Bethlehem. Alfredo Troisi originally proposed the star's construction at a height of 70 metres to decorate the 1984 Christmas ark contest. The world-famous Brutalist architect Rinaldo Olivieri built the structure, causing an immediate uproar, not unlike that which greeted Paris' Eiffel Tower. Yet a year later, it was once again assembled, soon to become a perennial favourite backdrop for wintertime pictures in Verona. Miniature versions of the star have been presented to the likes of Mikhail Gorbachev, Ronald Reagan, and Pope John Paul II.

Siempreverde22 (iStock)

Palazzo Barbieri

Piazza Bra 6, Verona
Giuseppe Barbieri 1836–1848,
Raffaele Benatti,
Guido Troiani,
1950 (reconstruction and rotunda)

003 A

Even the festive Corinthian order can't animate this reserved façade made for Austrian Empire army officials. In those days, they were occupants in Italy at the doorstep of Risorgimento. Giuseppe Barbieri – one of the protagonists of the urban renovation spurred by Napoleon – made his best effort to build a landmark portico near the Arena, looking as bureaucratic and precise as those of Vienna or St. Petersburg. Since 1865, it has been the site of the Verona City Hall. The building had to be rebuilt after it was destroyed during the Second World War. Benatti and Troiani added a stylish rotunda to its old volume, reminiscent of the visions of Boullée and Ledoux, who inspired Barbieri and his nineteenth century colleagues.

Sergey Nikitin-Rimsky

Palazzo Barbieri Extension

Palazzo della Gran Guardia

Piazza Bra 1, Verona
Domenico Curtoni 1610–1614,
Giovanni Barbieri 1819–1820,
1853

Why was the Gran Guardia, Verona's most impressive palace, built? 'The ground floor is to inspect the troops on rainy days, and the upper floor is an academy for chivalric exercises,' as explained by Giovanni Mocenigo to the Doge of Venice, Leonardo Donà. Soldiers hadn't cared much about the weather in Verona previously, but Mocenigo nonetheless sought to introduce an equestrian hall in Verona. These were popular aristocratic attractions in his hometown of Venice. Domenico Curtoni was invited to design this Versailles-esque structure. A mysterious figure among Veronese architects and the nephew of the great architect Michele Sanmicheli, Curtoni is credited with just two completed projects: the Gran Guardia and the Rosario Chapel in Sant'Anastasia. Some critics have even suggested that Curtoni merely recycled the designs of his grandfather, while

svarshik (iStock)

others argue that he developed his own variant of the neoclassical style. Indeed, Curtoni does not curate each individual element of composition, as his famed grandfather had. Instead, he focused on the whole of the work. Sanmicheli sanctified each stone and composition, while Curtoni is distinctly secular, even festive. He seems at total ease in his play with triangular tympans, which are jovially interspersed with columns. Perhaps this spirit is to be expected, having grown up in a family of such artistic renown. Thirteen rusticated ashlar arches and eight sections of the upper part (starting from the right) were finished in 1614, after which work was suspended. Only in 1819 did Giuseppe Barbieri, architect and restorer, finally add the long flight of steps at the building's entrance. It was not until 1853 that the Gran Guardia finally opened. By the time it was completed, not only did the Venetian Republic no longer exist, but the chivalrous tradition was quickly becoming obsolete. Thus, congresses, parties, and exhibitions are now hosted where it was once imagined that horses would be rearing.

Alexander Grenkow

giuliano2022 (iStock)

Portoni della Brà

Piazza Bra
1480

005 A

A medieval wall marked the border between Verona and its rural outskirts. During the short rule of Visconti (1387–1402) it was strengthened with the octagonal tower. Venetians moved the city walls far further and created these two scenographic arches in local marble – i Portoni della Bra. A clock was installed in 1872. Among the gorgeous palaces of Piazza Bra, pay special attention to n. 16, with its balcony and arched portico facing the Arena – this is Michele Sanmicheli's Palazzo Degli Honorij.

![image](Portico of the Theater)

Sergey Nikitin-Rimsky

Portico of the Theater with installations of the Museum

Sergey Nikitin-Rimsky

Sergey Nikitin-Rimsky

Museo Lapidario Maffeiano

Piazza Bra 28, Verona
Arrigo Rudi
1976–1982

006 A

After assisting his teacher Scarpa with the world-famous Castelvecchio Museum permanent collection, Arrigo Rudi grew into an artist in his own right. He went on to create permanent museum exhibitions in Brescia, Modena, and Piacenza. In the Museo Maffeiano – a vital part of Verona's intellectual heritage – Rudi employed all of his sensibility in stone,

concrete, and metal to create a marvellous archaeological installation where each element receives the deserved degree of light and attention. One of the oldest lapidary museums, it was established in 1738 by Scipione Maffei, an intellectual protagonist in Verona, who organised a collection of Etruscan, Greek, and Roman epigraphs. City leaders directed that the building house the collection in the Philarmony hall's courtyard, with its gorgeous ionic colonnade, creating a natural backdrop to the beloved sights of the ancient world.

Teatro Filarmonico di Verona

Via Roma 1, Verona
Francesco Galli da Bibbiena
1716–1732,
Giannantonio Paglia 1749
(reconstruction),
1975 (reconstruction)

Verona began to crave its own great hall in the eighteenth century, as musical theatre blossomed in Venice, offering the era's most complex entertainment. Europe's leading master of theatres, Francesco Galli da Bibbiena, who had already built Große Komödiensaal for Emperor Leopold I in Vienna, was asked to conceive this temple of art. Construction lasted from 1716 until 1732. For the theatre's opening, Antonio Vivaldi wrote the pastoral drama *La fida ninfa*, a libretto written by local Scipione Maffei. Soon after, the building was destroyed by a fire and then later reconstructed. It was once again destroyed in 1943, this time by bombs. The theatre did not reopen again until 1975 after profound reconstruction and some changes to the original project. The foyer is called the 'Hall of Mirrors' for the cheerful pastiche of mirrors and its gilded decor. Since reconstruction, the Great Hall holds three tiers of boxes – instead of the original five – each with a different golden decoration, balcony, and gallery. Pay special attention to the Sala Maffeiana, which survived both the fire and bombing, thus preserving the charming original atmosphere of a small court theatre. The frescoed architecture, chandeliers, and wooden floors were made by Filippo Maccari in 1779. The original entrance is no longer used as it is now part of the Museo Maffei. Its ionic portico covered by the three-pitch roof, however, is one of the loveliest in Northern Italy. The portico was likely constructed by Domenico Curtoni, who was also responsible for Verona's Gran Guardia. The street porticoes were begun by Adriano Cristofaldi (1772, alongside Via Roma) and completed much later by Ettore Fagiuoli (1927–1929).

Sergey Nikitin-Rimsky

Palazzo dell'INA

Corso Porta Nuova 11, Verona
Paolo Rossi de Paoli
1937–1938

In the 1930s, the city of Verona was busy developing a new central axis: Corso Vittorio Emanuele. Supervisor architect Paolo Rossi de Paoli imagined it laced with green flora and stretched wide enough for military parades and spacious condominiums – a Veronese Champs-Élysées, of sorts. The imposing Littorio Palace, the local headquarters of the Fascist party, was also featured here. However, it was never built due to scandals within the competition. To remind us of these ambitious plans is this stylish red and white brick palace with fancifully elevated corners that Rossi de Paoli designed for the National Insurance Institute (INA). It is now a condominium complex, where a kind guard might let you enter the lobby to immerse yourself in the subtle colour play of the walls, the geometric ornaments, and an elegant twisted staircase with a lantern. Two murals by Pino Casarini at the entrance tell stories of Verona's past. The devil is interestingly featured here: he has built the Arena, set the fire, and killed King Teodorico, appearing to the King as a deer. It seems the leaders at the insurance company were a

Sergey Nikitin-Rimsky

bit flippant about these subjects. Though other devilish forces visited here, too: the palace was the headquarters for the SS during the Nazi occupation, which is attested to by a plaque located outside. Palazzo GIL, another impressive building of the same period on this street, sadly did not survive the war. For a wonderful display of modern monumental paintings, however, San Luca Church across the street features an art nouveau memorial chapel dating back to the First World War (Carlo Donati, 1919).

Sergey Nikitin-Rimsky

Sergey Nikitin-Rimsky

House of the Invalids

Via dei Mutilati 22, Verona
Francesco Banterle
1931–1934

Sergey Nikitin-Rimsky

This austere building is the local site of Benito Mussolini's extensive system of philanthropic institutions for mutilated soldiers. Inside were Prosthesis workshops, libraries, and meeting rooms, each dedicated to the mother of an illustrious deceased soldier. Veterans of war have played a central role in the state religion of Italy since the days of Garibaldi in the nineteenth century. Accordingly, Mussolini urged celebrations of the fallen and the provision of assistance to ex-combatants. The architect of this building, Banterle, revisits the triumphal arch with sculptural groups of soldiers and a bas-relief of Victoria. A bit stiff on the outside, the inside is rather gloomy, reminiscent of some 1920s German architecture. The vast Hall of Meetings, with its apse, recalls a church: There is now a canvas there featuring Christ. Remarkably, the city of Verona has managed to maintain most of the original furniture from the 1930s. The art deco chandeliers in the shape of flames are also remarkable.

Former Fiat Garage

Via Daniele Manin 7, Verona
Ettore Fagiuoli 1919–1920,
Mauro Felice, Gaetano Lisciandra
2004–2009

This is one of the rare public buildings that features the art nouveau style. This magnificent entrance portal with eaves once invited visitors to a Fiat automobile garage. Fagiuoli, the city's most fashionable architect of the 1920s and 1930s, was invited to design the building. This was not altogether unexpected, as city laws demanded that any building in the city centre be ornately designed. Inside, however, the structure is dictated by rational simplicity. The building was abandoned for decades and only saved from demolition thanks to its recent conversion into a supermarket.

Fabrizio Mauro

Fabrizio Mauro

saiko3p (iStock)

Castelvecchio

Corso Castelvecchio, 2
Cangrande II della Scala
1354–1356,
Carlo Scarpa, Arrigo Rudi,
Carlo Maschietto (engineer)
1957–1974

011 A

Once the site of a Roman fortress here, Cangrande II della Scala, the seigneur of Verona, built this powerful and compact castle. Surrounded by a ditch with imposing M-shaped merlons, the castle's seven towers and fortified bridge were intended to accommodate an escape to Tyrol in the event of a rebellion or occupation. However, these measures couldn't protect the despot from being assassinated by his brother, Cansignorio. Under the Austrian Empire, Castelvecchio became a military barracks. Antonio Avena together with Antonio Fagiuoli created a new museum in 1923 partly using fragments of old frescoes. It was a Romantic representation of neogothic interiors, a living museum that could be rented for private events. Nazi troops blew up the bridge in 1945, but the building itself wouldn't be destroyed until the charismatic Licisco Magagnato

was appointed its director. The co-founder of the Ministry of Cultural Heritage, Magagnato believed that culture requires profound exposure and aesthetic preparation. The Avena's museum, therefore, must disappear. Together with the Venetian architect Carlo Scarpa, Magagnato founded a new museum, the concept of which was destined to become world-famous for exhibition creators. These were happy times for Verona, under the guidance of mayor Giorgio Zanotto. The city was not rich, but rather growing steadily and spending public funds wisely. The first part of restoration was completed in 1958: the new ground floor featured innovations for the display systems. Simple tuff shelves were designed for polyptychs. As for the stationary crucifixes, he used small tuff cube supports and put panel paintings into simple frames with a coloured background. Some pictures were exhibited on rotating supports, while others rested on easels or hung on side fixtures. It took more than 16 years to finish the second part of the project: the first floor, the library, and the garden adorned with two shallow pools of water, which became a recurrent element of Scarpa's compositions.

46

Fabrizio Mauro

Fabrizio Mauro

Cangrande statue – taken from his tomb (see Tombe Scaligere)

Fabrizio Mauro

Claudio Divizia/dreamstime

pidjoe (iStock)

Arco dei Gavi

Corso Cavour, Verona
Lucius Vitruvius Cerdo
1 CE

012 A

Those from the Renaissance era knew this arch by heart. Painters Bellini and Mantegna and architects Palladio, Sangallo, Serlio, Falconetto, and Sanmicheli all studied its proportional relationships and decoration, copying and introducing it into their own work. This profound inspiration was primarily because of the signature of Vitruvius – still legible on its river façade – which recalls the well-known Roman scholar, architect, and creator of the 'De architectura'. As it turns out, this was in fact the work of his namesake, Lucius Vitruvius Cerdo – most likely a former Greek slave freed by his master Lucius Vitruvius. The arch originally adorned Via Postumia, Verona's most important Roman road. The structure stood in the middle of the street at what is now Corso Castelvecchio 7, across from the Clock Tower of Castelvecchio. Interestingly, this is the only known arch in honour of an individual family: the Gavi family, who lived in Verona. Statues of family members once decorated its niches. The arch was integrated into the city's defensive system during the Middle Ages. Shops were built inside it in Venetian times. The arch's fortune declined in 1805 when the French command decided to have it disassembled as it was deemed to be interfering with local traffic. All the blocks were numbered and neatly stacked at Piazza Cittadella, then later moved to the vaults of the Arena for protection from thieves. It was not until 1932 when Roman glory played an integral part of Mussolini's rhetoric and Via dell'Impero was cut through the Forums of Rome that the regime changed the name of Via Filarmonico to Via Roma and reconstructed the ancient arch. Antonio Avena, who was then the director of the Castelvecchio Museum and author of the scenography of the House of Juliet, approached the project as confidently and quickly as possible. The leading architect those days, Ettore Fagiuoli, took the drawings of Palladio and Barbieri as models. Since some blocks were missing, they were restored in the same shape and same matter – limestone – but the surfaces were treated with a light hammering in order not to be confused with original pieces. The 13-by-6-by-11-metre structure was soon raised next to Castelvecchio. The façade that faces Corso Cavour is more preserved than the one that faces the river. The interior of the arch has a flat coffered ceiling featuring Medusa in a clipeus. A stretch of Roman pavimentation was placed at the base of the monument. The site also boasts the best view of the Castelvecchio Bridge and Borgo Trento.

Palazzo Canossa

Corso Cavour 44, Verona
Michele Sanmicheli 1530s,
Lellio and Vincenzo Pellesina
1662–1675,
1761

Sergey Nikitin–Rimsky

Canossa was the Pope's ambassador, Bishop of the Norman city of Bayeux, and personally acquainted with Erasmus of Rotterdam. He even organised the wedding of Louis XII and Mary Tudor. Canossa knew the world, and so when he returned to his hometown of Verona as the ambassador of King Francis I to the Venetian Republic, he chose Michele Sanmicheli as the architect for his project. This was actually the first palace commissioned to Sanmicheli, who was then mostly known for his fortifications and engineering works. For the first two floors, Sanmicheli proposed a superbly developed rustication with bands of varying heights, and Corinthian columns decorating the piano nobile. The magnificent palace's front arch presents a charming garden pavilion along the river's cool breeze. Sadly, the commissioner never saw the completed project, but his nephew, Galeazzo, continued the building. His descendants added protruding loggias to the villa's river façade in the seventeenth century. In the eighteenth century, the ceiling of a large hall was raised and decorated with a fresco of Tiepolo, though it was later destroyed by bombs in 1945. To hide the raised roof, they added a balustrade with allegorical statues, including dogs – a symbol of this ancient Italian family, prominent on their coat of arms. Inside there are still decorations from the Sanmicheli period, including Paolo Veronese's *The Stories of Joseph*. Napoleon Bonaparte, Alexander I of Russia, and Francis I of Austria, all stayed here at various different times. Recent restorations revealed the remains of the façade's polychrome, visible now on its pilasters.

Rooms Castelvecchio – Palazzo Canossa

Palazzo Portalupi

Corso Cavour 40, Verona
Giuseppe and Gaetano Pinter
1804

014 A

The last great palace on Corso Cavour is a neoclassical block by Giuseppe Pinter. Throughout his life, Pinter was busy either reconstructing or building something. However, this graceful palace is the only one of his remarkable works left in the world. Pinter did not live to see the masterpiece finished, but his son resumed construction in order to complete the project. The Pinter family confidently followed the pattern established by Sanmicheli's nearby palaces: sturdy rust for the first and second floors, piano nobile with a balcony and a colonnade of pilasters, and a mezzanine with dancing bacchantes. Portalupi's forms are slightly larger and juicier than his fifteenth century neighbours. Two wolves guard the clock: an allusion to its patrons' coat of arms. Unfortunately, the building's gorgeous interiors are closed to the public.

Sergey Nikitin-Rimsky

Sergey Nikitin-Rimsky

Basilica di San Lorenzo

Corso Cavour 28, Verona
12th century,
1877, 1945

015 A

Enclosed between cylindrical scalar towers, a small cosy temple hides its heroic façade in the courtyard of this basilica. The towers likely double as structural buttresses. San Lorenzo is a rare type of temple in Northern Italy, with its prominent 'matronei' – the balconies on the upper level initially reserved for women, which give the church the appearance of a theatre. Medieval builders used brick, limestone, and pebbles, which provide a dynamic pattern of stripes to both the interior and exterior. While this site has housed a church since the fourth century, the present building is from the twelfth century after its reconstruction following the 1117 earthquake. The church's Romanesque bell tower was added in 1468. The bright red and gold altarpiece depicts the Madonna and Christ with Saints and was made by Domenico Brusasorci.

Mario Rossi

Sergey Nikitin-Rimsky

Palazzo Bevilacqua

Corso Cavour 17, Verona
Michele Sanmicheli
1556–1559

016 **A**

Opposite the Palazzo Canossa, brothers Antonio and Gregorio Bevilacqua began work on their family palace. The Sanmicheli style here is radically different from the tectonic rigor of his early years. It is a magnificent festive façade: cut like a cake with lovingly drawn and carved details and ornaments. Most notable is the vigilant Caesar's head guarding the entrance gate. Through all the centuries, the palace was believed to be contemporary to Canossa's, but recent archival studies of Francesco Marcorin (2015) have corrected the date of the building to 1556–1591. This subsequently shed new light on its composition.

The treatment of the piano nobile for Bevilacqua is based on the famous façade of the Library of St. Mark (Biblioteca Marciana) by Jacopo Sansovino (1537). Here, Sanmicheli shows a total absence of voids, clearly inspired by Sansovino's usage of sculpture. The semi-columns with spiral fluting pay tribute to the famous Roman monuments of Verona, such as the nearby Porta Borsari, Porta Leoni, and arch of Jupiter Ammon. Bevilaqua is therefore a contemporary to Sanmicheli's other palaces – most prominently to Grimani on the Grand Canal in Venice, with whom it shares common traits in the piano nobile and rustication of the lower register. These are derivations from the Roman models, such as those in the Caprini Palazzo by Bramante, or Palazzo Vidoni Caffarelli by Raffaello. The building now houses the Technical Institute.

Porta Borsari

Corso Porta Borsari 57A, Verona
1st century BCE – 1st century CE

At two millennia old, the Porta Borsari stuns modern spectators, having survived unspeakable wars and earthquakes. It served as the main gate of Verona in Ancient Rome. The original name was Porta Iovia and it once stood beside a temple to Jupiter. Today, the name Borsari recalls medieval tax officers. The gate was built at the same time as the Roman Wall and Porta Leoni (see 048: Porta Leoni), around the second half of the first century BCE. Meanwhile, the richly decorated façade is from the imperial period of the first century CE. It was originally a double gate with a central courtyard, where travellers were stopped and checked. Thirteen metres high and wide, its walls are 93 centimetres thick. It was once enclosed between two tall towers, the remains of which are incorporated into the adjacent modern houses. Giovanni Caroto, Andrea Palladio, and numerous other Renaissance artists admired and studied this storied spectacle. The spiral-fluted pilasters of the second tier, also present on the Porta Leoni, have become a recurrent feature in Veronese architecture since the time of Sanmicheli. It was here that Matteo Bandello staged a fight between two bored youngsters, Romeo and Tybalt in the original rendition of Romeo and Juliet. Shakespeare, on the other hand, whose audiences would have known nothing of Verona, omits this particular location in his version.

Sergey Nikitin-Rimsky

Fabrizio Mauro

Sergey Nikitin-Rimsky

Stal de le Vecie

019 A

Corso Porta Borsari 32, Verona
14th century,
Libero Cecchini (restoration)
2009

Stal de le Vecie, meaning 'stable of the old ladies' in the Veronese language, is a carefully restored house that has been re-modeled several times over the centuries. It was used for storage and as a stable in the nineteenth century. There is a Ro-manesque relief featuring the Holy Trini-ty, Mary, and archangels over the portal. There are also three courtyards, including a noble arcade from the fifteenth century to humbler on-site lodgings, which have all been carefully restored in the twenty-first century. Next to the building is the eighteenth-century Palazzo Monga-Realdi (n. 36), which has been converted into a boutique hotel and shop. There is an orig-inal Palladio façade just across the street (see 019: Palazzo Dalla Torre).

Palazzo Dalla Torre »

019 A

Via Quattro Spade, 19, Verona
*Andrea Palladio 1555–1568,
Italo Mutinelli 1950*

For many years, the Dolci brothers dreamed of converting their fourteenth century palace into a cinema. The city preservation commission, however, was strongly against the conversion until the Second World War. After the war, Mutinel-li recycled the heavily bombed structure into a multifunctional hall with an or-chestra pit. It has a sober, though slightly gilded, rationalist style. The hall's main feature is the enormous openable ocu-lus. The palace also has another façade: in fact, the only work of the exalted ar-chitect Andrea Palladio in Verona is in the Vicoletto Cieco Padovano. The patron, Giambattista Dalla Torre, invited Palladio to redesign this inherited building. It seems, however, that work never pro-gressed much beyond the ground floor's portico and some decorations. Never-theless, Palladio included the design and floorplan of the villa in his book, *I quattro libri dell'architettura* (1570).

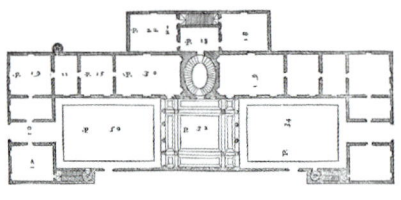

Fabrizio Mauro

Fabrizio Mauro

Corte Sgarzerie Archaeological Site

Corte Sgarzerie 8, Verona
14th century

During the Middle Ages, Verona was the European capital of fine fabrics thanks in large part to the city's small water-powered factories. Corte Sgarzerie is one such place where woollen clothes were once produced. In the fourteenth century, Mastino II della Scala erected this 'Loggia del Mangano' atop the red marble columns, which, according to scholars, operated as the office for quality control. The Corte Sgarzerie Archaeological Site is also here, holding the ruins of the tuff and limestone cryptoporticus in the Capitoline complex, an ancient temple dedicated to the Roman gods Juno, Jupiter, and Minerva. Additionally, the site shows the remains of an original Roman road in red marble. It is worth a visit, and not only on a rainy day.

Sergey Nikitin-Rimsky

Palaces around Piazzetta Monte

Via Francesco Emilei 20 & 22, Verona

A theatrical street dialogue: two balconies across from each other on via Emilei. Palazzo Dal Verme (n. 20) was built in 1475 on pre-existing Romanesque buildings. Its windows and balcony with putti strongly remind us of the Venetian Gothic fashion. Note the carved portal. At n. 22 is the sixteenth century Palazzo Negrelli-Giusti-Zamboni-Pindemonte-Camuzzoni, the birthplace of the Romantic poet and English park promoter Ippolito Pindemonte (see 152: Villa Mosconi Bertani). Two elegant façades create a metaphysical feeling at the Piazzetta Monte – the church of Monte on the left and the Catholic bank of Monte di Pietà with a clock raised over Christ. The Catholic banking machine in Verona has been composed of about 40 officials since 1490: notaries, clerks, accountants, estimators, auctioneers for unpaid pawns, checkwriters, and postcard writers. It was a happy day for the Veronese in 1630 when a fire in the building destroyed most of the pawns. The bank survived, of course. In the twentieth century, Monte di Pietà of Verona became Cassa di Risparmio di Verona, which joined the Unicredit banking group as a founding subsidiary and shareholder. The bank is still inside.

Sergey Nikitin-Rimsky

Fabrizio Mauro

Palazzo Pellegrini

Via Rosa 5, Verona
Domenico Curtoni
1610s

The Veronese justly dubbed this building 'el porton senza casa', the doorway without a house. With its massive entrance and key stone in the shape of a dangerous giant fist, it resembles the demonic fireplaces of Villa Della Torre. This exaggerated gem of mannerism is believed to have been made by Domenico Curtoni, the grandson of Sanmicheli and designer of the Gran Guardia Vecchia in Bra. Take a walk down the quaint Vicolo Raggiri towards the right side of the palace to catch a glimpse of old Verona. Here you will find the lovely Piazzetta Monte directly beside the Roman Capitolium.

Fabrizio Mauro

Palazzo Emilei Forti

Via Achille Forti 1, Verona
Ignazio Pellegrini 18th century,
Libero Cecchini (restoration)

023 A

One of the sweet, care-free façades of the Veronese eighteenth century is that of Ignazio Pellegrini – a nobleman and military man, but also the successful architect responsible for the northern wing of Florence's Pitti Palace. The building, with its rather heavy tympans and fat balustrade, includes the residence of Ezzelino III da Romano, a thirteenth century Veronese tyrant. The eastern façade and some frescoes inside still demonstrate these features. The building's last owner, Achille Forti, was a naturalist and collector of Jewish origins. Forti donated the entirety of his real estate and paintings to the municipality upon his death. His interesting art collection has recently been exhibited in the Palazzo Della Ragione (see 038: Palazzo Della Ragione). In the interior you may see a broken mirror that remains a testiment to the fist of Napoleon Bonaparte, who shattered it in 1796 when he received unfortunate news from the frontlines while staying on the grounds.

Fabrizio Mauro

Duomo

Piazza Duomo 21, Verona
1117–1187

024 A

It is possible to buy tickets to visit the cathedral, two other temples, and a magnificent cloister with antique mosaics. Christians began construction here in the fourth century. The buildings were devastated by an earthquake in 1117 and later rebuilt. The façade with a two-storey projecting porch is embellished with sculpture by Nicholaus. Two griffins support the portico of the Virgin Mary holding the young Christ. Only two centuries later it was already being decorated in the Gothic style with lancet windows. The interior is mostly from the fifteenth century. Naves are divided by tall pillars in red Verona marble, which supports the Gothic arcades. It's coming closer to the main altar to admire the architectural perspectives of the life of the Virgin Mary on the frescoes, according to a drawing by Giulio Romano. In front of them is a semi-circular colonnade by Michele Sanmicheli that celebrates one of his early patrons, Lodovico Canossa (see 013: Palazzo Canossa). The cathedral's 75-metre belfry is visible from nearly everywhere in the city. Construction began in the Romanesque style. It was then developed by Sanmicheli and followed by Ettore Fagiuoli's attempt to complete the project in the 1920s. However, construction has been halted since 1927. The baptistery is the triple-naved Basilica di San Giovanni in Fonte, built in the first half of the tenth century and rebuilt after the earthquake using older materials, such as pebbles, tuff, and bricks. An octagonal baptistery vase from the eighth century is carved with the story of Christ's childhood. The church of Sant'Elena, Romanic piece and part of the ensemble, stands where the first place of Christian worship in Verona was built by Bishop Zeno in the fourth century. The Chapter Library of Duomo (since V century), claimed to be the world's oldest library in continuous operation, is also here.

Vvoevale (dreamstime)

DEO · ALMAEQ · DEI · GENITRICI · MARIAE · ET · DIVIS ·
HIERONYMO · SEBASTIANO · THEODORO · PIA · SOCIETAS ·

Vvoevale (dreamstime)

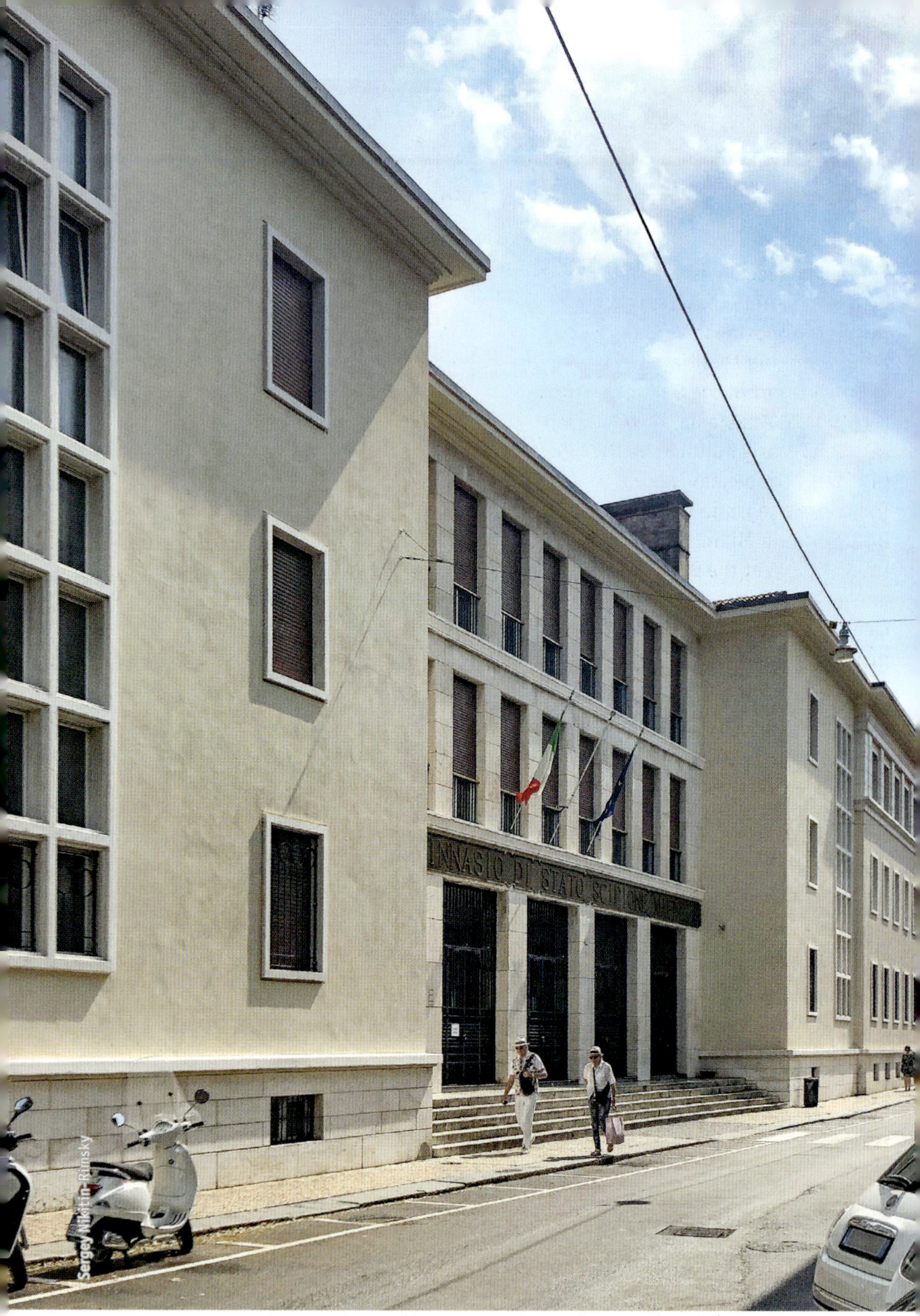

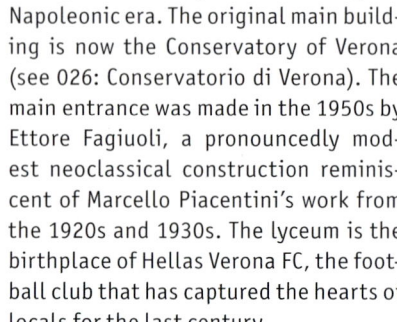

Istituto Maffei (Liceo Ginnasio di Stato 'Scipione Maffei')

025 A

Via Abramo Massalongo 4, Verona
Ettore Fagiuoli (extension)
1958–1963

A classical and linguistic secondary school, the most prestigious school in Verona is named after Scipione Maffei, the leading Veronese writer and scientist of the eighteenth century. It was the first lyceum in Italy created during the Napoleonic era. The original main building is now the Conservatory of Verona (see 026: Conservatorio di Verona). The main entrance was made in the 1950s by Ettore Fagiuoli, a pronouncedly modest neoclassical construction reminiscent of Marcello Piacentini's work from the 1920s and 1930s. The lyceum is the birthplace of Hellas Verona FC, the football club that has captured the hearts of locals for the last century.

Conservatorio di Verona (formerly Royal Lyceum)

026 A

Via Abramo Massalongo 2, Verona
Bartolomeo Giuliari
1808–1814

Sergey Nikitin–Rimsky

The royal lyceum is the most significant social and urban realisation of the Napoleonic period in Verona. It was created according to a Napoleonic decree. Originally part of the Dominican monastery of Sant'Anastasia, it was converted into a scholarly building by Bartolomeo Giuliari. A nobleman and a nephew of Ignazio Pellegrini, Giuliari completed his studies in Milan, where he matriculated in 1773 at the Barnabite college of San Saverio. Later, Marcellino Segrè became his teacher, one of the key figures in the Austrian Milan. Back in Verona, Giuliari wrote his modestly titled work, *Studi imperfetti d'architettura*. Encouraged by the challenges brought by Napoleon, Giuliari developed into a leading urban thinker, preservationist, and architect of the first half of the nineteenth century. While designing the lyceum, he carefully weaved the old, frescoed cloister into the new structure. A beautifully proportioned set of ionic half-columns create a great inviting façade. The building now houses the Conservatory of Verona, which sometimes hosts public concerts. Otherwise, it is entirely closed to visitors.

Sergey Nikitin–Rimsky

70

Chiesa di San Giorgetto o San Pietro Martire

027 A

Via Abramo Massalongo 2, Verona
1283–1354

Sant'Anastasia, the central church of the Dominican abbey, was officially dedicated to the local Veronese martyr Peter, a Dominican killed in Milan. However, la Signora di Verona did not take this inscription into account: the site was previously occupied by a small church of Saint Anastasia built by King Theoderic. Thus, the Veronese insisted on using this beautiful name for more than 500 years, even though inside Sant'Anastasia there is not a single depiction of this saint. Dominicans tried for a second time to rename the Gothic chapel adjacent to Sant'Anastasia, but the Veronese still call it the church of San Giorgetto. The chapel was initially erected for the Brandenburg guards of Cangrande II Della Scala, though there is some debate that the guards were in fact from nearby Tyrol. Inside, there are marvellous frescoes with kneeling knights, princesses, unicorns, and Saint George. To the right of the church, over the arch that connects it to Sant'Anastasia, is a Gothic arch with the tomb of Guglielmo di Castelbarco – a condottiere mercenary, ally of the Scaligers, and sponsor of the San Fermo Maggiore church. Scholars consider Castelbarco's tomb a prototype for the famous Scaliger Pantheon (n. 030 in this book).

Sergey Nikitin-Rimsky

Bernard Białorucki (dreamstime)

Basilica di Sant'Anastasia

028 A

Piazza Santa Anastasia, Verona
Fra' Benvenuto da Imola,
Fra' Nicola da Imola
1280–1440, 15th century (belfry)

Behind a nondescript, unfinished façade that blocks the Roman Via Postumia, the Scaligers erected the most beautiful Dominican basilica in memory of San Pietro di Verona. The Scala nobles were never able to see it completed, as they were overthrown by their Milanese relatives after fatal skirmishes broke out. In its soft aurorean glow, Sant'Anastasia offers a breath-taking collection of Veronese architecture and monumental painting. From the middle of the fifteenth century, the city's elite built their palaces for the afterlife here, reflecting their tastes and opinions at the hands of the masters from Verona, Venice, and Florence. A colourful contrasting ornamental ceiling recalls the proximity of the Alps and the Gothic interiors of Tyrol. The main altar has a special point of interest: a man on the horse, in the spirit of the Roman emperor Caligula,

who rides confidently, is the condottiere Cortesia (meaning 'favor') Serego, one of the assassins of Bartolomeo II Della Scala. His sarcophagus is empty though – it took more than 30 years to finish this tomb. To the right of the main altar, above the apse, there is a gorgeous courtesan scene – a Gothic Princess immersed in idyllic

Sergey Nikitin–Rimsky

cityscapes (Pisanello, 1433–1438). The apse below is lined with terracotta statues by Michele di Firenze. The joyful palette and Quattrocento taste of the family chapels of Manzini (built after 1482), Boldieri, Miniscalchi, and especially of Bevilacqua-Lazise, are thrilling to observe with their semi-circular pediment. In the Cinquecento period, everyone wanted an arch for themselves. A white marble triumphal arch with four Corinthian columns is created by Danese Cattaneo, a disciple of Sansovino and friend of Palladio. An honest and simple set of allegories surrounds a strong and handsome portrayal of Christ. Depictions of condottiere mercenaries, military virtue, glory, and eternity recount the hectic life of the ex-magistrate of Genoa, captain Giano II Fregoso. Giano's son Ercole was the tomb's commissioner and a friend of Matteo Bandello, the author of the original Italian version of Romeo and Juliet. The Pindemonte family came closer than anyone to reprising Gavi's arch almost entirely in 1541. Still, a painting of St. Martin in red steals the show. Romantic poet Ippolito Pindemonte was buried under the marble sarcophagus. To appreciate the grandeur of the whole building, it's worth getting a glimpse from the other side of the Adige River: the brick volume of the temple still towers above the residential buildings, villas, palaces, and gardens.

Sergey Nikitin-Rimsky

Sergey Nikitin-Rimsky

Vvoevale (dreamstime)

Sergey Nikitin-Rimsky

Due Torri Hotel

Piazza Santa Anastasia 4, Verona
Alessandro Polo (engineer)
reconstruction 1959

029 A

This historic hotel boasts two great sets of dreamy frescoes by Pino Casarino, the star of twentieth century Veronese murals. They can be found in both the lobby and meeting room. The building once housed Scaligeri's German guards and later became the Due Torri Hotel. Its notable guests include Mozart, Goethe, and other youthful travellers on 'the Grand Tour'. Giuseppe Garibaldi addressed the Veronese people from the hotel's balcony in 1866. During the days of the Republic of Salò, it was a ministry headquarters, but was later reincarnated as a hotel after its 1959 reconstruction. The terrace café offers breathtaking views over the town.

Detail of the Pino Casarino fresco in the lobby

Arche Scaligere (Scaliger Tombs)

Via Santa Maria in Chiavica 1a, Verona

Cangrande, Mastino II, Cansignorio, Bonino da Campione

1329, 1350, 1375

030 A

A

Any of the three monuments in the Scaliger Tombs would make for a beautiful canopy in a church altar. This is not, however, a temple of God, but rather a site on the streets in the very centre of the city of Verona. The Scaliger Tombs are monuments to a dynasty of secular leaders, tyrants who appealed to the Veronese masses. The Scaligers created the most striking, straight-talking, and propagandistic memorial of the Middle Ages. Two of its monuments especially – those honouring Cansignorio and Mastino II – resemble models of Gothic churches. Indeed, they are almost equal in height to Santa Maria Antica and feature far richer decor. With these intricate monuments, the Scala family aimed to flaunt their significance and earthly success to both their contemporaries and those who followed them. They constructed their lives as part of a large and sacred history, demanding recognition, admiration, and eternal peace in heaven. Like Cansignorio's inscription says: 'I, Cansignorio, rest in this shining ark. I who could have been monarch of many cities in Italy ... My value, added to the love for

Cansignorio and Mastino II tombs. On the right, over the entrance, is the tomb of Cangrande

samael334 (iStock)

peace and not detached from my faith, will give me fame for centuries to come.' The tomb of Cangrande I was the first of the ensemble, positioned by the entrance to the Santa Maria Antica Church, of which Cangrande was especially fond. It is richly carved from all sides with scenes from the life of the great warrior, including the mystic finale – the body of Cangrande exiting the gates of Treviso upon his death. A huge sword of Cangrande, sound inside the tomb, is currently on display in the Museum of Castelvecchio. After the tomb for Cangrande was built, Mastino II began to think about his own sepulchre. It is a freestanding and rectangular composition. Four high reliefs with scenes from the Bible are in the tympanums of the tabernacle: the temptation of Adam and Eve, the work of the progenitors, the killing of Cain, and the mockery of Noah. Mastino is depicted lying serene and satisfied. The ark is surmounted by his figure on horseback, prepared for battle, completely enclosed in armour. At just 24 years old, Cansignorio della Scala had already called on the craftsman Bonino da Campione to construct his tomb. Bonino also made the memorial to the husband of Cansignorio's sister, the Lord of Milan Bernabò Visconti, in the church of San Giovanni in Milan. This memorial caused a scandal because it was claimed to be too close to the church altar. In Verona, however, Cansignorio was able to construct the memorial on the central square, spending more than 10,000 florins (the equivalent of about 35 kilogrammes of gold). The construction revolves around the number six: six pillars rise from a hexagonal base to support six Gothic tabernacles with six saints – Quirico, Martin, Sigismund, Valentin, George, and King Louis IX of France. Scenes from the New Testament are carved into the sarcophagus, featuring Cansignorio himself at the coronation of Mary. Historian Licisco Magagnato (see 011: Castelvecchio) called Cansignorio's tomb 'the hexagonal machine', stressing the dynamism of its image. Beyond the glimmering tombs of Trecento, it's a challenge to note the modes and simple tomb of Mastino I (1277), the founder of the dynasty, and that of his brother Alberto (1301).

Tomb of Cansignorio

Sergey Nikitin-Rimsky

The staircase (scala) is a heraldic sign of the Scaligers family

Sergey Nikitin-Rimsky

Chiesa di Santa Maria Antica

031 A

Via Arche Scaligere 3, Verona
1185

The current three-naved Romanesque church was built after the earthquake of 1117 destroyed its predecessor. It was a private chapel of Verona's ruling Scaligeri family, comfortably located between their palaces on Piazza dei Signori and surrounded by the family cemetery. The church was redecorated in the baroque style in the 1630s. At the turn of the nineteenth and twentieth centuries, however, it was restored to the severe 'original' design. The exterior has alternate bands of tuff and cotto, with small windows that were discovered during the restoration process. The entrance is dominated by the tomb of Cangrande I della Scala. A small tuff bell tower with bifora windows and a brick-covered spire is quintessentially medieval Verona and Tyrol.

Sergey Nikitin-Rimsky

Andrea Bertozzi

Prefettura (formerly Palazzo Scaligeri)

032 A

Piazza dei Signori
1308
Antonio Avena (reconstruction)
1927–1930

Gothic historicism captured rich cities of Europe in the nineteenth century, often damaging original monuments. Verona spent a lot on Gothicising its structures, too. Yet the office of the prefect, once a palace of Cangrande I Della Scala, remained shabby and unadorned until the 1920s. The long-standing museum director Antonio Avena proposed refreshing the charms of the house where the Seigneurs of Verona received Dante and Giotto. He decorated the façade with a large, deliberately decorative merlature and opened one arcade to the right of the entrance, opting not to open the other on the left. Avena knew that medieval buildings are pleasing with their picturesque unevenness and

Portal by Sanmicheli

Sergey Nikitin-Rimsky

asymmetry, so some of the windows here were made arched, while others became small and square, not unlike those of a dungeon. A beautiful white marble portal by Sanmicheli (1503) was under threat, since it was so out of tune with the Gothic trend. In the end, though, it was kept, as Vasari was an ardent admirer.

ARTECO srl

Palazzo del Cansignorio (also known as Palazzo del Capitanio or Palazzo del Tribunale)

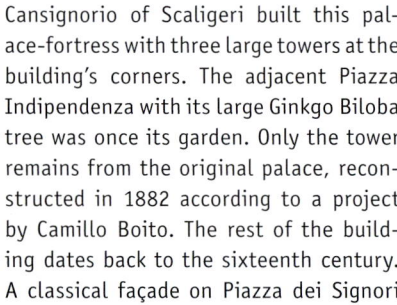

033 A

Piazza dei Signori 22, Verona
1363 (?), 16th century

Cansignorio of Scaligeri built this palace-fortress with three large towers at the building's corners. The adjacent Piazza Indipendenza with its large Ginkgo Biloba tree was once its garden. Only the tower remains from the original palace, reconstructed in 1882 according to a project by Camillo Boito. The rest of the building dates back to the sixteenth century. A classical façade on Piazza dei Signori boasts lion heads in its coats of arms – reminding us that we are, indeed, in what was once the Venetian Republic. A magnificent marble Corinthian portal was likely crafted by Michele Sanmicheli around 1530. Corinthian semi-columns rest on square bases to support the palace's elegant architrave. Within the site's internal courtyard rests the elegant three-layered Loggia Barbaro, built in 1476, with its happily alternating Gothic and round arches. The pageant Gate of the Bombardiers (1687, Bernardino Miglioranzi) showcases a playful still life of weapons: barrels with gunpowder and cannons. It underwent a renovation by Verona-based Arteco between 2013 and 2021.

ARTECO srl

Loggia del Consiglio

Piazza dei Signori
1476–1492

When Verona lost its independence to Venice, the town establishment built a meeting place for its council using a rigorous classical style. A characteristic memorial, the lodge praises the town through antique characters who were then considered Veronese, including architect Vitruvius, poet Catullus, naturalist Plinius the Elder, poet Aemilius Macer, and historian Cornelius Nepos. Sometimes it is erroneously called Loggia Frà Giocondo after the famous Veronese architect who was active in Paris and Rome, but never Verona. Supported by eight arches on slender columns, the first floor is decorated with biforas and stucchi, reminiscent of the delicate designs of Mauro Codussi, an early Renaissance master. A statue on the arch between the Loggia and Café Dante is perhaps the oldest personal memorial to Girolamo Fracastoro, a sixteenth century

Sergey Nikitin–Rimsky

doctor known for his monograph *Syphilis, or French Evil*, and much esteemed by the international Catholic establishment. He was the official doctor of the Council of Trento until his death.

Daniel Ouellette (dreamstime)

Palazzo Domus Nova

Piazza dei Signori, Verona
13th century, 1659,
1731 (restoration)

035 A

Here is a bombastic neoclassical building between triumphal arches. It is a surprisingly high (six floors!) and slightly disproportionate Palladian condominium. Domus Nova was built in the Scaligeri's times, then rebuilt and raised in the times of the Venetian Republic as a place for judges. Now you can stay in the guesthouse inside or eat at the café. Busts, plaques, and obelisks abundantly ornate its walls and entrance, making it another element of this incredible memorial square. A late seventeenth century postcard praised the building for a (now gone) 'clock showing the hours transparently at night' and its statues of illustrious Veronese on the roof. The statues were likely smashed by French troops in 1797, aiming to end Verona's subordination to Venice. There are, however, still statues on the arches that connect it to other houses on the piazza: Cardinal Enrico Norris (on the left) and the erudite scientist Scipione Maffei (to the right). Maffei's monument (1756, Giovanni Angelo Finali) was erected just a year after his death – only monarchs could expect recognition at such a speed. Check: Museo Maffeiano next to Arena – his creation!

Meinzahn (dreamstime)

Torre dei Lamberti

Via della Costa 1, Verona
12th century, 1448–1464

036 A

At 84 metres tall, the Torre dei Lamberti is Verona's most prominent tower. It may help you imagine the city's medieval environment in the times of Montecchi and Capuleti – when the noble families of Verona lived not in a palace, but rather in a small, fortified house where they were defended against the rest of the world with turrets. 'My home is my castle' as was once said. It was the Lamberti family who built this tower, which was originally much lower than it is today. One can witness the history of the building's architectural progress by inspecting the varying layers of tuff and cotto. The tower became the city's belfry in

1140. Since then, the Marangona bell tells the time of day, while the largest bell, the Rengo, was used to schedule council meetings and alert people in the event of fire, war, or public decapitations. In those original days, the tower was also a place to live – for bell ringers and a prison was located here, too, since it was annexed by Palace of Justice (see 038: Palazzo Della Ragione). The tower was struck by lightning and damaged in 1404 – perhaps an omen, as the following year Verona lost its independence when it became part of the Venetian Republic. Seemingly no one cared about the city's belfry anymore, as its restoration took 60 years. The clock was added in 1798 through a philanthropic motion by Count Giovanni Sagramoso. The tower provides a stunning view of town, but the surrounding protective net makes it a challenge to capture in a photo.

Sergey Nikitin–Rimsky

Piazza delle Erbe
Piazza delle Erbe

037 A

The gorgeous Piazza delle Erbe, or Green Market Square, sits exactly on the site of the Roman Forum. Here, the Palazzo Maffei stands over the remains of the Roman Capitolium. Medieval towers, the Mazzanti Palace, and the high-rises of the Jewish ghetto all contribute to the special atmosphere. In 1523, Venetians erected a pillar with the winged lion of St. Mark – the symbol of the Venetian Republic. Adjacent to the Piazza delle Erbe is Piazza dei Signori, which is home to the palaces of the Scaliger family.

Palazzo della Ragione » (also known as Mercato Vecchio)
Piazza Erbe 12, Verona
1193–1196;
Giuseppe Barbieri
(façade of Piazza delle Erbe) 1800s,
Camillo Boito 1894;
Afra and Tobia Scarpa
(interiors for the exhibition) 2007

038 A

The current Palazzo della Ragione was initially a private building built near the ancient Roman forum (now the Piazza delle Erbe) on one of the blocks formed by the cardo and decumans of Roman Verona. In the twelfth century, after an earthquake razed Verona, the municipality erected the Palacium Communis Veronae. This building served as a hall for city council meetings, the salt warehouses, the silk-duty office, a pawn shop, and later the tax office and prison. It was a sober, simple, and fortified structure with four corner towers, one of which is Torre dei Lamberti. During the fifteenth and sixteenth centuries, under Venetian control, the palace became a justice hall and its name was changed to Palazzo della Ragione (Palace of Justice). The complex was enriched with the Scala della Ragione (Stairway of Justice), followed by the Cappella dei Notai (the Notaries' Chapel), the Chapel of Santa Maria della Neve, and finally the Torre dei Lamberti. The grain market was placed in the building's courtyard at around the end of the sixteenth century. In the nineteenth century, Italy's leading restorer (and horror writer) Camillo Boito suggested eliminating all of the superstructures and additions to the building, considering them deformations to the medieval original. Erroneously, Boito thought the roof of the staircase was a late addition and thus destroyed it. Boito standardised all the façades, introducing an arched cornice and Romanesque mullioned windows. The walls of the palace were re-laid with alternating rows

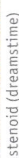

Castenoid (dreamstime)

Sergey Nikitin-Rimsky

Sergey Nikitin-Rimsky

of terracotta and marble, except for the Renaissance piece of Piazza dei Signori, which is decorated with eighteenth century memorial busts. However, the building's original, pre-Boito state can still be seen at the intersection of Via della Costa and Piazza delle Erbe. In 2007, Afra and Tobia Scarpa transformed the palace into an exhibition space for the Gallery of Modern Art, now showcasing a valuable collection of local paintings and a chance to witness the interiors of long-gone eras.

Filippo Carlot (dreamstime)

Ghetto Nuovo buildings on Piazza delle Erbe

039 A

Piazza delle Erbe 3-5, Verona
16th – 18th centuries

These houses grew to quite a considerable height when this area became Verona's new Jewish ghetto. The ghetto's perimeter was decreed and delimited in 1604, but because the community was growing steadily, the only option was to go high. Curiously, the result resembles the medieval towers of Verona. There are nine towers between Via Mazzini and the Domus Mercatorum. These towers all stand tall and narrow, each with the same typology: two windows and one room per floor. The highest tower has eight floors, the lowest five. They seem to stand by each other in solidarity. The rest of the new ghetto was destroyed in the 1920s. Unexpectedly, the ghetto's skyscrapers inspired merchant Andrea Scalabrini to build his two-window, eight-storey house across the road (Via Cappello 3a) in 1856. At first, city hall's Ornate Commission refused the house, but later allowed it on the condition that the balconies be limited to no more than 80 centimetres. Scalabrini decorated the upper floor with arched windows, a clock, and a swallowtail merlature – all Veronese classics.

Domus Mercatorum or Loggia dei Mercanti

Piazza delle Erbe 17, Verona
1301
Camillo Boito (restoration)
end of the 19th century

040 A

Marina113 (iStock)

Originally a wooden structure on the central market, it was ordered to be rebuilt in stone by Alberto I Scala, the first real Scaliger to rule the city as 'Seigneur'. Its name 'Merchants' Lodge' is a common reference for public buildings in Italy that provided meeting places for merchants. Today, we see the Romantic-Gothic restoration of the nineteenth century that spoiled the façade; introducing swallow-tail merlature, for instance, instead of the original belvedere. Banca Popolare di Verona, the city's last major bank, had offices here until they were eventually absorbed by the Milanese. Another crucial sight is the fountain, built in 1368 by Cansignorio della Scala and crowned with a Roman statue called Madonna Verona.

Newlander90 (iStock)

Aliaksandr Antanovich (iStock)

Palazzo Maffei
Piazza delle Erbe 38, Verona
1626–1663

multi-function use – shops at the bottom and rooms rented out by the hotel, just as it is now. The top has a balustrade with six statues of ancient deities: Hercules, Jupiter, Venus, Mercury, Apollo, and Minerva. It is believed that the figure of Hercules (first from the left) is Roman, probably from the temple of the Capitol on whose foundations Palazzo Maffei was built (see 020: Corte Sgarzerie). Here, too, there is a unique helical staircase that climbs from the basement to the rooftop. In 2019, the Baldessari e Baldessari studio adopted the piano nobile of the palace for a new privately owned Carlon museum featuring Boccioni, Kandinskij, Magritte, Braque, and others.

It should have been an architect from sunny Rome to adorn the most popular façade in Verona with confectionery generosity. Marcantonio and Rolandino Maffei, uncle and nephew, were wealthy Veronese money changers who had a bank at the Piazza delle Erbe. They wanted to raise the height of the old house. Work went on until 1663 when one document ironically mentions that 'the palace is almost reduced to perfection'. The structure was intended for

Strenghtofframe (dreamstime)

Omnipresent winged lion: symbol of the Venetian Republic that ruled Verona for three centuries

Case di Mazzanti e Volto Barbaro

042 A

Piazza delle Erbe 24–26, Verona
1200–1500

With its charming multi-layered façade, relaxed rhythm, and galleries under sweeping cornices, the Houses of Mazzanti are classic landmarks in photos of Verona. The site's main features are the allegoric frescoes by Alberto Cavalli (sixteenth century), stylistically reminiscent of those of his teacher, Giulio Romano. Since the sixteenth century, Verona earned its Latin nickname: *Urbs Picta,* or 'painted city'. Its many painted façades were highly visible in town until the unfortunate contamination of car pollution. This site features one of the city's rarest still-visible examples. Here, too, is a picturesque courtyard façade, which was saved by the conservative restoration trend that triumphed in Verona following the Second World War. The court maintains this stylish and ungentrified look with its steep staircase connecting galleries. It is easy to imagine how just 100 years ago people flocked to this marble well to retrieve fresh water. Now known as Case Mazzanti, it was referred to as Scaligeri's Place in the thirteenth century. The Scaligeri lord Mastino I Della Scala was stabbed to death in 1277 in the charming and narrow passage called Volto Barbaro. Today, a plaque memorialises this event. At this site, too, is a lovely neo-Gothic iron streetlamp featuring a staircase from the late nineteenth century – a symbol of the Scala family and Verona.

Courtyard with a dwell

Sergey Nikitin–Rimsky

Sergey Nikitin–Rimsky

Evgenia Fezenko (dramatina)

Sergey Nikitin-Rimsky

Fontana della Madonna Verona

Piazza delle Erbe 26, Verona
1368

 043 A

Cansignorio not only built his own beautiful Gothic tomb, but also left behind a fountain named 'Madonna Verona' in the main market square where his beloved citizens could wash their hands. The fountain, though, is surprisingly modest, and is in fact half recycled. A Roman bath made of red marble was repurposed and crowned with a Roman female torso.

The statue's missing head, arms, and crown were later added when the fountain was finally erected. Under the queen that symbolises the city itself, you may see faces of the four rulers of the city: the legendary Vero, Alboino of the Lombards, Berengario, and, again, the Madonna. In today's Verona, there is a lady endearingly called Madonna di Verona, whose nickname originated from her identical appearance to the statue. She owns a cult bar with a dark antiquarian-styled interior (Via Don Bassi 4) which is open at night.

Sinagoga di Verona

Via Portici 3, Verona
Ettore Fagiuoli
1864, 1929

044 A

Beginning in 1600, Jewish people in Verona were forced into a ghetto, just as they were in Venice, where the term 'ghetto' was coined. The densely populated neighbourhood with its small streets, next to Piazza delle Erbe, fell victim to gentrification processes during the late 1920s. Verona's most popular architect, Ettore Fagiuoli, was invited to rebuild the city's synagogue. He raised a barrel vault, adding its current enigmatic façade with a marble triumphal portal decorated with six bas-relief panels, which are surmounted by the Tablets of the Law.

Sergey Nikitin-Rimsky

Banca Nazionale del Lavoro (BNL) Verona Headquarters »

045 A

Via Giuseppe Mazzini 18, Verona
Ettore Fagiuoli
1938

This superbly sculpted four-storey cube, with three identical façades and a menacing eagle, is the former headquarters for the local labour bank. With its protruding cornice, supported by closely spaced indents, it is one of the city's most imposing architectural additions from the 1930s. With a synagogue just behind it (see 044: Sinagoga di Verona) and ancient Jewish tower-houses not far off, the bank was the last piece of the ghetto reconstruction that began in 1924 and concluded after the imposition of Mussolini's racial laws.

Sergey Nikitin-Rimsky

A

RnDmS (iStock)

Casa di Giulietta (Juliet's House)

046 A

Via Cappello 23, Verona
Antonio Avena (reconstruction)
1300, 1937–1940

Hollywood's MGM Studios came to Verona to shoot *Romeo and Juliet* in 1935. In essence, they were shown a shabby old house in the courtyard on Cappello Street, which guides traditionally called 'Juliet's House'. According to local historians, a certain Dal Cappello family lived here in the Middle Ages, which is where Via Cappello gets its name. It's likely that these were the descendants of the Cappelletti family that Dante met in his *Inferno*. The name was later used in Bandello's original version of *Romeo and Juliet* and was eventually turned to the 'Capulets' in Shakespeare's legendary play. At this historical site, however, the Americans did not find anything suitable for a romantic movie. The court was a horse stable, with a strong odour and cheap lodgings. Thus, the Californian cineastes departed, choosing instead to shoot everything in Hollywood. Professor Antonio Avena, director of city museums from 1915 to 1955, watched the Hollywood movie and believed it was time to create something for the city's tourists to enjoy. He changed the round arch doorway into the blunt one. He closed some windows and redesigned others as two-cusped Venetian arches. To send it home, he put a Gothic rose window on the ground floor. And the balcony, of course! Instead of a twentieth-century shaky structure with railings, he assembled a new stone one using original Gothic pieces, which he found in the courtyard of his museum. Historically artificial, but lovely nonetheless. The city's cultural elites were weary of this pastiche, and the Supervisor of the Cultural Heritage protested. But Avena was faster. His creation turned out to be the most famous and popular place in the city – beating even the ancient Arena – and it continues to attract tourists from all over the world. A statue of Juliet by Nereo Costantini was installed in 1969 and visitors touch her breast for good luck. Curiously, a balcony never appears in Shakespeare's version of the play – this detail was actually reimagined later by performers and directors. But where would the story be without it?

Statue of Juliet in the centre (under green bush); Avena's balcony and windows on the right

sphraner (iStock)

Street façade of Juliet's House (before Avena)

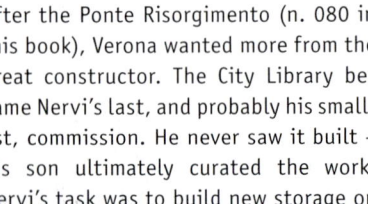

Sergey Nikitin-Rimsky

Biblioteca Civica

Via Cappello 43, Verona
Pier Luigi Nervi
1973–1980

047 A

After the Ponte Risorgimento (n. 080 in this book), Verona wanted more from the great constructor. The City Library became Nervi's last, and probably his smallest, commission. He never saw it built – his son ultimately curated the work. Nervi's task was to build new storage on a site where the Church of San Sebastiano stood before bombings during the Second World War. The façade has already been transported and attached to San Nicolò in 1951 by Pietro Gazzola. Nervi proposed a six-storey block on conical pillars, leaving the ground floor open, following the Le Corbusier principle. The building might be good to hold books, but its rugged and anaemic appearance spoils the view of such a beautiful and old street like Via Cappello, especially given its location next to one of the city's main tourist attractions: Juliet's House. The Veronese cultural elite protested against it, yet city hall believed in Nervi's brand. Recently, the space between the pylons has been glazed – now looking more commercial than aggressive. Inside the library, the interiors vary from classicism to postmodernism. Visitors do not require a card to peruse the library's books.

Sergey Nikitin–Rimsky

Sergey Nikitin–Rimsky

Sergey Nikitin-Rımsky

Porta Leoni (Gate of Lions)

048 A

Via Leoni 1, Verona
1st century BCE (built),
1st century CE (embellishment),
Libero Cecchini 1977–1982

Only half of this ancient gate's façade is now visible. It was originally part of the Roman defence system on Via Claudia Augusta, a road that connected the Alps to Central Italy. The gate had a square-plan structure of 17 metres on each side and a rectangular central courtyard. The corners of the structure had two towers of 16 sides with a diameter of 7 metres each,

guarding the surroundings. The lower part is similar to that of Porta Borsari (see 017: Porta Borsari). An upper exedra is decorated with twisted columns, which are also present on Borsari gate. Originally built almost completely in tuff and bricks, it was monumentalised with Valpantena marble during the empire period. Excavations began in the area in 1974, followed by the creation of an archaeological zone to better understand the organisation of the walls. The Vicolo Leoni features a wonderful portico of Palazzo Verità (then Bianchini, Salgari, Tedeschi). Some murals still remain in the tiny courtyard.

Sergey Nikitin–Rimsky

Dogana di San Fermo

Via Dogana, Verona
Alessandro Pompei
1746, 1792 (pier)

049 A

The area between Stradone San Fermo and the river stands in silence, as if it is somehow outside of time. This is the site of the city's epic neoclassic customs house. It was designed by Alessandro Pompei, a lover of ancient architecture who worshiped Michele Sanmicheli and even lived in a palace he constructed across the river (see 117: Palazzo Pompei). At the customs house, Pompei designed a magnificent peristyle featuring tall columns at its front, with a two-storey portico on each of its minor sides. Eighteenth century Verona's greatest public building, it was originally intended as a sanitary control for goods delivered along the river. Completed in only a year, it managed to

Sergey Nikitin-Rimsky

A pier on the Adige

cause a dramatic scandal with the Venetian government. According to a story recently discovered by historian Arturo Sandrini, Venetian officials insisted on cost efficient and pragmatic buildings. Not only did the Verona City Council completely ignore this, but they even built the customs house without their leaders' knowledge and inscribed it with celebrations of local pride – with no mention of Venice. Upon visiting the site, Venetian supervisors found the building's layout inappropriate for its needs – there were too many small rooms for private merchants, and it lacked the expected infrastructure for a public building. The fury of Venice was such that work on the pier on the Adige River was halted and not finished until half a century later in 1792 when river commerce was in decline. The superintendence of cultural heritage now maintains an office here, and a canoe school uses the pier.

Sergey Nikitin-Rimsky

svarshik (iStock)

San Fermo Maggiore

050 A

Via Dogana 2, Verona
1065 (lower church),
mid-14th century (upper church, ceiling), 7th–8th centuries (bell tower)

Located right at the bustling crossroads of the old town, the Gothic apses of San Fermo strike viewers with the playfulness of a fairytale magician. The interior is dominated by a magnificent ceiling, one of the city's great architectural triumphs. Appearing like the hull of an overturned ship – symbolising the ship of salvation – the ceiling houses 416 portraits of saints. It took 35 years to complete. It was built from the wood of alpine larch and shaped by hundreds of carpenters under the direction of Fra Daniele Gusmerio. The patron saint, Guglielmo da Castelbarco, is portrayed together with Gusmerio on the triumphal arch over the altar. On the right by the entrance is a surprisingly whimsical rendition of the Resurrection: cheerful cherubs and the archangel seem almost indifferent to Christ. This sculpture is a monument to Nicolò Brenzoni by Nanni di Bartolo (1426), who fled to Verona from Florence because of his debts. Pisanello's dreamy Gothic fresco, featuring the Annunciation and urban fantasy, surrounds the sculpture. The lower church was built two centuries before and retains some of its striking original frescoes, like that of the Christ's Baptism. According to Shakespeare's story and Matteo Bandello's Italian original, this is where Romeo and Juliet died. Since Friar Laurence was a Franciscan monk, San Fermo Maggiore would have been his place of practice.

Sergey Nikitin-Rimsky

Monument to Nicolò Brenzoni

Andrea Bertozzi

Main entrance to the upper church

Sergey Nikitin-Rimsky

Upper church

Palazzo Beccherle

Stradone San Fermo 12, Verona
Giuseppe Barbieri
1818

Verona is famous for its beautiful court-yards, many of which are well-re-stored and open to visitors. Here at the Beccherle palace, it is possible to look into stunning two-level porticoes drowning in ivy and featuring a charming collection of old cars. The building was designed by Barbieri (see 003: Palazzo Barbieri), uniting several earlier structures.

Sergey Nikitin–Rimsky

Sergey Nikitin–Rimsky

Palazzo Turchi

Via S. Cosimo 4, Verona
15th century,
1571–1579 (façade)

052 A

Irony is not a common dialect in old architecture. The Moors decorated Campo do Mori in Venice for a long time, while Giulio Romano, with his Hall of the Giants in the Te Palace in Mantua, legalised it for patrician use. In Verona, it went out into the streets. A jurisconsult and humanist, Pio Turchi built a new façade at his family palace immediately after the battle of Lepanto against the Turks. He pompously decided to decorate the palace with puppets donned in turbans – a pun on his own surname, Turchi. Scholars believe that he followed the concept of the Palazzo Omenoni ('big men') in Milan, which was built only slightly earlier by the sculptor Leone Leoni. Turchi's attempt at humour didn't bode well for him. One hot summer night, people cut the heads off his puppets and brought them to the Piazza delle Erbe, where the heads of criminals were normally flaunted. The jokesters were never caught.

Sergey Nikitin–Rimsky

Sergey Nikitin–Rimsky

Sergey Nikitin–Rimsky

Cristina Romanello

Banco Popolare di Verona (now Banco BPM)

053 A

Piazza Nogara 2, Verona
Carlo Scarpa, Arrigo Rudi
1973–1981

Unhurried and meditative, Carlo Scarpa was not concerned with money. He started his career building a bank office in the small town of Tarvisio. Though in 1973, when he received this commission – one of his last – the Veneto region, Italy, and indeed the world were all different places. What reigns over this complex is its resemantisation of materials and elements, meaning employment of good, old, and valuable materials, such as a red marble, but treating them to look like concrete or even plastic elements. An example is the industrial-looking railings for the stairs. Scarpa tried his best to surprise his fellow bankers, for example, by making a futuristic corridor wrapped with wooden finishes. Scarpa's thoughtful manner hardly corresponds with the nature of the cash flow.

The thoughtfully odd façade tries to speak out this indigestion with an impossible set of unevenly-located round windows and sporting glass boxes. It was an enormously expensive project, but you have a feeling of a fish humming on the sand. The façade was finished when Scarpa was still alive, but his pupil and assistant Arrigo Rudi had to complete the rest. How did the town react? Very well. Architect Scarpa was an international superstar, and his illuminated client, ex-mayor Giorgio Zanotto, was the chief of the bank.

asquimo/tumbex

Palazzo dei Diamanti (Palazzo Cappella Sansebastiani, Bellini, Carnesali)

Via Enrico Noris 1, Verona
1582

054 A

From Cremona to Moscow, diamond-cut ashlar façades were one of the favourite themes at the turn of the fifteenth and sixteenth centuries. A century later, this trend reached Verona, where Camillo Cappella was building a house for his family. His anonymous builders laid a friendly three-storey block, clearly inspired by the palace of Sigismondo d'Este in Ferrara (Biagio Rossetti, 1492). Even the balcony at the corner was neatly copied. Tropical generosity reigns over the entrance, with its bouquet of Ionic and Doric pilasters and flying Victorias. Today, however, only one is left to imagine how lively it must have looked when the façade was freshly painted.

Fabrizio Mauro

Loggia Arvedi »

Via Giuseppe Mazzini 48, Verona
Giuseppe Barbieri
1816

055 A

Sergey Nikitin-Rimsky

Connecting the Arena and Piazza delle Erbe, Via Mazzini is the high street of Verona. It was cleaned and cobbled at the beginning of the nineteenth century. One of its highlights is this elegant lodge by Giuseppe Barbieri (see 120: Monumental Cemetery and 003: Palazzo Barbieri). The owner, Arvedi, was a wealthy wool merchant. A slightly advanced portico with the ground floor and the god Mercury in the keystone is surmounted by the elliptical loggia with ionic columns. Here, Hercules fights the Nemean lion in the tympanum. To feel the difference between Barbieri's French precision and the old Veronese neoclassicism, pay a visit to the relaxed volumes of 1750s Palazzo Sambonifacio Tedeschi, which is now Hotel Accademia (Adriano Cristofali, Via Scala 12, 1750). It is owned by the Zenatello family, whose ancestor, the tenor singer Giovanni Zenatello, created and sponsored the Arena di Verona Opera Festival 100 years ago.

Sergey Nikitin-Rimsky

Palazzo Mosconi (formerly Headquarters of Banca Cattolica del Veneto)

056 A

Corte Farina, Verona
Adriano Cristofali 18th century,
Libero Cecchini, Silvano Zorzi (engineer)
1969–1973

Behind the narrow marble windows of the block on Via Catullo 3 lies what is likely Verona's most famous brutalist interior. It boasts a magnificent atrium with spiral walkways and oculi that open in the ceiling. Enormous windows reveal intriguing suprematist compositions, which can now only be viewed from the courtyard. Libero Cecchini took a bombed eighteenth-century palace with Roman remains in the basement and reinvented it for Veneto's leading bank institution in the brutalist marble style. The Catholic Bank of Verona, however, has abandoned the building for the past ten years now. New owners have since attempted to adapt it for apartments, despite protests from influential architects and the architectural public at large. The fate of the interiors remains unknown.

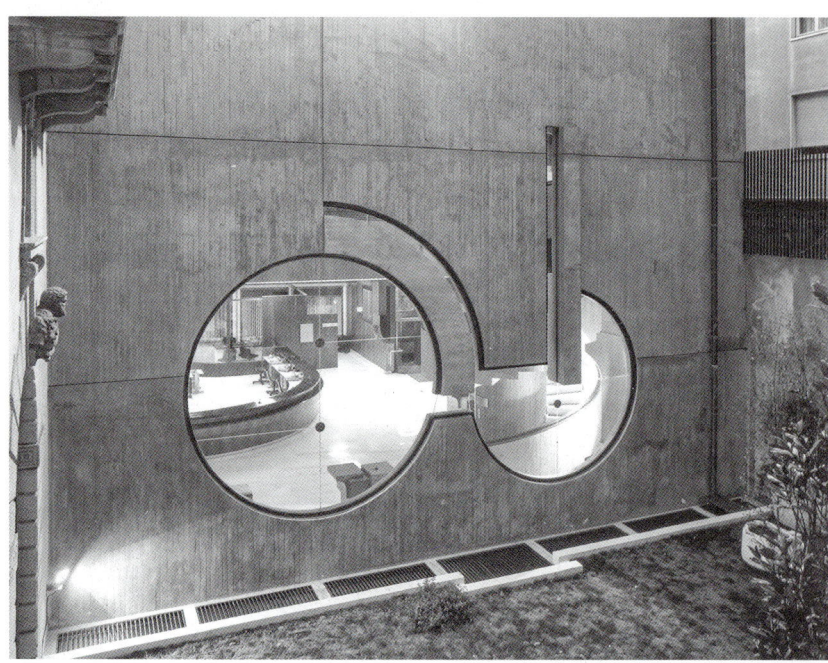

Studio Cecchini

Cecchini

Studio Cecchini

Palazzo Supercinema

Via Giuseppe Mazzini 6, Verona
Francesco Banterle,
Mario Dezzutti (interiors)
1928

 057 A

While it may have once been common to claim Italy lacked art deco, scholars have more recently begun to recognise traces of the style's poetics and palette in the architecture of cinemas and public buildings from the 1920s and 1930s. On the site of the old Verona ghetto, one such building is the Supercinema that opened in 1928 to seat 2,300 spectators. Today, as department stores continuously replace each other inside of the building, one is left to only imagine its once-glittering interiors painted in lemon, blue, and silver. A Turinese man, Mario Dezzutti, created these interiors for the company's owner, who was also from Turin. This success earned him another commission for the red-and-white Ponte delle Navi (1934). It was Francesco Banterle's first experience in the neoclassical style, and the façades seem rather lifeless for such a grand construction. A graceful chest adorns the Supercinema's roof, which was originally conceived as a rooftop bar. Sadly, it has since forgone this original function.

Ingus Kruklitis (dreamstime)

Palazzo Ridolfi-Dalisca

Stradone Maffei, 3
Bernardino Brugnoli (likely)
16th century

Begun in 1545, this whitewashed palace was likely completed by Bernardino Brugnoli, the nephew of Michele Sanmicheli. It is now a State Scientific Lyceum named after Carlo Montanari. Destroyed by bombings on the night of 23 February 1945, the central hall and its fifteenth century fresco were spared. The fresco *Cavalcade of Pope Clement VII and Charles V, Holy Roman Emperor* by Domenico Riccio, however, was recently transferred to the Museum of Frescoes at Juliet's Tomb. A richly sculpted fireplace featuring a shy and playful Venus and Cupid – likely by Bartolomeo Ridolfi – has remained in the Aula Magna at the Lyceum.

Sergey Nikitin-Rimsky

Verona City
Route 2

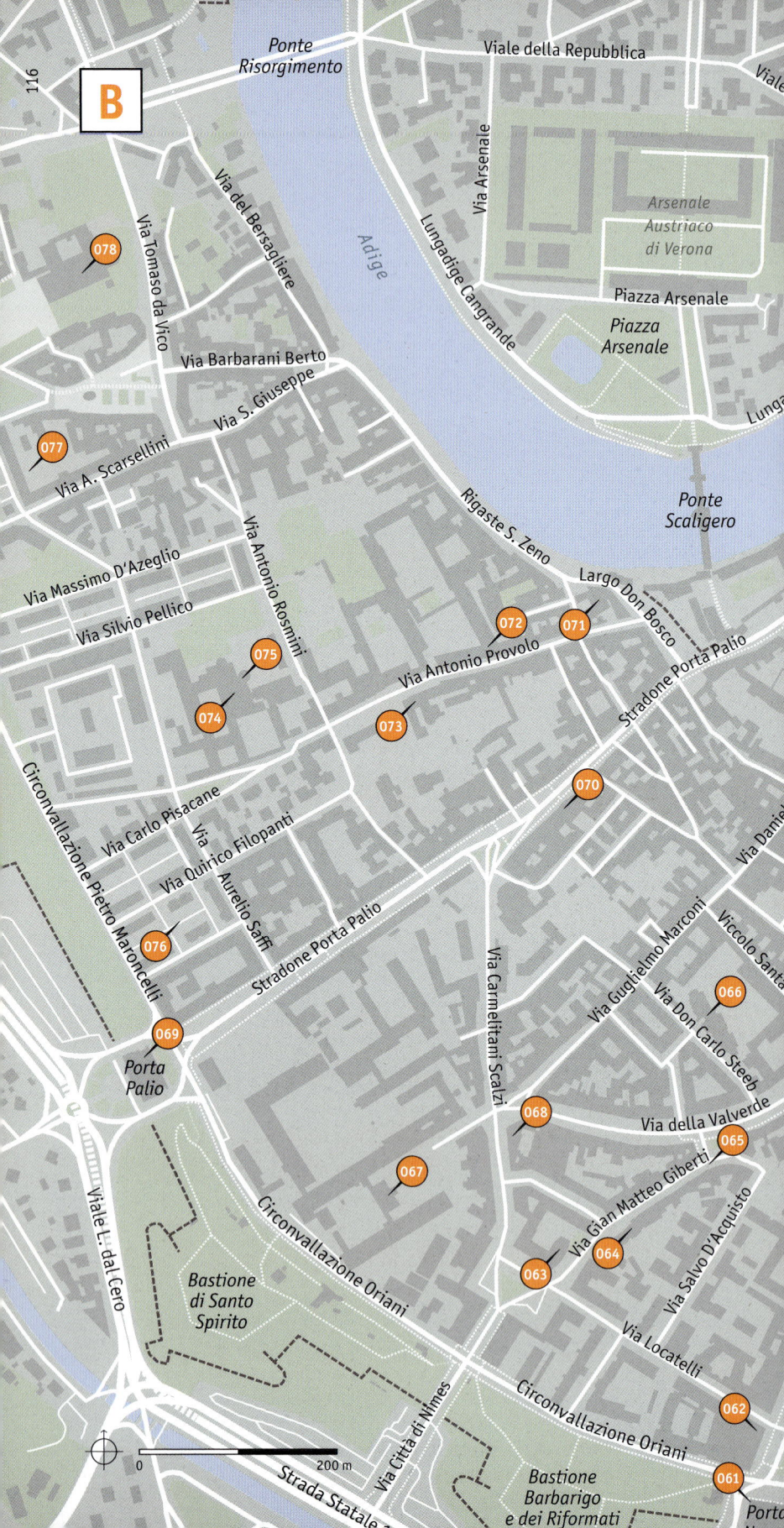

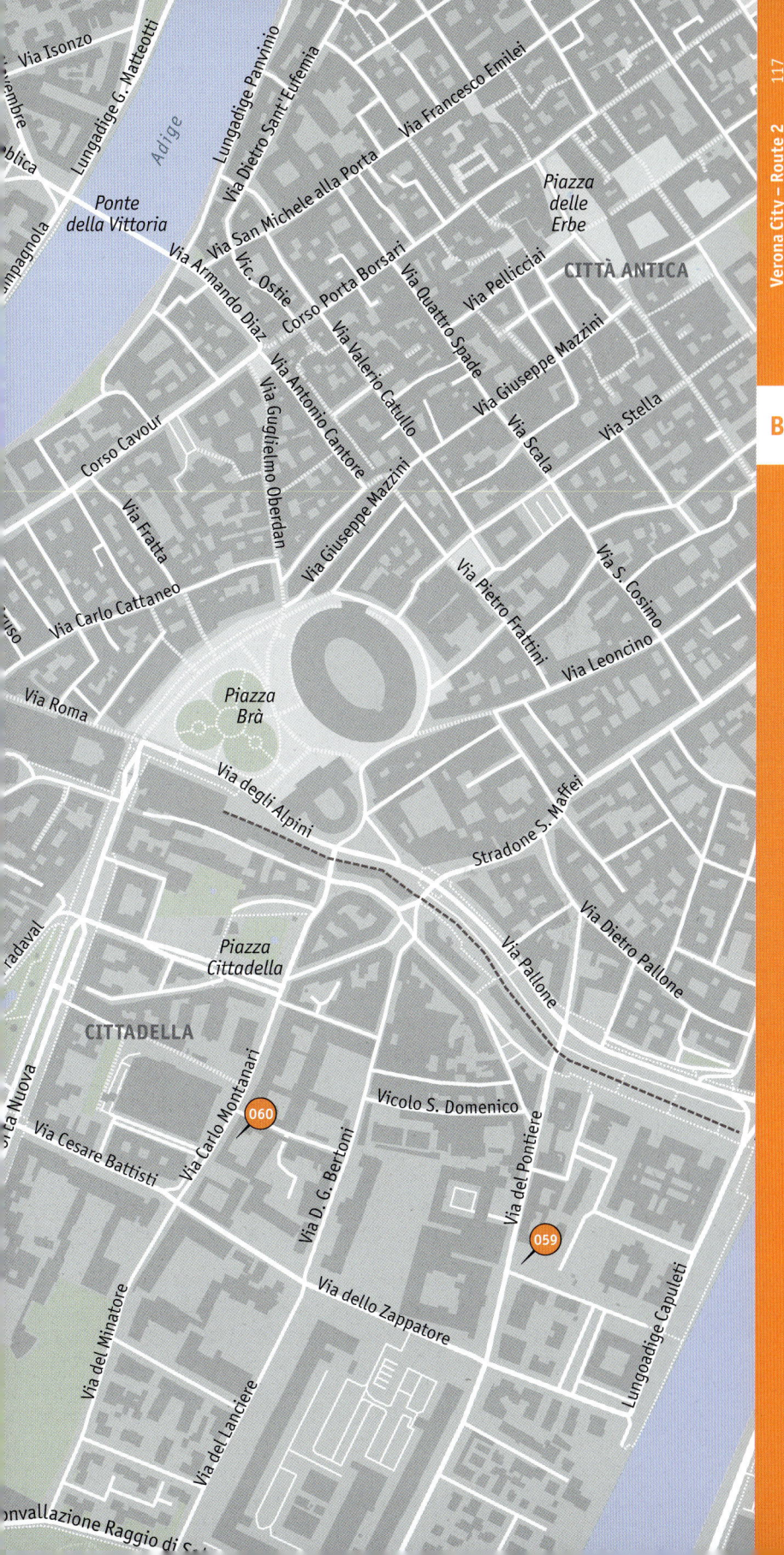

Adige

Via Isonzo

Lungadige G. Matteotti

Ponte
della Vittoria

Lungadige Panvinio

Via Dietro Sant'Eufemia

Via San Michele alla Porta

Via Francesco Emilei

Piazza
delle
Erbe

CITTÀ ANTICA

Via Armando Diaz

Vic. Ostie

Corso Porta Borsari

Via Quattro Spade

Via Pellicciai

Via Valerio Catullo

Via Giuseppe Mazzini

Via Antonio Cantore

Via Scala

Via Stella

Corso Cavour

Via Guglielmo Oberdan

Via Giuseppe Mazzini

Via Fratta

Via S. Cosimo

Via Carlo Cattaneo

Via Pietro Frattini

Via Leoncino

Via Roma

Piazza
Brà

Via degli Alpini

Stradone S. Maffei

Via Dietro Pallone

Piazza
Cittadella

Via Pallone

CITTADELLA

Via Carlo Montanari

060

Vicolo S. Domenico

Via Cesare Battisti

Via D. G. Bertoni

Via del Pontiere

059

Via dello Zappatore

Lungoadige Capuleti

Via del Minatore

Via del Lanciere

Sergey Nikitin–Rimsky

Tomba di Giulietta
(Juliet's Tomb)

Via Luigi da Porto 5, Verona
Antonio Avena (tomb installation)
1937

059 B

The double suicide of Shakespeare's heroes became the epitome of Romanticism, an era that thoroughly enjoyed celebrating glorious losers and bloody endings. Educated people from all over Europe wanted to see this site, including Madame de Stael, Lord Byron, Heinrich Heine, and Alfred de Musset. Those were the days when the remains of Abelard and Héloïse were brought to Paris, their tombs becoming a money-maker for the new Père-Lachaise cemetery. Nuns of the San Francesco al Corso convent were happy to show foreigners an empty and anonymous marble sarcophagus – perhaps of Roman origin – but that was enough to drive Romantics crazy. Byron took some pieces for his daughter, while Napoleon's widow,

Maria Luisa of Habsburg Lorraine, had earrings and a necklace made using pieces of it. Archduke John of Austria reportedly bought the sarcophagus lid for a steep price. However, this was not enough for mass tourism in the twentieth century. Verona's museum director Antonio Avena realised this when he met Holliwood director George Cukor, who came to Verona to shoot *Romeo and Juliet*. Thus, Avena created a new noble entrance to the cloister and moved the tomb underground. 'Probably a cellar, disguised in imitation of the crypt,' as it was disdainfully described by the Superintendent of Cultural Heritage who was Avena's enemy in those days. Yet millions of tourists sent a different message. Licisco Magagnato also opened the Museum of Frescoes here in 1973 – a parade of painted walls brought from various palaces of the town once known as the Urbs Picta, or 'Painted City'. Valter Rossi, a colleague of Scarpa and Rudi, redesigned the museum in 2012.

Palazzo Verità Montanari – Accademia di Belle Arti

Via Carlo Montanari 5, Verona
1583
Libero Cecchini 1950s
Otto Tognetti, Giorgio Vincita 1985

060 B

Here is a lovely suburban villa. With the main house tucked away from the main road, the house is enclosed by a wall decorated with playful satyrs. It transmits a harmonious extravagance. Its architect was a representative from the artistic circle of Domenico Curtoni or Bernardino Brugnoli, both nephews of Sanmicheli. The keystone of the main entrance has a bust of Hieronimus Veritas, a famous member of his family, which the original owner,

Count Giacomo Verità, wanted to establish as a central symbol for his family. Built in the same period as the Turchi Palace, this structure, with its masks and cherubs at the keystone and consoles, demonstrates a sense of light-hearted humour. Traces of frescoes between the windowsills indicate that the façade was initially fully frescoed. The liberal patriot and Risorgimento supporter Carlo Montanari lived here until he was captured and killed by the Austrians in 1853. Later in the nineteenth century, the house became an art institute and has since been renovated several times. Libero Cecchini restored the façade and rebuilt the stables. Otto Tognetti and Giorgio Vincita were involved in reworking the interiors of the second floor of the main house.

Verona In

Porta Nuova

Corso Porta Nuova, 1
Michele Sanmicheli
1532–1540, 1852

061 B

After Sanmicheli returned to his hometown to become superintendent of military construction, he received orders to construct three gates, the first of which was Porta Nuova. The Renaissance biographer and brilliant architect Giorgio Vasari asserted that there was 'never before another work of greater grandeur nor better understanding'. Today, however, only the central section is the Sanmicheli original, while the two side gates were built in the nineteenth century

to accommodate increased local traffic. Along with construction of the Porta Nuova, Sanmicheli opened a new street heading directly to the Arena. After 400 years, in the 1930s, this became a central new axis of the city known as Corso Porta Nuova.

Fabrizio Mauro

Sergey Nikitin-Rimsky

Camera del Commercio
Corso Porta Nuova, 96
Libero Cecchini
1965

062 B

The brick rationalist block of the Fascist Party's youth wing (the GIL, Gioventù Italiana del Littorio), built by Ettore Fagiuoli, once stood just across the street from Porta Nuova. Bombed but not destroyed in the Second World War, it was nonetheless later dismantled to ruins. The leading architect of post-war Verona, Libero Cecchini, won the heart of the developer. Legend has it that it was intended to be a condominium, but when construction began in 1966, it was ultimately bought by the Chamber of Commerce for new offices. The new owners demanded a big hall to host a stock exchange, as well as another meeting hall for members. Ready to please his customers, Cecchini found a solution: he excavated a part of the courtyard in order to host meeting halls underground, with the stock exchange on top of it. Inside the peaceful courtyard there is a view of the reverse of the building's curvy volumetrics, as well as a more modest condominium from the same period. With 3 by 3 metre panels made of marble, the façade pays tribute to Verona's most successful trade. In fact, Cecchini's own family were marblers.

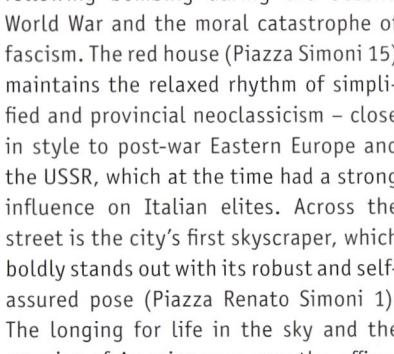

Fabrizio Mauro

063 B

First skyscraper and other buildings on Piazza Simoni

Piazza Renato Simoni, Verona
Lucio Arneri, Luigi Sabelli
1959

This piazza is named after Renato Simoni, a Verona-born critic, playwright, and co-writer of Puccini's *Turandot*. The square is a bit like an architectural theatre, with popular styles representing a variety of political sentiments. Most of the buildings here are from the 1950s and 1960s, when the square became the new access gate to town thanks to its reconstruction following bombing during the Second World War and the moral catastrophe of fascism. The red house (Piazza Simoni 15) maintains the relaxed rhythm of simplified and provincial neoclassicism – close in style to post-war Eastern Europe and the USSR, which at the time had a strong influence on Italian elites. Across the street is the city's first skyscraper, which boldly stands out with its robust and self-assured pose (Piazza Renato Simoni 1). The longing for life in the sky and the promise of America won over the offices that first agreed to call this building

Sergey Nikitin–Rimsky

Residential buildings on Piazza Simoni 15

Fabrizio Mauro

Verona's first skyscraper on Piazza Simoni 1

Piazza Simoni, via Gian Matteo Giberti 11 on the background

home. After 70 years, it is now the highest residential condominium in Verona at 55 metres: 15 floors above ground and two levels below, which act as cellars and garages. The slender eight-angle plan resembles Italy's most famous skyscraper and the symbol of *il boom economico*: Milan's Pirelli Tower made by Gio Ponti. Here, however, Arneri and Sabelli opted to add brick in an effort to make the building more Veronese and to distinguish it from other, more 'Western' shopping centres. The brown building across the square (Piazza Simoni 31) gives the vibe of a serious technocrat from the 1970s, though slightly poisoned with Roberto Venturi's smile. The porch connects the brown house to n. 40, a heavily balconied structure vested in marble. There is an office building with an elegant arched passage (Via Gian Matteo Giberti 11) on the corner with Via Locatelli. Its square façade is entirely white, while its other – along Via Locatelli – is made of red brick. The building's architect remains unknown. Nonetheless, its well-balanced neoclassicism broadcasts nostalgic tones from the ambitious 1930s when Italy proclaimed itself an empire. Indeed, before the war, the whole of the Arsenal and Borgo Trento area in Verona was once planned to be built with similar white palaces with porticoes.

Sergey Nikitin–Rimsky

Sergey Nikitin–Rimsky

Residential building on Piazza Simoni 31

Fabrizio Mauro

Hotel Giberti

Via Gian Matteo Giberti 7,
Verona
Anonymous 1980s,
*Antonio Munarin and
Giampietro Pavan (renovation)*
2013

064 B

Glazed in dark burgundy glass, this hotel (formerly Montresor) still seems an unlikely fit for a small city like Verona. A legacy of the Italian 1980s, it emits sentiment of wealth, self-confidence, and ambition. Originally a school building, it was converted into a hotel to be influenced by great masters from Verona and beyond. Postmodernism reigns prominently over the whole structure. On the right is a ground floor window modelled after Boullée's unbuilt masterpiece, the Cenotaph for Newton. The lobby has a fabulous golden door assorted with white marble Cubist bas-reliefs, making its 1980s origins unfathomable. At last, the courtyard offers a lovely vision of the metal terraces and stairs that adorn the structure. It is rumoured among hotel staff that the building is awaiting reconstruction. One can only hope to witness this treasure before then. Verona-based architects Antonio Munarin and Giampietro Pavan gave this postmodern building's interior a new face in 2013.

Hotel Giberti/M&P Architetti

Largo Carlo Caldera
1960s

065 B

Via Luigia Poloni 1

Sergey Nikitin-Rimsky

To get a feel for the Verona of the 1960s, try this small square dominated by the Veronese headquarters of the Automobile Club d'Italia, once an envied organisation. The dynamism and welcoming spirit of the façade with loggias are juxtaposed to the slightly curved condo on the other side of this largo (Caldera 11). The ULSS hospital (Via Luigia Poloni 1) fits in with its red brick walls. A monument to the fallen motorist, in a paradoxical pose, stands in the middle of the largo. The Don Steeb Retirement Home is across the corner.

Automobile Club d'Italia

Fabrizio Mauro

Largo Carlo Caldera 11

Fabrizio Mauro

VETRO

Don Steeb Retirement Home

Via Don Carlo Steeb 4, Verona
Luigi Calcagni, Luciano Cenna
1958

066 B

This piece of architecture is not exactly lucky: in London or Milan, its brutalist spirit and rough brick would have announced itself as a manifesto. In Verona, however, it appears as an outcast. Rather unexpectedly for its brutal appearance, it houses a catholic charity institution. Religious authorities were known to commission quite interesting constructions throughout the 1960s and 1970s. The plan here is nervously carved out on an uneven plot: balconies pile up on top of each other like honeycomb. This is one of the first realisations, and perhaps the most expressive work, of the Cenna-Calcagni duo. It was inspired by their favourites: James Stirling and Alvar Aalto. As Cenna explained to me, 'In the second half of the 1950s, only condominiums were built, and the projects were in the hands of architects much older than us. Fortunately, we won the competition to build the Don Steeb nursing home and we started to work'.

Fabrizio Mauro

Fabrizio Mauro

Sergey Nikitin–Rimsky

Ministry of the Defence Offices

067 B

Piazza Santo Spirito 13, Verona
1850s–1860s

Just a few steps from Via Giovanni della Casa is a quaint piazza-turned-carpark, embraced by a military structure in the yellow colour that was characteristic of Austrian military structures. This building is another survivor from the late days of the Austro-Hungarian Empire, when Verona had become a crucial point for the defence of the southern borders. A porch and turret now watch over pedestrians with a toyish seriousness. With some imagination, one might be able to picture a garrison marching here, even though national armies are a thing of the past given that Italy's neighbours are now its Schengen allies.

Condominium Red Brut

068 B

Via Giovanni della Casa 23, Verona
1970s–1980s

Sergey Nikitin–Rimsky

What a building! Its concrete façade is painted in Pompeian red – the only wink to its brick neighbours. Yet its heroic and masculine appearance doesn't care to please its middle-class surroundings. Instead, it flaunts rhythmic variations and rounded corners. This is evident of an architectural epoch when computer-assisted design could be only imagined, but inspired and organic compositions could still be found. In those days, provincial developers dared to manifest their artistic ambitions. Now, the paint on this building is left crumbling, which somehow strengthens its brutal appearance. 'Barbaric, robust, abandoned to the impetus of feeling' were the words of Giancarlo De Carlo in his praise of Mario Ridolfi's Viale Etiopia complex in Rome. These same words might also celebrate this house by an unknown Veronese designer.

Sergey Nikitin–Rimsky

City façade

Country façade

Porta Palio

Piazzetta Porta Palio, Verona
Michele Sanmicheli
1550–1571

069 B

Michele Sanmicheli was born to a family of Veronese stonemasons in 1484 in the days of the Venetian Republic. He lost both his parents when he was 19 years old. With his only surviving brother in a convent, he sold his property and moved to Rome, probably to work as an assistant to Antonio Sangallo. He subsequently gained recognition for both church and military architecture in various towns in the Papal State. In 1527, he decided to visit his hometown and Venice, partly out of an interest in Venetian fortifications. Legend has it that soon after he was arrested on suspicion of being a Roman spy. At that time Venice was in a period of difficult relations with the Papacy, so a visitor from Rome would certainly have seemed shady. As soon as his intentions became clear, however, he planned not to return to a Rome destroyed by Charles V. Instead, Sanmicheli was nominated to be the Venetian superintendent for military construction. He created three gates in his hometown of Verona: Palio, Nuova, and San Giorgio, two of which are considered Renaissance classics. But Sanmicheli was a slow-working man. The Porta Palio gate, for instance, inched forward in construction and, to this day, has never been completed as planned. Sanmicheli intended to add an upper deck to overlook the surroundings, though it has never come to fruition. Nevertheless, with its epic rusticated columns and chiaro-scuro effects, the Porta Palio drives architecture lovers crazy. Its fanbase begins with his contemporary Giorgio Vasari, who claimed it to be 'architettura nuova, bella e bizzarra'. Porta Palio has managed to survive throughout the centuries without alterations, and for a very specific reason: this fantastic entrance to the city turned out to be rather unnecessary and has thus been unused for most of its existence. This has earned it its local nickname, *porta stupa*. The name 'Palio,' however, comes from an ancient game by the same name: a famous race through the streets of Verona, mentioned in Canto XV of Dante's *Inferno*.

B

Palazzo Orti Manara

Stradone Porta Palio 31,
Verona

Luigi Trezza

1784

This palace might be the main attraction in almost any other town in Veneto, but here in Verona, the Palazzo Orti Manara is just one of many eighteenth century patrician homes. Soon after its completion, architect Luigi Trezza became the leader of Verona's neoclassicism. Francesco Zoppi and Angelo Sartori sculpted idyllic reliefs and giants that pretend to support the balcony. The carefully restored lobby can be visited during regular opening hours. The piano nobile is well-frescoed and filled with statues of Roman Emperors. The building's rear façade (Vicolo Carmelitani Scalzi) is in an entirely different style, however, with its whitewashed walls and baroque balustrades – perhaps reminiscent of Spain. The palace's patrons, the Orti Manara family, were serious collectors of coins and other archaeological finds. Giovanni Girolamo Orti Manara was the city's mayor from 1838 to 1850. They are still remembered today in Verona.

Sergey Nikitin-Rimsky

Sergey Nikitin-Rimsky

Sergey Nikitin–Rimsky

Chiesa di San Zeno in Oratorio **071** **B**

Via S. Zeno in Oratorio 13, Verona
7th–8th centuries

A seemingly tiny and cosy basilica, this church includes a gothic rose, three naves, and even an atrium-garden with olives. The church coolly reminds one of early Christian times. San Zenetto, as locals endearingly call it, was probably built over a Roman sepulchral building and rebuilt after the 1177 earthquake. The church houses the river stone on which, according to tradition, Saint Zeno used to fish.

Sergey Nikitin–Rimsky

Fabrizio Mauro

B

Fabrizio Mauro

Istituto Don Bosco

072 B

Stradone Antonio Provolo 16,
Verona
Architect and year unknown

This long, laborious façade is not a factory,
even if it looks like one. The brickwork presents a geometric version of art nouveau
with simplified Moorish ornamentation – a
style you may find popular with synagogues
in Italy. It is possible to enter the idyllic courtyard, pass a graceful pavilion, and
witness an arcade twined with ivy. There is
even a basketball court. Sadly the name of
the architect is unknown, as in many other
twentieth century ecclesiastical buildings.

Sergey Nikitin–Rimsky

Virgin Mary Institute for the Deaf and Mute

073 B

Stradone Antonio Provolo 43,
Verona
1960s

Here is a classic example of the high modernist style that dominated Verona in the 1960s and 1970s: constructed with top-quality materials and delicate finishes. While the main façade is relatively simple, the institute's more extravagant upper tiers one may explore in the adjacent school courtyard. Its balconies perch out of the walls and enter into the green cool of the garden. The street's namesake is Antonio Provolo, an Italian educator and singer who founded a Catholic school for deaf children here in 1830. This later evolved into the present building, the Virgin Mary Institute.

Sergey Nikitin-Rimsky

Sergey Nikitin-Rimsky

Sergey Nikitin–Rimsky

First cloister

Chiesa di San Bernardino

Stradone Antonio Provolo 28,
Verona
15th century

074 B

Occupying an entire quarter with three cloisters, blossoming with cypresses, and roses, the Franciscan convent of San Bernardino welcomes guests with an entrance gate reminiscent of De Chirico's paintings. Inside this late-Gothic church are frescoes by Giolfino and Morone, as well as the Pellegrini Chapel. Ask to see Sala Morone with its celebrated frescoes showing beautiful friars (all martyred in various ways) across the landscape. It took nine years for Domenico and Francesco Morone to complete these masterpieces.

Sergey Nikitin–Rimsky

Sala Morone

Sergey Nikitin-Rimsky

Cappella Pellegrini
in chiesa di San Bernardino

075 B

Stradone Antonio Provolo 28,
Verona

Michele Sanmicheli,
Antonio and Jacopo Marastoni,
Bartolomeo Giuliari
1527–1538, 1538–1559, 1793

Margherita Pellegrini, a noblewoman, lost her 18-year-old son Nicolò de Guareschi, who was the only male heir of her family. To leave a memory of the De Guareschi family, she invited Michele Sanmicheli, just back from Rome, to produce a funeral chapel that would 'overshadow all those built in the city'. Sanmicheli's proposal was a success, but he was slow and meditative and always had many other projects going on simultaneously. She fired him in 1538. Two stone masters, Antonio and Jacopo Marastoni, were employed to continue, but the task wasn't an easy one: it took 20 years to complete the chapel and dome. Margherita never lived to see it completed. Two centuries later, Bartolomeo Giuliari, a Pellegrini relative with enormous respect for Sanmicheli, arrived to finally realise a radical restoration. This immaculate white space recalls both the Pantheon and Tempietto of Bramante in Rome. Remember, however, that we are in Verona, and thus the architect adorned the chapel with elements of the city's famous Roman monuments. These include twisted columns and niches of the Borsari gates and the pediment of Arco Dei Gavi, believed to be created by Vitruvius. On observing the chapel from the outside, from Via Antonio Rosmini, it looks a bit like an industrial cistern propped up against the church.

Complesso residenziale di Porta Palio

076 B

Via Angela Brofferio,
Via Carlo Pisacane,
Via Aurelio Saffi, Verona
1913

Here is a group of ten four-storey residential buildings, still owned by the city and provided to people in need of housing. Its only decorations are shutters and humble stucco detailing. Behind the simple fences and closed gates are the green courtyards curated by the municipality. Next door is the San Bernardino Complex, built from 1926 to 1934 (Via M. D'Azeglio, 1-29).

Sergey Nikitin-Rimsky

Fabrizio Mauro

Fabrizio Mauro

Fabrizio Mauro

B

Fabrizio Mauro

Fabrizio Mauro

Palazzo ATER (formerly IACP) 077 B
Vicolo Fossetto, 1/c,d,e, Verona
Otto Tognetti
1986

It might be said that public institutions should be kept modest. But not in Verona. This residential construction company preferred to construct a magnificent headquarters: two marble battleships clashing over a vast atrium. Quintessential of postmodernism, it was designed by Otto Tognetti, who has managed to keep it local by playing with layers of white and red marble, characteristic of the Romanesque and Gothic styles that define the city's Scaliger roots.

Fabrizio Mauro

Fabrizio Mauro

Fabrizio Mauro

Abbazia di San Zeno

Piazza San Zeno
10th–12th centuries,
1178 (bell tower),
Libero Cecchini (restoration)
1984–2000

078 B

This cathedral must be viewed from different angles. It appears elegant and compact when witnessed from the elongated multifaceted apse. From Via Pontida, however, it is long, striped, and utilitarian – not unlike a mill. Finally, the façade blooms, featuring a huge rose that locals call 'the Wheel of Fortune'. While Verona, of course, has the Duomo, its main cathedral, San Zeno has and still acts as the city's most important church. Interestingly here in Verona, the most revered and precious temple was, throughout the

Middle Ages, built beyond the city walls. This is no coincidence, as the Abbey of San Zeno was a base for the German emperors. From the nineth to the twelfth centuries, they enthusiastically sponsored its operations, and even stayed in the monastery during their visits to Verona. The abbey's independent status ended, however, under the rule of the Scaligers, who included it in their ring of fortifications. San Zeno is a glorious feat of Romanesque style that transcended borders and united Europe. The colossal marble basilica is dedicated to its holy patron, San Zeno, the eighth bishop of Verona, who was born in what is now the Maghreb region of Northern Africa. Founded in the fourth century over San Zeno's tomb, the abbey grew in the ninth century with the help of the Frankish King Pepin of Italy, son of

bbsferrari (iStock)

Charlemagne. A century later, Bishop Ra-terio embarked on creating the site's most prominent temple, which was speedily finished around 1138. Master Niccolò decorated the prothyrum with scenes from the Bible as well as the legendary hunts of Theodoric the Great and his damnation. The scene in the lunette from 1138 still maintains its original colouring. The bronze doors were a fashionable feature in the seventh century, similar to the Bernward Doors in Hildesheim, Germany, or the doors of the Gniezno and Novgorod St. Sophia cathedrals. Here in Verona, the masters were also German. While there are still traces of some of the original paint, originally the church would have looked quite different. The Universal Judgment, for instance, was painted in the pediment of the façade. All of the church's sculptures, including those in the interior, were entirely frescoed. At 64 metres tall, the elegant belfry was one the highest in Italy at the time of its completion in 1178. It reflected the city's elevated status in the Middle Ages, which it maintained even until the eve of the Renaissance. The church's duotone is characteristic of the Veronese Romanesque style. Strolling around inside the church, the calm rhythm of its arches emits a spacious atmosphere. Inside, too, are touching ex-voto frescoes, dotted with graffiti. No to mention the magnificent Andrea Mantegna triptych in the altar, ornamental carvings and palatial stairs, and a high-stretching wooden ceiling that dates to the end of the fourteenth century. As in Istanbul's Hagia Sophia, here, it is the open space that conquers us.

B

Verona City
Route 3

C

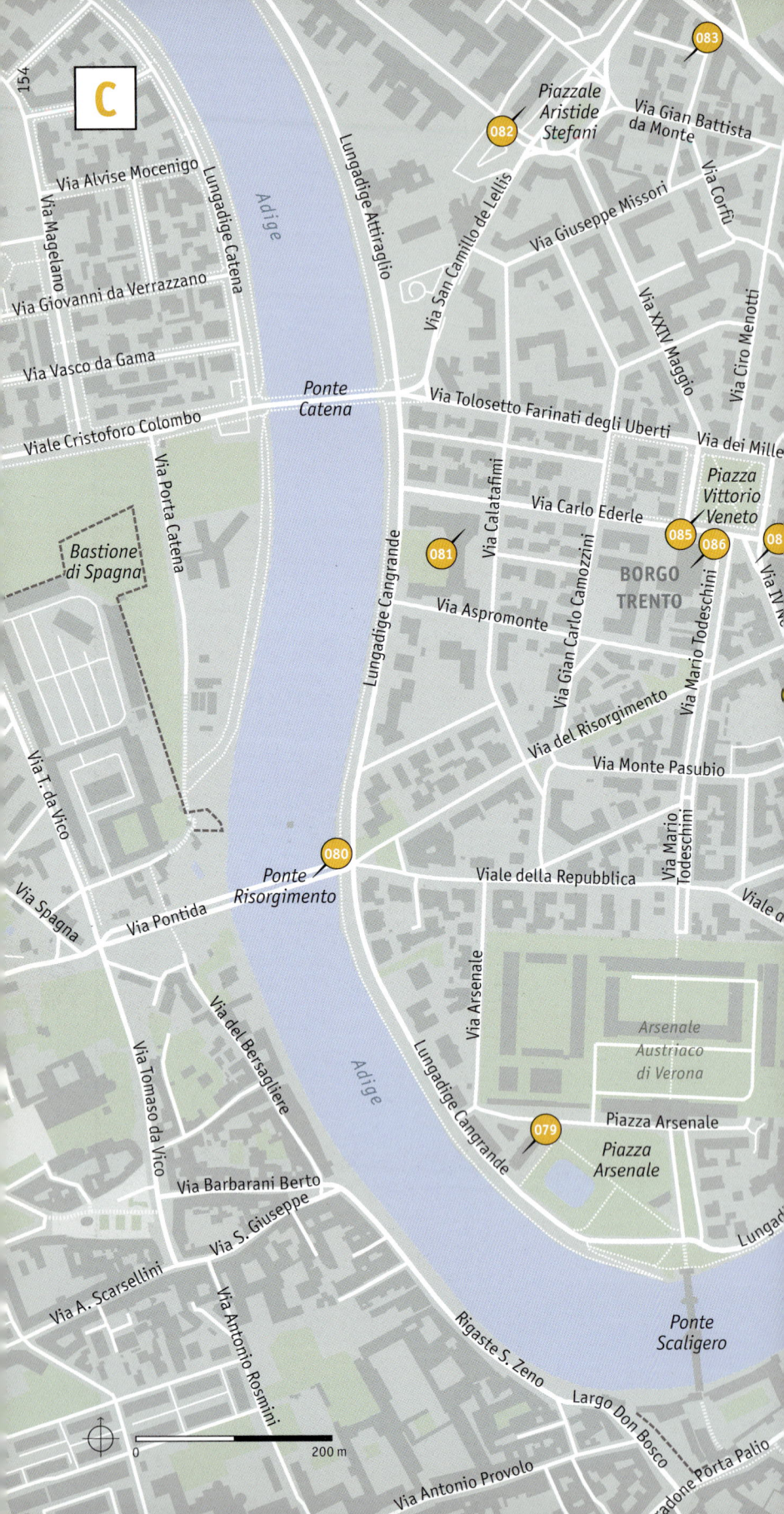

C

Via Alvise Mocenigo

Via Magelano

Via Giovanni da Verrazzano

Via Vasco da Gama

Lungadige Catena

Adige

Lungadige Attraglio

Piazzale
Aristide
Stefani

083

082

Via San Camillo de Lellis

Via Giuseppe Missori

Via Gian Battista
da Monte

Via Corfi

Via XXIV Maggio

Via Ciro Menotti

Viale Cristoforo Colombo

Via Porta Catena

Ponte
Catena

Via Tolosetto Farinati degli Uberti

Via dei Mille

Bastione
di Spagna

081

Via Calatafimi

Via Carlo Ederle

Piazza
Vittorio
Veneto

085 086 08

Lungadige Cangrande

Via Aspromonte

Via Gian Carlo Camozzini

BORGO
TRENTO

Via Mario Todeschini

Via TV No

Via del Risorgimento

Via Monte Pasubio

Via T. da Vico

Via Spagna

Via Pontida

Ponte
Risorgimento

080

Viale della Repubblica

Via Mario
Todeschini

Viale a

Via Tomaso da Vico

Via del Bersagliere

Via Arsenale

Adige

Lungadige Cangrande

Arsenale
Austriaco
di Verona

Piazza Arsenale

Lungadi

Via Barbarani Berto

079

Piazza
Arsenale

Via A. Scarsellini

Via S. Giuseppe

Via Antonio Rosmini

Rigaste S. Zeno

Ponte
Scaligero

Largo Don Bosco

Via Antonio Provolo

radone Porta Palio

0   200 m

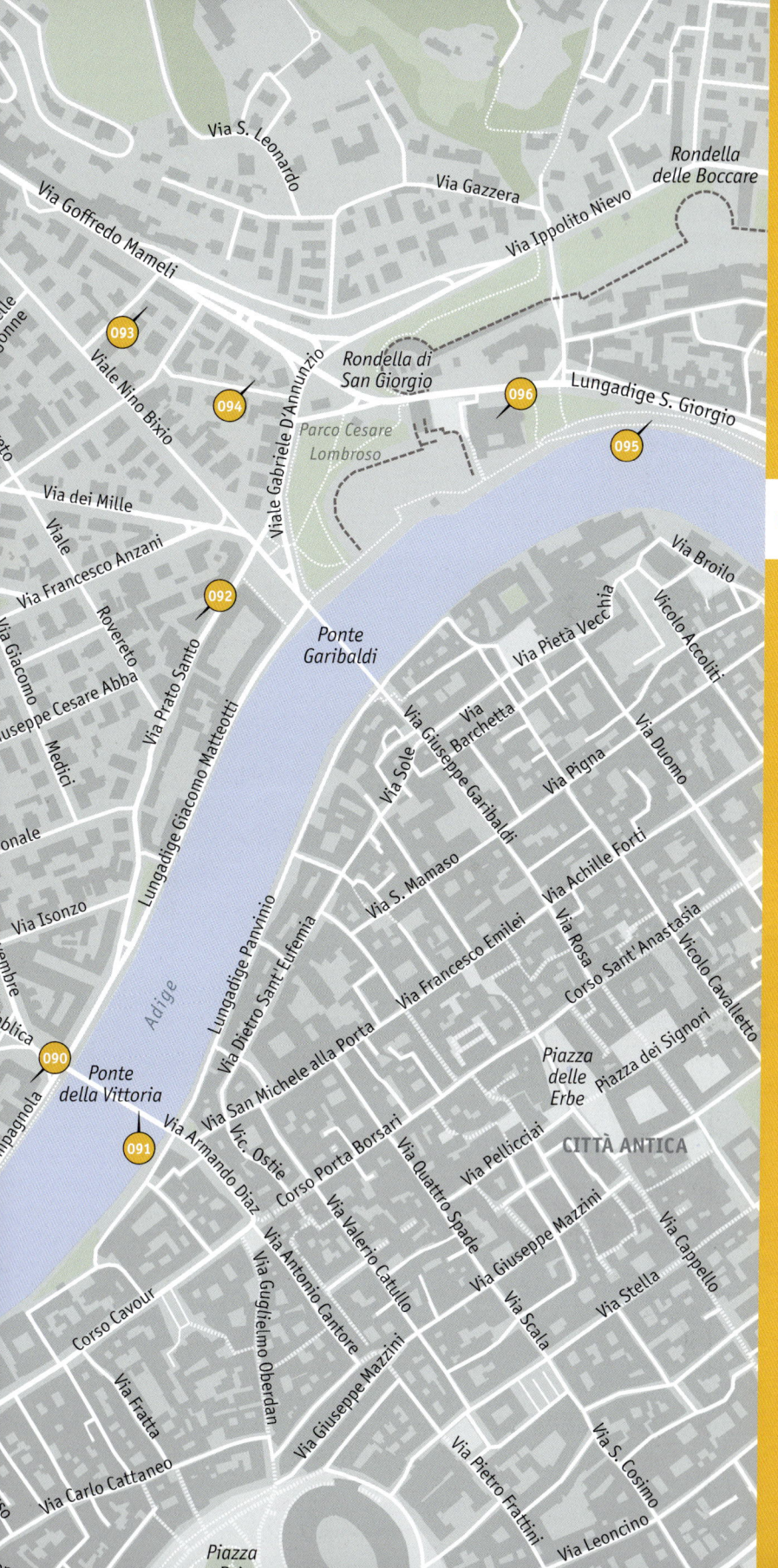

Via S. Leonardo

Via Gazzera

Rondella delle Boccare

Via Goffredo Mameli

Via Ippolito Nievo

Viale Nino Bixio

093

094

Viale Gabriele D'Annunzio

Rondella di San Giorgio

096

Lungadige S. Giorgio

Parco Cesare Lombroso

095

Via dei Mille

Viale

Via Broilo

Via Francesco Anzani

Vicolo Accoliti

092

Rovereto

Via Prato Santo

Via Pietà Vecchia

Via Giacomo

Giuseppe Cesare Abba

Ponte Garibaldi

Via Duomo

Via Barchetta

Medici

Lungadige Giacomo Matteotti

Via Sole

Via Pigna

ionale

Via Giuseppe Garibaldi

Via Achille Forti

Via Isonzo

Via S. Mamaso

Via Rosa

Corso Sant'Anastasia

Vicolo Cavalletto

Lungadige Panvinio

Via Francesco Emilei

Adige

Via Dietro Sant'Eufemia

Piazza dei Signori

090

Ponte della Vittoria

Via San Michele alla Porta

Piazza delle Erbe

CITTÀ ANTICA

mpagnola

091

Via Armando Diaz

Vic. Ostie

Corso Porta Borsari

Via Pelliccai

Via Quattro Spade

Via Giuseppe Mazzini

Via Cappello

Corso Cavour

Via Antonio Cantore

Via Valerio Catullo

Via Scala

Via Stella

Via Fratta

Via Guglielmo Oberdan

Via Giuseppe Mazzini

Via S. Cosimo

Via Carlo Cattaneo

Via Pietro Frattini

Via Leoncino

Piazza

Residential Building with Basin

079 C

Lungadige Cangrande 1, Verona
Sperandio Casali (house) 1950s,
David Chipperfield Architects
(reconstruction of the basin and park)
2008

When looking from the basin, surrounded by stone pines, it feels as though one is in Rome's EUR district looking at the Palazzo della Civiltà. Given the building's 1950s origin, it is surprising to see such a clear nod to Mussolini, as this kind of architectural style was then highly connotated with the fascist regime. The restrained marble façades are contrasted by the joyful mood of living by the water. Sadly, we don't know of any other works by this engineer, Sperandio Casali. On one side, the house overlooks the Adige River, and on the other there is a legendary vasca, or 'basin' of Arsenale – a bustling attraction during hot summer days. The basin of the Arsenale was initially built as a swimming pool for soldiers, and in 1898 it opened to civilians. Having degraded over time, David Chipperfield Architects of Milan began redeveloping the basin and the surrounding park in 2012. Their solution was to decrease the water's depth down to only a few centimetres, which became a hit for teenagers, tourists, children, and critics (Architetti Verona Award 2013). Nearby, at n. 5, is Francesco Banterle's Villa Galtarossa (1941).

Fabrizio Mauro

Ponte Risorgimento »

080 C

Pier Luigi Nervi
1963–1968

Reluctant and small before the Second World War, Verona desired to work with architectural stars in the 1960s. After his success with the pavilions of Italia 1961 exhibition in Turin, Pier Luigi Nervi was invited to build a bridge celebrating 100 years of Risorgimento. He accepted the bid on the condition that he would curate both its engineering and architecture. The Verona City Hall asked Nervi to use Ponte Catena as a reference. Nervi slightly remodelled and lowered the structure to create a dramatic effect of the vicinity of the roaring waters. The design was ready and approved by the City Hall in three months, but talk of the possible negative impacts of the new bridge slowed the process. It took four more years. Nervi chose a structural pattern with a continuous beam on four supports, with a span of 35 metres for the two side spans, and a span of 62 metres for the central part. The brick structure in the river before the bridge is the remains of the medieval turret that once controlled the passage of ships.

Fabrizio Mauro

Cattolica Assicurazioni Headquarters ⌃

081 C

Lungadige Cangrande 16
Via Carlo Ederle
Luigi Caccia Dominioni 1968–1971,
Mario Bellavite (reconstruction)
2007

One of Italy's largest insurance companies, Società Cattolica, invited an extraordinary architect to build its headquarters: the Milanese-born and unhurried Caccia Dominioni, who is now venerated for his furniture. It's likely that Giorgio Zanotto, a protagonist in the city government and society, was behind this commission. Every Caccia Dominioni construction undoubtedly has character. This one, however, is a bit controversial: its wings open wide with a garden that is closed by a merrily painted red fence, somehow holding a reserved official appearance. A bench goes along the façades, reminiscent of the Renaissance palaces by Michelozzo and Sanmicheli. Yet everything is moderate, almost to remind guests that this is not Milan, but rather a Catholic institution in provincial Verona. You'll find Caccia Dominioni's trademark sophisticated details: a beautiful twisted staircase creeps between floors with the same picturesque asymmetry of his famous condominium at Via Ippolito Nievo. But he wouldn't be Caccia Dominioni without a Milanese touch, namely the urban noise and busy rhythm that make his works so special. In Verona, Caccia Dominioni also designed the gorgeous housing estate, Atrio del Palio (Via Albere 8), which was finished after his death. Also red, the Atrio del Palio is near the Palladio Estate. Remarkable condominiums are next door: one brutalist (Lungadige Cangrande 14), one neoclassical (Lungadige Cangrande 15).

Sergey Nikitin-Rimsky

Main Hospital of Borgo Trento 082 C

Piazzale Stefani 1, Verona
Giovanni Tempioni, Pio Beccherle
1911–1927

Villa Padovani » 083 C

Via Cefalonia 4, Verona
Mario Semprebon
1935

Initially built only for children, by the late 1920s this hospital was transformed into Verona's general hospital. It is now nearly 150,000 square metres in size, with edifices from various epochs. The heroic portico, with stucco and marble details, stands somewhere in between art deco and Piacentini's neoclassical tastes. The lobby contains a portion of the original Secession-inspired decorations. Pio Beccherle is the man behind the Great Fridge of the Magazzini Generali.

Roman and Milanese schools presided over the rationalist movement in Italy, but its world-famous alumni never built anything in Verona. Yet, a few houses did appear close to the northern version of rationalism. Here, we see a small two-family villa commissioned by Giovanni Padovani. It resembles the Frankfurt of Ernst May's years with its confident and compact composition and complete absence of décor, except for windowsills and a small cornice.

Sergey Nikitin–Rimsky

Sergey Nikitin–Rimsky

Fabrizio Mauro

Villa Pasetto

Salita Monte Grappa 7, Verona
Eugenio Gallizioli
1934

084 C

Around the time that Bauhaus closed its doors in Berlin, this small villa grew up on a hill above Borgo Trento among vineyards and orchards. In Italy, it is a rare example of pure northern rationalism with the typical cubic shape, portholes, and angular vertical windows. The roof was originally a flat terrace, but in the 1980s it was partially built up; as a result, the asymmetric composition became even more convincing. One of the building's tenants, Anna, who lived on the third floor, proclaimed that she would rather move to a nursing home than alter this beautiful house with a lift for a wheelchair.

100 Years of Italy Fountain

Piazza Vittorio Veneto
Aldo Montù,
Franco Foso (sculptor)
1961

085 C

It was a lovely idea: a fountain in honour of the national anniversary amid the tall and shady trees on the main square in Borgo Trento. Three streams of water represent each of the three wars for independence that Italy passed on its way to becoming a modern nation state. The Milanese Aldo Montù won the national competition, creating a contemplative piece of babbling brutalism – almost Scarpaesque – that is so dear to the hearts of Venetians. Meditating over the slabs of Prun stone, one might also recall the Karl Liebknecht and Rosa Luxemburg Memorial by Mies van der Rohe – and, of course, Frank Lloyd Wright's Fallingwater.

Parrocchia
San Pietro the Apostolo

Piazza Vittorio Veneto
Bruno Milotti, Luigi Rosa
1958–1965

086 C

With its red colour and dynamic, industrious composition, this church is reminiscent of 1930s advertisements. Even the rose on the concave façade seems like a porthole, a favourite feature of Art Deco. By 1958, the Borgo Trento neighbourhood was already quickly populating and was thus in need of a church. Monsignor Marini, professor of sacred art at the seminary, requested it should be high enough 'not to disfigure next to the new buildings', and that it ought to have a single, large nave, solemn access steps, and a large churchyard. The asymmetrical façade solution of this basilica democristiana, meaning a church sponsored by the Christian Democrat government in Italy, was made as the customers insisted on installing the baptistery as its own separate building. The same architects created the Geriatrics Hospital of Verona (Via Goffredo Mameli).

Roberto Bianconi

C

Fabrizio Mauro

Fabrizio Mauro

Borgo Trento – From Liberty to *Il Boom Economico*

087 **C**

Via Nino Bixio, Piazzale Cadorna, Via IV Novembre
1911–1939

The liberty style in Italy is all about details and ornaments, the flight of fantasy, the will to travel. All of this was reflected in the development of Borgo Trento between 1911 and 1939. It is a bourgeois paradise, with a fleur of international exhibition, a collection of various cottages, and a flood of flowers and orchards. The neighbourhood wraps around Via Nino Bixio from the Garibaldi Bridge to the Monumental Hospital. After the Second World War, a second part of Borgo Trento grew around Via IV Novembre, starting from Piazzale Cadorna. It arises like a great 'Avenida' of the 1960s. With its many unusually tall buildings, the neighbourhood was at first heavily criticised by the local press. Nonetheless, the area has since matured into what is now the most fashionable area in all of Verona.

Villa Rossi Pavesi

Via IV Novembre 26, Verona
Italo Mutinelli
1930

Fabrizio Mauro

The central arteria of Borgo Trento is called patriotically Via IV Novembre after Victory Day for Italy in the First World War. It later became the main street of the area. The first house erected here was this villa. Symmetrical in a Neoclassical manner, but ultimately of Central European tastes, the villa hosts frescoes by Pino Casarini and sculptures by Giuseppe Garonzi. The owners, the Rossi Pavesi family, also sponsored the construction of the local fascist group's headquarters, 'Cesare Battisti', just a few blocks away. Though this building was done in a rational brick style and was recently converted into housing.

C

Sergey Nikitin-Rimsky

Condominio II (Casa a Sparasi)

Via IV Novembre 3, Verona
Gianfranco Bari
1952–1954

What if we made a house of villas? This exact idea came to the architect's mind. The villas – each for several families – are set one on top of the other, each with its own small, protected area where its residents could relax and decorate their space to their own tastes. Judging by the pictures, this experiment worked quite well.

Ivy already entangled the columns by the 1960s and local residents pitched up umbrellas to unwind. Bari, who also lived in the house, even put a parrot outside. Condominio II, which was developed around a heavily bombed four-storey house, earned mentions in the local press and public folklore. The Veronese nicknamed it the 'Asparagus House'. City leaders proudly brought delegations from the USSR and Great Britain to visit this curious location. Bari was also the architect of the condominiums on Via Tonale, just next door.

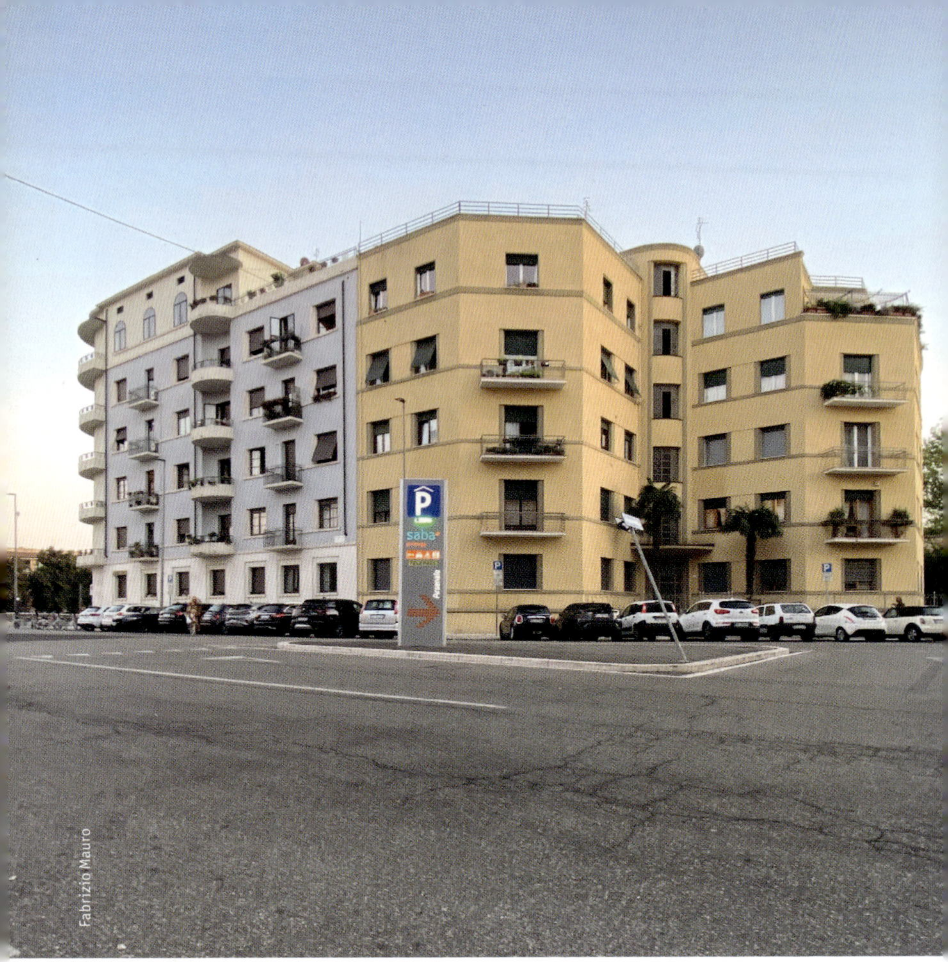

Fabrizio Mauro

Piazzale Luigi Cadorna

Ettore Fagiuoli

1930s

090 C

Visitors can find traces of all the leading trends of the 1930s here. A towering and calm condominium by Ettore Fagiuoli overlooks the area (Piazzale Cadorna 4-6), spanning over Viale Della Repubblica. At Cadorna 1, there is an elegant condominium building by Antonio Tonzig that features a rounded balconied solution for its corners – a popular-in 1930s Verona. The atrium shows off a lovely iron design. Across the square is a nicely designed, if grotesquely squeezed, rotunda, which marks an entrance to the offices of a civil engineering building (Cadorna 2). The rotunda was once a turret, but a fourth floor was added after the Second World War. Not far from here, Lungadige Campagnola 6 offers a graceful marble gateway, staged as a modernised triumphal arch.

Fabrizio Mauro

Fabrizio Mauro

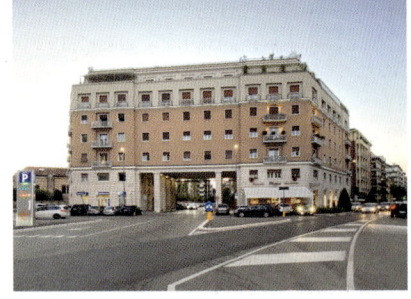

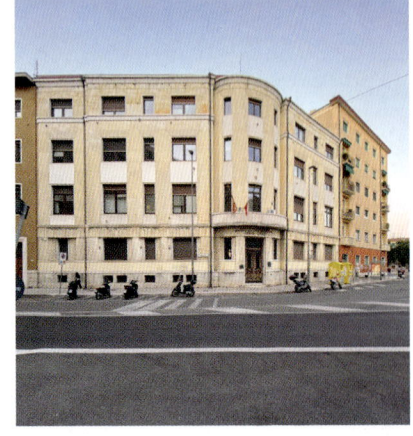

Sergey Nikitin-Rimsky

Ponte della Vittoria
Ettore Fagiuoli
1928, 1955

 091 C

This bridge was inaugurated three times: first when it was originally completed in 1928, then when it was partially restored in 1945 after Nazi troops destroyed it, and finally in 1955 when it was fully restored. In 1924, the Verona City Hall organised a national competition calling for a project to design the bridge-monument, which was won by Ettore Fagiuoli. The most successful architect in Verona with the ability to build in any style, Fagiuoli opted for an Ancient Roman approach. The interesting sculpture groups present here are not part of an original project, and perhaps to some extent disrupt its aesthetic. Ponte della Vittoria was originally in celebration of victory in the First World War, which led to the seizure of Trento, making it easier to then develop Verona's Borgo Trento residential district (see section n. 087: Borgo Trento). The neighbourhood starts across the river with a nice ensemble at Piazzale Luigi Cadorna. From here, one can enjoy the beautiful views over the Adige River and Castelvecchio.

Sergey Nikitin-Rimsky

Via Tonale and Prato Santo Condominiums

Via Tonale 6 and 24,
Via Prato Santo 4, Verona
Gianfranco Bari
Late 1950s

092 C

Via Tonale – stretching from Viale della Repubblica to Prato Santo – is a pleasant, shady promenade of condominiums from the late 1950s and 1960s, three of which were built by Gianfranco Bari. Things became starkly serious in Verona following the Second World War, and architecture received particular emphasis and notable attention from local newspapers. Via IV Novembre – a new route just across the river from Porta Borsari – was expected to become the new face of town, resurrecting the Veronese after war and poverty. Developers and some members of the city administration tried to get the most from the plots, while local critics labelled their production as simply 'barriers of cement'. At the same time, they praised Bari for his extensive research. To diversify his façades, for instance, he played with texture and even laid some tiles at right angles. His most central accents are found on his balconies, where he employs metal fixtures that recall houses for the poor with galleries, called *casa alla ringhiera*.

Sergey Nikitin–Rimsky

Via Tonale 6

Via Prato Santo 4

Fabrizio Mauro

C

Sergey Nikitin–Rimsky

Villetta Tosadori

093 C

Via Anita Garibaldi 3, Verona
Ettore Fagiuoli
1922

The tireless Fagiuoli had an uncommon fantasy. In Borgo Trento – named in commemoration of taking Trento from the Austrians – he erected a painted farmhouse in the Austrian and Bavarian styles, with idyllic wall paintings and a wide rustic cornice. The commissioner, Nicola Arturo Tosadori, was a developer of the City Hospital and the first to build condominiums in here on the corner of Via dei Mille and Via Anzani. He also owned Villa Tedeschi in Borgo Trento, which was made by Fagiuoli.

Sergey Nikitin–Rimsky

Villino Brugnoli »

094 C

Via Caprera 2, Verona
Tommaso Contini
1911

An epitome of Veronese liberty with its will to travel and explore, this cottage looks like a bubbling Victorian invention jumping over the hills of San Francisco. Tommaso Contini, a 'modest master builder', designed the house for a certain Drusilla Pomari, who sold it soon after. Veronese critics see it as a mix of 'medieval, Nordic, Arab-Norman, and local references'.

Fabrizio Mauro

San Giorgio Embankment
1935–1938

Sant'Alessio was the last historic working-class neighbourhood in the centre, where houses hang over the Adige River. It was demolished, just like the ghetto next to Piazza delle Erbe. As with houses next to the Roman Forum in the 1920s, this was explained as being for hygienic reasons. A gracious tongue of marble, alternating with rectangles of green, was born. It is a fantastic two-level promenade to gaze out over the Duomo area of Verona. And who was the designer of this lovely piece of rationalism? Believe it or not, city hall engineers!

Alberto Masnovo (iStock)

Chiesa di San Giorgio in Braida ⩗

Piazzetta S. Giorgio, Verona
Michele Sanmicheli,
Bernardino Brugnoli,
Paolo Farinati
15th–17th centuries

096 C

Its silhouette, topped with obelisks, a dome, and unfinished bell tower surrounded by obelisk cypresses, has lured spectators ever since the seventeenth century. Originally a Benedictine monastery when Verona became a part of the Venetian Republic, the building was transferred to the rich Augustinian order of San Giorgio in Alga. The city's leading architect, Michele Sanmicheli, was invited to rebuild the premises and construct the dome in the middle of Quattrocento. Roam around this paradoxical complex to gaze at the Old Romanesque belfry absorbed by the northern wall and the dreamy metaphysical arcades of the cloister, dating back to the sixteenth century. The façade initially boasted more decoration than it now shows. San Giorgio's excellent pieces of Paolo Veronese and Tintoretto are well-known, but here you can discover some great local finds, including the altar by Giovan Francesco Caroto and a graceful Christ in Noli me tangere by Francesco Montemezzano. A small door on the left leads to a small oratory with a remarkable collection of ex-votos – the real folk art of Italy.

C

Strenght of Frame (iStock)

Verona City
Route 4

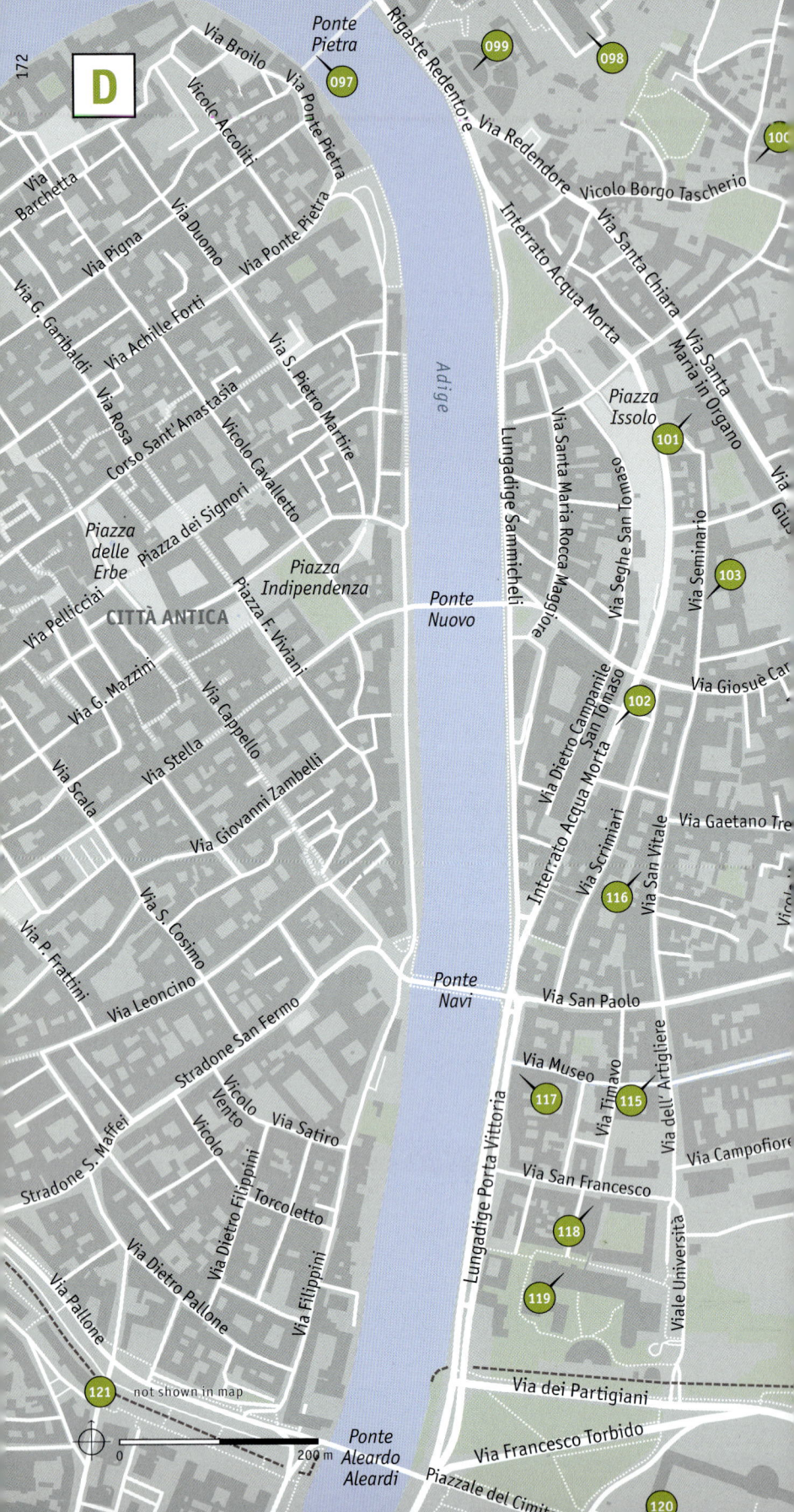

172

D

Ponte Pietra

Via Broilo

Vicolo Accoliti

Via Ponte Pietra

Rigaste Redento're

Via Redendore

097

099

098

100

Vicolo Borgo Tascherio

Via Barchetta

Via Duomo

Via Pigna

Via G. Garibaldi

Via Achille Forti

Via Ponte Pietra

Via Santa Chiara

Via Santa Maria In Organo

Interrato Acqua Morta

Via Rosa

Corso Sant'Anastasia

Via S. Pietro Martire

Vicolo Cavalletto

Piazza dei Signori

Adige

Piazza Issolo

101

Piazza delle Erbe

Piazza Indipendenza

Piazza F. Viviani

CITTÀ ANTICA

Via Pellicciai

Via G. Mazzini

Via Cappello

Via Stella

Via Scala

Via Giovanni Zambelli

Via Santa Maria Rocca Maggiore

Via Seghe San Tomaso

Lungadige Sammicheli

Ponte Nuovo

Via Seminario

103

Via Giosuè Car

Via Dietro Campanile San Tomaso

Via San Tomaso

102

Via Gaetano Tre

Via S. Cosimo

Interrato Acqua Morta

Via Scrimiari

Via San Vitale

116

Via P. Frattini

Via Leoncino

Ponte Navi

Via San Paolo

Stradone San Fermo

Via Museo

Via dell'Artigliere

Vicolo Vento

Vicolo

Via Satiro

117

Via Timavo

115

Stradone S. Maffei

Via Dietro Filippini

Torcoletto

Lungadige Porta Vittoria

Via San Francesco

Via Campofiore

Via Dietro Pallone

Via Filippini

118

Viale Università

Via Pallone

121

not shown in map

119

0   200 m

Ponte Aleardo Aleardi

Via dei Partigiani

Via Francesco Torbido

Piazzale del Cimiter

120

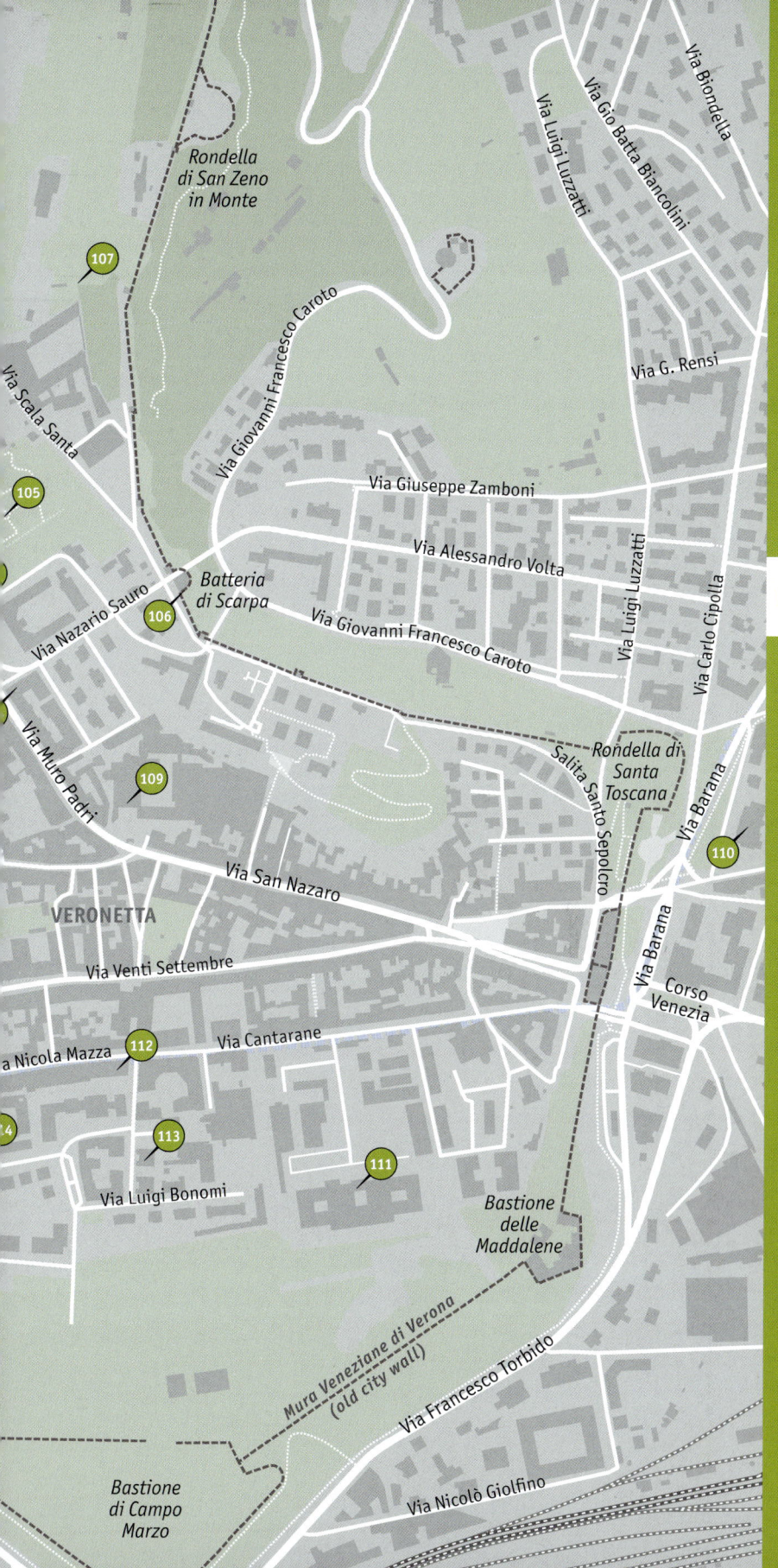

D

Rondella
di San Zeno
in Monte

107

Via Scala Santa

Via Gio Batta Biancolini

Via Luigi Luzzatti

Via Biondella

Via G. Rensi

Via Giovanni Francesco Caroto

Via Giuseppe Zamboni

Via Alessandro Volta

105

Batteria
di Scarpa

106

Via Nazario Sauro

Via Giovanni Francesco Caroto

Via Luigi Luzzatti

Via Carlo Cipolla

Salita Santo Sepolcro

Rondella di
Santa
Toscana

Via Barana

110

Via Muro Padri

109

Via San Nazaro

VERONETTA

Via Barana

Corso
Venezia

Via Venti Settembre

a Nicola Mazza

112

Via Cantarane

4

113

111

Via Luigi Bonomi

Bastione
delle
Maddalene

Mura Veneziane di Verona
(old city wall)

Via Francesco Torbido

Bastione
di Campo
Marzo

Via Nicolò Giolfino

Ponte Pietra (Stone Bridge)
100 BCE
Piero Gazzola, Libero Cecchini (reconstruction) 1957–1959

097 D

Stone Bridge is one of two Roman bridges in Verona, the second of which was destroyed by the Adige River. Looking down at the river, one can see and hear just how turbulent the water is. It is understandable how difficult it was for the bridge to hold. The Stone Bridge was completed around 100 BCE and used for the Postumia Road, which led from Genoa to Aquilea. It was originally made of marble in opus quadratum and composed of blocks of Valpolicella stone arranged without mortar in horizontal rows, held together by metal clamps. In the Scaligeri and Venetian times, brick was used to restore it, which explains why it is now red and white. Just like the Ponte Vecchio in

D

Sergey Nikitin-Rimsky

Florence or any other bridge in the Middle Ages, Verona's Ponte Pietra was filled with huts and various businesses. A watchtower stood on the San Giorgio side. However, these were all demolished during the so-called 'enlightened' nineteenth century because it supposedly looked offensive next to the majesty of the Roman monument. Only the first section, next to the city, is original, and the rest was reconstructed after being bombed by Nazi forces in April 1945. Professor Piero Gazzola, Superintendent of Monuments in Verona and one of the authors of the Venice Charter, elected to rebuild the bridge as it was – piece by piece, brick by brick, employing all original materials. This was the first great accomplishment of Libero Cecchini, who was soon to become Verona's leading architect throughout the twentieth century. The bridge is now 93 metres long and 7 metres wide.

Castel San Pietro

`098` `D`

Piazzale Castel San Pietro, Verona

Conrad Petrasch

1852–1858

Verona's perfect panoramic point was, of course, always of military interest. The first castle here dates back to Berengario I in 890. In 1393, Gian Galeazzo Visconti built a new citadel, which later became military barracks. In 1801, the French army destroyed much of the Visconti fortifications before giving this part of the city to Austria. Between 1852 and 1858, Austrian Field Marshal Radetzky ordered the construction of new barracks on the hill. Conrad Petrasch supervised the design. Wishing to adopt a new structure to fit harmoniously in the beautiful medieval town, they chose the Rundbogen – a round arch style – of Romanesque, which was then popular in Austria and Germany. It features exposed brick and polychrome arch rings. In the twentieth century, gardeners planted cypresses on the edge of the hill, adding a Gothic silhouette to the square volumes of the building. It currently awaits its new role – most likely as a luxury hotel.

D

Sergey Nikishin-Rimsky

Xbrchx (dreamstime)

Museo Archeologico al Teatro Romano

Rigaste Redentore 2, Verona
1 BCE

099 D

Verona was born in Veronetta: the initial pre-Roman settlement situated on the slopes of San Pietro hill. Urbanisation inside the loop of the Adige River freed up new space here, offering a natural setting for a theatre. During the Middle Ages, an entire neighbourhood landed on top of the ancient substructures, with staircases used to access buildings. Theodoric, King of the Ostrogoths and known as 'Diederich von Bern' in German folklore, built his palace here, giving the hill its unofficial name, which is still in use today. The loving eyes of the Renaissance could see the ancient grace of it: Giovanni Caroto and Andrea Palladio bestowed inspired reconstructions, which Palladio later applied to his Teatro Olimpico in Vicenza. Finally, in 1834, a doctor and lover of archaeology, Andrea Monga, bought the land and started to excavate. The works continued until the 1970s, when the archaeological museum was settled here. Try either Vicolo Botte or Scalone San Pietro, the two paths left of the theatre that climb up the hill. They offer breathtaking views of Verona and the well-restored pieces of the urban environment.

Alexander Grenkow

D

Chiesa di
San Giovanni in Valle

Via San Giovanni in Valle, Verona
7th century,
1120–1164 (current building),
1300 (façade)

100 D

A few hundred metres up from the bustling embankment, this temple radiates the severe strength and tranquillity of the early Christian churches. One of the oldest in Verona, it stands where a pagan necropolis with a temple once was – perhaps dedicated to the sun god. It has been suggested that San Giovanni was initially the church of the followers of Arianism, since the castle of King Theodoric the Great was not far away (see 099: Museo Archelogico al Teatro Romano). It was rebuilt to its current state after a succession of tragedies: the destructive 1117 earthquake, the later collapse of the bell tower and cloister, and finally bombings during the Second World War. Typical for Romanesque churches, the internal space here has three levels: three naves divided by the red-marble columns with carved capitals, the presbytery, which is accessed via monumental stairs, and finally a crypt located underneath. Walls, capitals, columns – everything was once frescoed, but today only a few fragments of the paintings survive. The vault contains a sublime sarcophagus from the second or third century CE, with two spouses atop a two-level carved tomb with bas-reliefs depicting rural scenes and philosophers. In the back, there is a house with a late Gothic porch, one of the oldest civil buildings in town. Ask for the key at the church and check out the apses behind the fence. The left one is a masterpiece of Roman Verona: the first to be built, it has the grace of an ancient pavilion. It is laid of precise cuts of large tuff blocks alternating with thin rows of bricks along with Corinthian-styled pilasters. Classical Veronese trattoria Ropeton is next door, as well as a recently restored public park, Corte del Duca, near the San Pietro castle.

Sergey Nikitin-Rimsky

D

Santa Maria in Organo

Via Santa Maria in Organo 1b,
Verona
7th century
Michele Sanmicheli,
Paolo Sanmicheli,
Adam and Battistino di San Giorgio,
Fra Giovanni da Verona
1546–1594 (façade)

101 D

This unfinished snow-white arched portico would catch anyone's eye. As it happens in Verona, Michele Sanmicheli designed but didn't complete the façade, which was inspired by Leon Battista Alberti's Tempio Malatestiano in Rimini. In truth, the monks made another attempt to complete the fabric 50 years later, inviting stonecutters Adam and Battistino from San Giorgio di Valpolicella, to whom we owe the laconic Corinthian pilasters (1590–1594). The main volume was built after the 1117 earthquake and was later embellished throughout the fifteenth to seventeenth centuries. This renovation was primarily under the direction of Olivetan Abbot Cipriano Cipriani, who involved Sanmicheli and Fra Giovanni da Verona, the great master of wooden inlaid works. Fra Giovanni is responsible for the witty allegorical compositions in the central apse (1494–1499), the wardrobes in the sacristy (1519–1523), and the bell tower. A touchingly cluttered interior is torn between its medieval foundations and colourful accents of the Renaissance and Baroque styles. A large thermal window was installed over the entrance as a means of providing the shrine with more light.

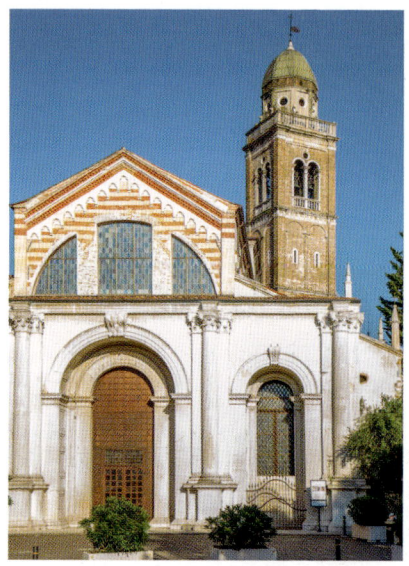

azoth22 (iStock)

Sacristy

Associazione Rivela/Maurzio Marcato

D

Detail of the sacristy by Fra Giovanni

Main vault

D

Interrato dell'Acqua Morta ⩥
Via Interrato dell'Acqua Morta, Verona

102 D

Until 1882, the houses along this route have been standing on the river. The street is laid over the second branch of the Adige River, which, unlike the turbulent main section, was distinguished by its slow movement. The resulting island is called 'Isolo' and its centre Piazza Isolo interspersed with monuments to the victims of Holocaust (Pino Castagna) and Christian missionary Daniele Comboni. The marble decor of the piazza attempts to reconnect today's visitors with Verona's stone tradition and Carlo Scarpa's legacy. Here stands the glittering marbles of Santa Maria in Organo, but also the wine bar 'ai Preti' – a meeting place for intellectuals.

Sergey Nikitin-Rimsky

Seminario Vescovile di Verona »
Via del Seminario 8, Verona
Ludovico Perini, Ottone Calderari
1700, 1779–1789

103 C

A century of work and dreams were poured into realising this magnificent neoclassical ensemble on a back street in Veronetta. It began when Bishop Gianfrancesco Barbarigo entrusted this design to some Venetian architects. Ludovico Perini elaborated the grandeur of the project in 1713, building the right wing with a library and the monumental atrium and clock. But Bishop Barbarigo soon left Verona, and ambitions for the project went with him. In 1786, Goethe wrote that the façade of the seminary was still under construction. Vicenza-born Palladianist Ottone Calderari was invited to style this flawless façade with 80 square metres of ionic-style lodge. Napoleon's troops were already on their way to Italy when Marco Marcola finished frescoing the lodge's ceiling, with its 12 zodiac constellations featuring, among others, the winding Eridano River, the Ursas, and Hercules slaying Cerberus.

D

Sergey Nikitin-Rimsky

Sergey Nikitin-Rimsky

Palazzo Giusti »
Via Giosuè Carducci 41, Verona
Francesco Perotti
End of 17th century

With a charming façade from the turn of the seventeenth and eighteenth centuries, this palace hums of knightly tournaments and bends along Carducci Street (pictured right) as if waiting to be saved from decades of abandon. The decaying mascaron is the remains of the wall painting, peeking out from under the eaves. There is also a small garden with firs and loquats, and remains of the old spinning mill. Across the street is a marvellous portal, thought to be made by Michele Sanmicheli (Vicolo Cieco Pozza 11).

Sergey Nikitin–Rimsky

Via Giosuè Carducci 41

Villa Giusti Giardino

Villa Giusti del Giardino ⌄

Via Giardino Giusti 2, Verona
End of 14th century,
1570

105 D

Italy is rich with gardens, yet this small urban villa, once at the end of town, hosts what is probably one of the most conspicuous. Its popularity is in part thanks to its dramatic composition: the garden storms up a steep hill. The whole setting is abundantly emphasised with cypresses, which drove travellers from over the Alps absolutely mad. It is possible that the poet Johann Wolfgang Goethe spent a relaxing afternoon under one of these monumental cypresses, which are almost 600 years old. Deeply inspired in his novel *Elective Affinities*, Goethe compared cypresses to 'a self-willed man, out of whom we can obtain all which we desire if we will only treat him his own way'. Obviously, the garden's fame doubled throughout Central Europe thanks to Goethe. The villa was founded in the late 1300s, but what we most admire now was modelled in 1570 for the diplomat Agostino Giusti, a gentleman who managed to work for both the Venetian Republic and their rivals, the Medici. Upon its completion, the villa was praised as a 'Second Paradise' by British traveller Thomas Coryat. The labyrinth of hedges was designed by Luigi Trezza (1786). Upstairs, there is an enormous mannerist mascaron and a breath-taking view over Verona.

D

Franco Cogoli

Riccardo Gasperoni

Terrace with panoramic view

Entrance to the villa

Riccardo Gasperoni

Riccardo Gasperoni

Riccardo Gasperoni

Art installations in the palace

Torricelle – Fortification around Veronetta

Salita San Sepolcro,
Via San Zeno in Monte
1321–1324

A vast resource of stunning green panoramas and the Trecento military legacy rests over the hills, just above Veronetta in what locals call Torricelle. It's great to walk or ride a bike here any time of day. Cangrande I of Scaligeri erected this thrilling rampart that marches up the hills with its 14 towers and nine-metre-high, one-metre-thick walls. The hills consist of tuff, so after the deep mote was dug, the excavated material was used to make the fortification itself. Don't miss the impressive Austrian defensive buildings from the 1850s nearby, for instance, Fort Sofia.

Sergey Nikitin-Rimsky

Sergey Nikitin-Rimsky

Sergey Nikitin-Rimsky

Illuminated Cross of Buoni Fanciulli

Via Torricelle
Francesco Banterle
1934

Although Mass services are often empty, the Catholic Church still holds great importance in the political, economic, and cultural life of Verona. The bishop's opinion is instantly transmitted by word of mouth. Ecclesiastic power, weakened by the Italian Kingdom that fought the Church to capture Rome in 1870, again raised its head when Mussolini and Pope Pio XI arrived to facilitate the Treaty Conciliation, establishing Vatican City as an independent state in 1929. Among various celebrations, the Pope proclaimed 1934 as a holy year to remember 1,900 years of the Holy Cross. To remind themselves anew, Veronese elites decided to erect a large and luminous cross. Its designer, Francesco Banterle, also curated the construction of the religious Istituto Don Calabria – an imposing complex on a huge platform that dominates the town. The cross may be reached from Torricelle to enjoy a stunning view over the city and the nearby church San Zeno in Monte, which was also reconstructed by Francesco Banterle.

Sergey Nikitin-Rimsky

D

Casa Madre Don Calabria

194

Casa Erlotti »

Via Nazario Sauro 2, Verona
Italo Mutinelli
1928–1931

D

Italy was on the winning side of the First World War but paid a terrible price. To mark this, city leaders in Rome and Milan painted triumphal façades for the middle-class, with intricate roofs, composite plans, and simplified baroque embellishments. This might be understood as the Italian answer to the German Heimat-schutzstil, or to the romantic gigantisms of American cities in the early twentieth century. There are a number of lonely islands of architectural style in Verona. This elegant Erlotti House with its 76 apartments, for instance, was built for Cavalier Erlotti by the engineer Italo Mutinelli. Upon the building's completion, it had been assumed that Veronetta would eventually feature other houses in a similar style.

Sergey Nikitin–Rimsky

Chiesa dei Santi Nazaro e Celso, featuring la Cappella di San Biagio ♪

Largo San Nazaro 1, Verona
1464–1483

D

This church's elegant façade of the mid-fifteenth century radiates confidence and tranquillity. Once a Benedictine monastery under the Castiglione Hill in the heart of Veronetta with two vast cloisters, it flourished under protection of the German emperors from the twelfth century onward. When Verona became part of the Venetian Republic, the monastery was linked with a rich confraternity in Padua. Using their money, the Veronese demolished the Romanesque basilica and erected the current temple in record speed. Still, they didn't want to entirely lose its rose-laden Gothic façade, which suddenly transforms into a rather ordinary Renaissance interior. The collection of paintings here is outstanding. Palma the Younger, Mocetto, Morone, Brusasorci, Farinati – all local celebrities who painted for the friars. The Feast in the House of Simon, the Pharisee by Veronese was originally hung in the church's refectory. On the left, next to the altar, is the stunning Chapel of San

Biagio (Beltrame Iarola, 1529) covered with a Venetian-styled dome and magnificent illusionistic frescoes. The bell tower was built in 1550. The streets around are full of charming buildings from the eighteenth and nineteenth centuries. From here, one can follow Via San Nazaro until it joins with a pleasant piazza at Porta Vescovo.

Fabrizio Mauro

D

Fabrizio Mauro

Villa Rossi
Via Barana 8, Verona
Italo Mutinelli
1934

110 D

Engineer Italo Mutinelli lived in an era of rapidly changing tastes and styles that he, like his wealthy customers, freely demonstrated. Rossi's brothers were perhaps Mutinelli's main commissioners, entrusting him with the design of his shoe factory. A luxurious villa for one of the brothers, Attilio, stands here at the gates of Porta Vescovo. The heavy symmetry reminds us that Mutinelli started his career in the neoclassical style – la Casa Erlotti, which can be found a few hundred metres from this spot (see n. 108). As in the other Rossi family villa (in Borgo Trento), Pino Casarini frescoed the interiors. Inside and out, the building provides a severe coolness, like the films of its 1930s origin. The Borgo Venezia neighbourhood begins just behind the villa's walls.

Fabrizio Mauro

Mario Campi/Carmassi Studio Di Architettura

Mulino di Santa Marta

111 D

Via Santa Marta 6, Verona
Andreas Tunkler,
Ferdinand Artmann,
Anton Naredi Rainer (military engineers),
Massimo Carmassi (restoration)
1863–1865, 2009–2015

D

With all these mid-century liberation movements and bourgeois revolutions in the empire, Verona was destined to become the military bridgehead for the Austro-Hungarians in Italy. The imperial army erected an enormous mill to supply flour to the Austrian garrisons in Northern Italy in Veronetta at the city's outskirts. Only a few months later, the troops of Victor Emmanuel II captured Veneto for the Italian forces. The mill became a warehouse and even a prison before eventually being abandoned. The university began its restoration at the silo tower and then took over the mill's main structure. Architect Massimo Carmassi won an Italian architectural gold medal prize for this restoration project in 2015. The former mill's opening sparked the regeneration of this previously sleepy and neglected corner of Veronetta. Since the university faces a shortage of dormitories, it is expected that students living here will soon replace the local population. Perhaps these new inhabitants will continue to rejuvenate the local offerings.

Mario Campi/Carmassi Studio Di Architettura

Complex of the ex-mills of Santa Marta

Fabrizio Mauro

Sergey Nikitin-Rimsky

Home for the Elderly
(formerly military barracks)
Via Nicola Mazza 54
Arrigo Rudi
1974–1975

Sergey Nikitin-Rimsky

Wooden shutters and cornices play leading roles in the traditional façades in
Veneto. Architect Arrigo Rudi, a pupil of
Scarpa, was inspired to work with these
shady elements and animate the bare and
concrete surfaces in the courtyard of this
senior home. Rudi was able to preserve
the original neoclassical façade of the
building, which had previously been used
as military barracks.

Sergey Nikitin-Rimsky

Sergey Nikitin-Rimsky

D

Residential Houses ⌃ in Veronetta
Via Luigi Bonomi 2–6, Verona
1929

113 D

Nations have been searching for their architectural identities since the late nineteenth century. Britain was balancing between Queen Anne and Gothic Revival; Germany enjoyed their Heimatschutzarchitektur as well as Gothic

Complesso Campofiore »
Via Campofiore 29, Verona
Antonio Tonzig
1935

114 D

This building was celebrated as the first public housing in town to be equipped with all the modern amenities: kitchens, gas, water, and electricity for all. The sophisticated Antonio Tonzig (Villa Tiberghien) chose a traditional Veneto house as his inspiration but eliminated some of the usual bourgeois excess. Instead, he employed proportions, rhythm, and shutters to create a practical and harmonious block. A pleasant, traditional, family-owned grocery store is located on the ground floor, where great sandwiches are offered. Across the street is a row of simple, yet tastefully decorated two-storey houses from the 1920s, with a subtle touch of art nouveau.

styles; Russians dived into neo-Russian and byzantine. At this time, the Veronese people justly saw the neoclassical villa as their architectural DNA, slightly embellished with baroque dressings. City hall commissioned an unknown architect to build these six three-storey apartment complexes to house its employees. A similar neoclassical vein can be seen in the public housing at Via Santa Marta 1–6, developed by an unknown architect.

Roberto Bianconi

Palazzo Giuliari (Rectorate of the University)

115 D

Via dell'Artigliere, Verona
16th century,
Ignazio Pellegrini 18th century,
Bartolomeo Giuliari,
Luigi Calcagni, Luciano Cenna 1965

In February 1959, the city council approved 'the institution in Verona of a University Faculty of Economics and Commerce'. Countess Giuliari Tusini subsequently gifted her famous palace to the new institution. It was the first commission for the firm Calcagni & Cenna, which continued to build up the university over four decades. Initially built in the sixteenth century, the palace was redecorated by the renowned architect and artist Paolo Farinati. The building was embellished with stuccoes in the late eighteenth century, and soon after the beautiful oval staircase was constructed by Ignazio Pellegrini. These additions were followed by the work of Pellegrini's nephew, Bartolomeo Giuliari. The two charming cabins projecting over Vicolo Passere were once bathrooms. The university has played a crucial role in the revitalisation of the Veronetta neighbourhood – an old and mostly working-class district – and maintains its influence in the area with its new operas. On the left is a rose-coloured palace from the seventeenth century with a lazy double-columned portico, belvedere, and a massive keystone (Via dell'Artigliere 10).

Stefano Aloe

Stefano Aloe

Stefano Aloe

Sergey Nikitin-Rimsky

Railroad Workers Cooperative «

116 D

Via San Vitale 19, Verona
Architect unknown
1919

Here is a unique interpretation of the rigid neoclassical scheme. An unknown architect from the Railroad Workers Co-operative created this emporium in 1919, and it was later converted into a gym. The five-axis façade of the three-storey house is richly decorated. Humanised animal heads hold a connecting ribbon in their mouths. Bundles of grain and fruit are another element of architectural richness. The workers' cooperative was obviously having a good time.

Sergey Nikitin-Rimsky

Palazzo Pompei (Museo di Storia Naturale) «

117 D

Lungadige Porta Vittoria 9, Verona
Michele Sanmicheli
1535–1540

The local aristocratic family Lavezzola commissioned this Renaissance palace to Michele Sanmicheli. Sanmicheli built the façade, contrasting severe rustic ground floors, and a festive piano nobile with fluted doric columns and huge windows, surmounted by quirky Dionysian mascarones. Inside, the courtyard features an arcade. One of the owners was Alessandro Pompei, an architect and scholar, who rigorously studied Sanmicheli's legacy. In 1833, the last member of the Pompei family gifted the palace to city hall, which later converted the building into the city's Museum of Natural History. In the eighteenth century, the palace's façade was copied by Carl Ludwig Hildebrandt for a beer house in Potsdam.

Biblioteca Centrale Arturo Frinzi & Chiesa di San Francesco di Paolo

Via S. Francesco 20, Verona
Luigi Calcagni, Luciano Cenna
1987

118 D

The order of the Minims erected this church in 1596 as well as the cloister in the seventeenth century, partly with money received from the municipality. In 1810, a Napoleonic decree established the suppression of convents, so when Calcagni and Cenna – both previously assistant professors of architectural history – first came to see the building, it was operating as a dusty military storage unit and had suffered heavy damaged during the war. Their visit inspired them to install a steel frame, so it could become a storage space for books. This honest and robust steel frame became the main feature both for the interiors and exteriors – connecting the floors and the cloister to the church and strengthening the galleries over the arcade. The director of the Castelvecchio Museum, Licisco Magagnato, blessed the young masters. The space immediately became one of the campus' central landmarks.

Sergey Nikitin-Rimsky

Sergey Nikitin-Rimsky

D

Sergey Nikitin-Rimsky

University of Verona –
Main Building and Polo Zanotto
Luigi Calcagni, Luciano Cenna
1987–1993, 1999–2002

119 D

One of the youngest universities in Italy, the University of Verona began as a branch of the Faculty of Economics at the University of Padua. Students initially studied in Giuliari Palace (see 115: Palazzo Giuliari). Fifty years later, the school has grown into an independent university with well-respected departments in philology, medicine, engineering, philosophy, and art history. Today it occupies many central buildings in Veronetta as well as in the Borgo Roma neighbourhood, located in the city's south. The heart of campus, however, still stands in the old convent of San Francesco. The university's main building is a postmodernist spectacle. The main building emerges from the cloister and the Frinzi library (see 118: Biblioteca Centrale Arturo Frinzi). The building is entirely designed by the architectural studio Cenna & Calcagni, founded by earlier students of Giancarlo De Carlo who have favoured brutalist and bare concrete styles. While aesthetically successful, visiting the building in the summertime is an infamously stuffy experience. The Polo Zanotto extension's big hall demonstrates a return to the basic volumetric of the 1920s and 1930s. It is named after the mayor Giorgio Zanotto, who contributed to the founding of both the university and the Castelvecchio Museum, among a number of Verona's other modern achievements. The university campus' beautiful landscape, laden with magnolias and elms, makes for a pleasant spot to sit with a book or a bite to eat. Spot the two rotundas on site from here: a minor nineteenth-century military building that houses the university sports club, and a second semi-rotunda of the cafeteria by the same architects, where all are welcome for coffee or prosecco.

Sergey Nikitin-Rimsky

D

Sergey Nikitin–Rimsky

Sergey Nikitin–Rimsky

Sergey Nikitin-Rimsky

Cimitero Monumentale di Verona (Monumental Cemetery)

Piazzale del Cimitero
Giuseppe Barbieri
1828–1838

120 D

The protagonist of nineteenth century Veronese architecture, Giuseppe Barbieri, is mostly remembered for his work on city hall, located next to the Arena. However, with this lifetime commission of the cemetery, it was as if he worked on it eternally. Remember that real classicism is about time and the temple, not offices for bureaucrats. It was Napoleon in 1804, who decreed to build the Empire's cemeteries according to the principles of sanity, secularism, and equality. Before this, noble families were simply buried in churchyards. Verona immediately decided to have a cemetery, but it took 24 years of debates to finally begin building on the ancient territory of the Field of Mars. Verona was already under Austrian rule by this time. The Napoleonic principles of equality has been lost. The aristocracy and military were to be buried in the doric galleries. Common folk, on the other hand, had a place in the bare earth. Designing the City of the Dead in the neoclassical style, Barbieri introduced Verona's traditional burnt red colour,

cotto, creating a dichromacy. It was soon adapted for the Austrian military architecture in town. In the eyes of scholars, there's something in this composition reminiscent of Revolutionary France, such as Boulée or Ledoux. Barbieri had a rectangular plan, with two semi-circle wings. Later, one of the wings became another rectangle to house a cemetery from the First World War. The Garden Cemetery was added in the 1930s for Verona's emerging middle-class families who didn't have chapels in the old building, the Monumental Cemetery. In the nineteenth century, cemeteries were considered a public space for a promenade, and thus the opening of the new monument was an urban event. A gorgeous Erbisti monument depicting the deceased Maria Smania with her children provoked criticism in *L'Adige* newspaper for being 'too elegant and too polished'. Indeed, there are many striking monuments here from the turn of the nineteenth and twentieth centuries. A particularly interesting one is the pre-Raphaelite styled Dolci tomb, which shows a family crying over the loss of their daughter Carolina. The sculptor Ettore Ferrari, then famous for the Giordano Bruno monument in Rome, placed the ensemble in the Gothic interior and decorated it with golden mosaics. For a mystic touch, there is an art

nouveau bas-relief for the Falceri family. To see the plaque of Italy's most celebrated futurist painter and sculptor, Umberto Boccioni, one must visit the new part of the cemetery, designated for the military. Boccioni died after falling from his horse during the First World War. Futurists praised the war as a purification, and Boccioni followed what he preached. There is no decoration, but there are interesting inscriptions on the tomb by his friend, the futurist Gino Severini, who came to visit the site several decades later. From here, one might continue to the cemetery garden, through the vaulted interiors of the Church of the Saviour.

Tomb of futurist painter Umberto Boccioni

Christ Saviour Church interior

Carolina Dolci tomb

D

FAMIGLIA

GIVLIO CAMVZZONI ...
NATORE DEL REGNO, SINDACO DI
VERONA PER SEDICI ANNI, GRAN-
DE VFFICIALE DELLA CORONA D'
ITALIA, DA GIOVANE RIDVSSE AB
VBERTA' IL LATIFONDO DI VILLA-
BELLA, DA VECCHIO SPLENDIDA-
MENTE RESTAVRO' IL CASTELLO
DI SOAVE, E NEL CORSO ...
SVA VITA FV PADRE ...
CITTADINO ESEMPL ...
TI PREZIOSE DI MENTE ...
BILISSIME DI CVORE ...
M. XVI AGOSTO MDCCCXXII
M. VII APRILE MDCCCXCV
LA VEDOVA ANTONIETTA ...
PANIZZO ... CORSO ...
ED VN ...
AFFE ...

Monumento to Giulio Camuzzoni

Sergey Nikitin-Rimsky

Sergey Nikitin-Rismky

Cimitero Monumentale – Extension with 20th Century Chapels (Edicole)

121 D

Entry via Cemetery Temple
or from Viale Caduti Senza Croce, 5
Various architects

This is perhaps the best spot in Verona to appreciate contemporary architecture. Who could imagine that the city's most elite, conservative families would have experimented on their deathbeds? A walk through the garden cemetery, or the *cimitero giardino*, as it was called in the 1930s, is highly recommended. This cemetery came to be when the cemetery galleries ran out of space for the newly emerging middle class. One first finds the high-tech tomb of Bianchi Parladori, with its irregular enigmatic form in glass, concrete, and stone. Turning left, there is a miniature two-storey rationalist building with a dome. Perhaps the owner was a cement producer. The Cassetta family made their tomb following Verona's specialty: decorative brutalist forms made with local marble. The Sesini family enriched their bare concrete volume with an art deco à la Chinoise portico. The Biscaro family put their marble cenotaphs inside the stylishly darkened windows, reminding one of the Egyptian temple located in the Metropolitan museum. Navi preferred a nude concrete pavilion with an almost prefabricated appearance. A smaller version of Verona's most important San Zeno cathedral was constructed for the Pomari family. Verona's own Ettore Fagiuoli designed the Roncari tomb, which was the first in this area. He also created a white marble chapel for Montresor with Enea Ronca. Ronca, an engineer, built a lovely brick and marble temple for Napoleone Paon, including sculptures by Mario Salazzari. A graceful arched portico with byzantine mosaics is for the Faccioli family. In the northern part, Gilberto Barbesi created an open space for the Bonazzi family with evergreen trees and the sky as its ceiling. The Conforti family's dark-coloured art deco chapel is one of the first operas by Luigi Calcagni and Luciano Cenna, a duo who later built the local university. The client wanted to put

D

Sergey Nikitin-Rimsky

the coffin in the basement and also in the suspended volume of the first floor. Cenna doesn't deny that 'the race for space conquests of those years may have been partially responsibility for its look'. Finally, the striking, yellow-coloured Cappella Bregola looks a bit an Italian sportscar.

Verona Surroundings

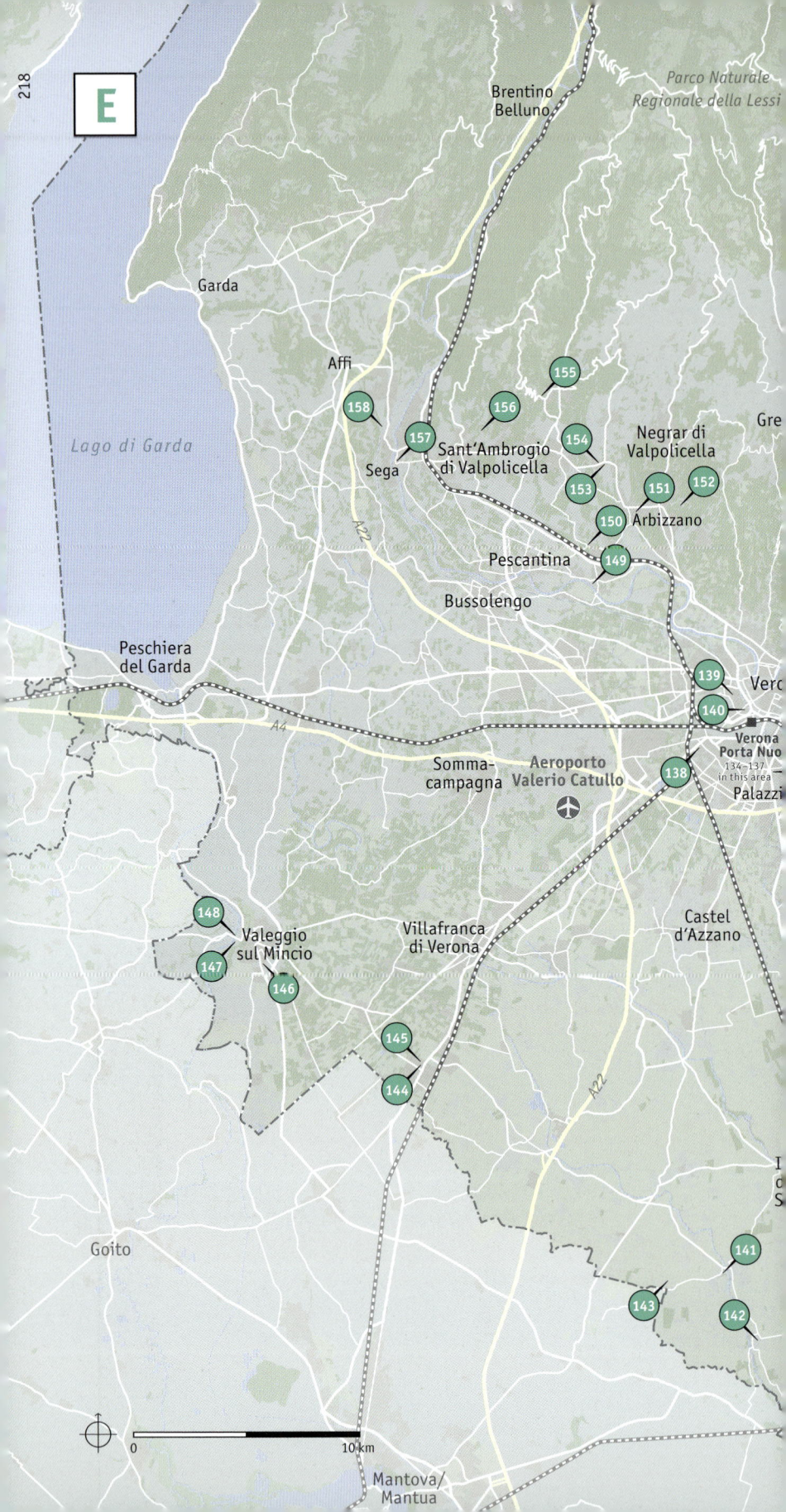

E

Parco Naturale
Regionale della Lessi

Brentino
Belluno

Garda

Affi

155

158

156

157

Sant'Ambrogio
di Valpolicella

154

Negrar di
Valpolicella

Gre

Sega

Lago di Garda

153

151

152

150

Arbizzano

Pescantina

149

Bussolengo

139

Ver

140

Peschiera
del Garda

Verona
Porta Nuo
134–137
in this area

138

Palazzi

Somma-
campagna

Aeroporto
Valerio Catullo

Castel
d'Azzano

148

Valeggio
sul Mincio

147

146

Villafranca
di Verona

145

144

A22

I d
S

Goito

141

143

142

0   10 km

Mantova/
Mantua

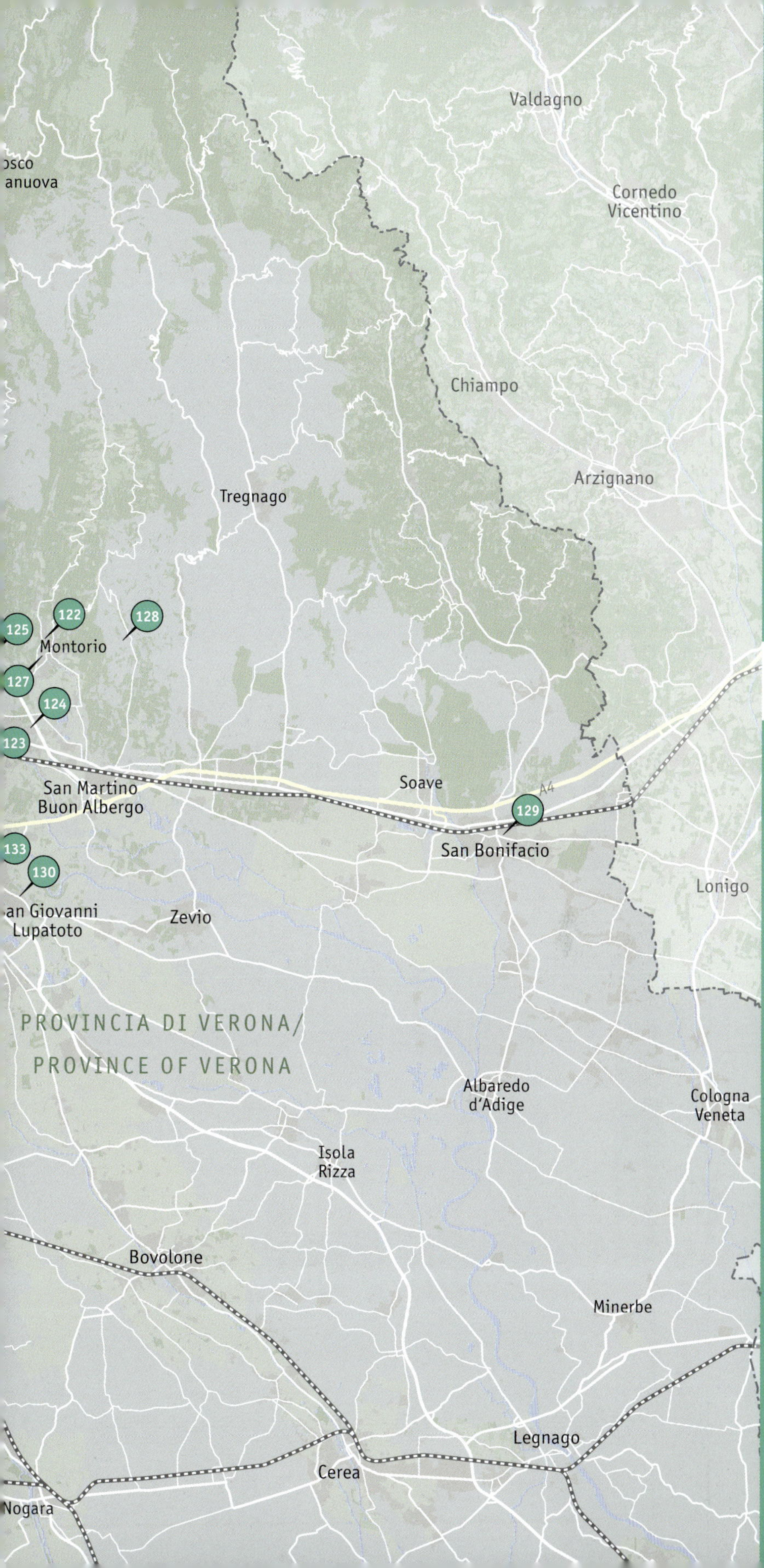
Valdagno
Cornedo Vicentino
osco
anuova
Chiampo
Arzignano
Tregnago
122
125
128
Montorio
127
124
123
San Martino Buon Albergo
Soave
A4
129
San Bonifacio
Lonigo
133
130
an Giovanni Lupatoto
Zevio
PROVINCIA DI VERONA/
PROVINCE OF VERONA
Albaredo d'Adige
Cologna Veneta
Isola Rizza
Bovolone
Minerbe
Legnago
Cerea
Nogara

Mulino Sartori
Via Villa 29, Montorio
16th century

122 E

The history of Montorio is linked to harnessing the driving force of water through the mills, which was first documented at this site in 920 CE. Immersed in flowers, moss, and cacti, the Sartori Mill looks like something out of a fairytale. Originally intended for cleaning grain, it holds the nickname Furia, meaning 'furious', because of the water's speed when it reaches this point. The Battaglia family built the structure and then sold it to the Cozza family, to whom the water rights also passed. Sartori was the name of the last renter, who used it to grind the plaster from one of his quarries.

Sergey Nikitin-Rimsky

Mondadori Workshops

Via Arnoldo Mondadori
(formerly Via Giovanni
Verardo Zeviani)
Armin Meili, Mario Mazzarotti
1956–1959

123 E

Arnoldo Mondadori, the founder of Italy's book empire, is widely associated with Milan. Yet his first big printing house was, in fact, in Veronetta. The new 40,000-square-metre premises was built for a few thousand workers on the outskirts of Verona in the late 1950s.

Mondadori invited Armin Meili, the leading Swiss master who broke Milanese hearts for building the Casa Svizzera, to decorate the huge and unpretentious workshops. The post-war town's first skyscraper was built when the city was still in ruins after the Second World War. A vast portal on mushroom-shaped columns with a spiral staircase and lamps, it resembles a giant musical instrument. The 50 stairs celebrate the 50th anniversary of the company. Unfortunately, miscalculations meant the staircase soon stopped being used. The factory is now closed.

Sergey Nikitin–Rimsky

Sergey Nikitin–Rimsky

Telecom (Iritel) Tower ⌄

San Michele, Verona East
Via Pietro Confortini 12, Verona
1991

124 E

At 149 metres, this is the tallest building in the city of Verona. According to a former staff member, it almost had an even bigger spire that would have reached up to 210 metres. The four-trunk tower is surmounted by the thinner square tower split by six discs. Two of them are turquoise octagonal rings, stitched by square windows. The first ring housed the TACS and GSM stations for TIM cell phones. The upper ring was used for technical staff offices, telephone equipment, and television transceivers. A paradoxical element becomes clear: the concrete tower is actually rusticated. However, the tower has become obsolete and was abandoned ten years ago. It still functions perfectly well as a common referent.

Stefano Aloe (Mo-KultProg)

Lime Kiln «

Via Ponte Florio 37, Montorio
19th century

125 E

Sergey Nikitin-Rimsky

This dramatically set structure featuring a crank is one of the highlights of Montorio's industrial legacy. Rails once connected the furnace with the quarry across the road, while wagons transported the raw material inside to transform it into lime. One of Montorio's patriots converted the building into a villa a few years ago.

Castello di Montorio

Via Castello, Montorio, Verona
Francesco Ronzan
10th, 14th, and 19th centuries

126 E

A kilometre outside of the city limits of Verona near the lovely Lessinia mountains, Montorio is a charming town that offers an industrial legacy and panoramic views overlooking the Squaranto Valley. One of its highlights is a medieval castle emerging from the fields and olive groves. There are just towers and walls, nothing more. Most are from the Scaliger times in the second half of the fourteenth century, but there are also some massive fortifications from the Austro-Hungarian period. The powder keg, walls, and the towers were restored in 2010. For a pleasant walk, you might start from Eurospin, where parking is available, and continue your trip up to the impressive Villa Guerrina.

Silvana Veneri

Sergey Nikitin-Rimsky

Spinning Wheel
Via Laghetto Squarà 34,
Montorio
1854

127 **E**

A gracious suburb of Verona, Montorio was once a laborious centre for silk production. This huge factory still dominates the area, surrounded by smaller villettas and a pleasant green space. The driving force here was powered by a sevenhorsepower hydraulic cast-iron wheel. The skeleton of the wheel is still visible over the small pond, which is one of the happiest public spaces in the village. This factory provided jobs to hundreds of people from neighbouring villages. Production halted shortly before the outbreak of the Second World War, and it was recently converted to an apartment building.

Sergey Nikitin-Rimsky

Villa Girasole
(San Martino Buon Albergo)

Via Mezzavilla 1, Marcellise
Ettore Fagiuoli, Angelo Invernizzi
(engineer)
1931–1935

A steel and marble cruiser lost in the cypress hills, Villa Girasole was built for and by engineer Angelo Invernizzi around 1929. In those days, Invernizzi was busy building multi-storey garages. Gazing at cars as they spun on ramps seems to have made him think a lot about rotation. Eventually, he called his army friend, architect Ettore Fagiuoli, to build a rotating two-storey house. Ever since, this 1,500-ton villa has been moving at 4 millimetres per second around the tower. Two electric motors powered by less than three horsepower can complete the 360-degree turn in nine hours and 20 minutes. Visionary! Villa Girasole was fuelled by the manic spirit of innovation that our great-grandfathers so cherished more so than by electricity or dominant futurism. Henry Ford would launch the first assembly line in 1913, 20 years before Invernizzi made the immovable first move. The villa has a concrete carcass with brick walls. The turning part was covered with sheets of aluminium alloy that gave a shiny 'aeronautical lightness' to the building, a trait so adored by art deco. Surrounded by 11 hectares of park with a tennis court and swimming pool, the Girasole family lived here happily until the foundation soil developed small subsidence, deforming the rails. This mysterious house has no longer moved since the 2000s. Swiss architect Botta has organised a foundation to restore it, giving a glimmer of hope to its admirers. Invernizzi's idea to build a house that follows the sun was revisited in popular revolving restaurants, first launched by the Florianturm Tower in Dortmund. All the rooms of the Dynamic Hotel in Dubai, too, are intended to rotate. And let's not forget the precedent set by Emperor Nero, whose spinning dining room on the Palatine Hill was recently discovered by archaeologists.

Roberto Bianconi

Roberto Bianconi

San Bonifacio Istituto Tecnico

**San Bonifacio
Istituto Tecnico
"Luciano Dal Cero"**
Via Fiume 28/bis, San Bonifacio
Rinaldo Olivieri
1966

129 E

Geometric concrete piles rise from the ground. When Rinaldo Olivieri first came here, there was nothing but abandoned suburbia. It seems he was quite inspired by this chaos, however, as he sought to create a picturesque composition displaying both the artistic and functional qualities of cement. Today, the institute includes a public library. The entrance's Pyramidal pylons with an oculus remind us that Olivieri's next big project was soon to be the world-famous La Pyramide in Abidjan, Ivory Coast. There is also the gorgeous, Romanesque Abbey of San Pietro (Piazza S. Benedetto 1).

Sergey Nikitin-Rimsky

226

E

San Giovanni Lupatoto
Piazza Umberto I

130 E

You'll find Italian architecture on parade here. This 500-metre-long main piazza of the suburban town of San Giovanni Lupatoto is immediately next to Verona's city limits. It tells the whole Italian story, from true liberty to commercial postmodernism. Piazza Umberto I, referred to simply as 'Liston' in Veneto, is a beloved public space featuring condominiums, cafes, hotels, and minor villas surrounded by gardens. One landmark is Villa Palazzoli (Piazza Umberto I 109–111) with its two turrets, a huge garden, and a nostalgic Austro-Hungarian feeling. The cinema-theatre Astra from the 1970s (Via Roma, 3/b) is behind the main church. A lovely villa, touting its swinging 1960s seaside modernism with a solarium atop it, is located at number 101. For one hundred years, the promenade area in the middle has been, in avant-garde fashion, overlooked by the water tower with two tiers of belvedere. The local administration decided to preserve it as a symbol of the town, and recent plans aim to convert the site into a museum.

Santuario della Madonnina dei Tedeschi

Via Madonnina 1,
San Giovanni Lupatoto
1630

131 E

The soldiers of Emperor Ferdinand II who marched to Mantua brought destruction and plague to this area. The plague killed two-thirds of the population, but this town was somehow spared by fate, as German troops never entered its limits. The survivors thus erected this church with the name 'Madonna of the Germans'. Outside, there are stunning stained-glass windows, probably from the 1960s, and inside there are wooden futurist sculptures. Frescoes from 1945 depict airplanes from the Second World War, meant to thank the Madonna who saved San Giovanni from German soldiers for the second time.

20th century wooden sculpture in the church

Sergey Nikitin-Rimsky

Threecharlie (wikipedia)

Church of Christ the Divine Worker

Piazza Papa Giovanni XXIII 2,
Verona South
Gelindo Giacomello
1964–1968

132 E

The Diocese of Verona built many churches in the 1950s and 1960s, both in town and in the province. All of them followed modernist architectural trends. The Second Vatican Council simplified the language of the ritual and encouraged architectural innovation. This suggestion may have remained on paper only if it weren't for the intervention of the Italian government. Dominated by the Christian Democratic party, the Italian state began financing new ecclesiastical construction with public money. Even the church's dedication to 'Christ the Divine Worker' reminds one of stiff competition for the votes of the working class – between communists and right-wing parties. After analysing this productive period, architect Federica Guerra proposed the term 'ecclesiastic structuralism' to describe it. This church was the first significant public building in this part of Borgo Roma. It had also tennis courts and the Don Baldo nursery school. Bruno Ghiettj, one of the Vatican's favourite masters, proposed using the parabolic vault – common in industrial buildings – in the interior of the Church of the Canadese Martyrs in Rome (Our Lady of SS. Sacramento). Gelindo Giacomello brought this tune here, as well as to some of his other creations in Verona. Its geometric severity contrasts with the childish manner of the mosaics by Scopini.

E

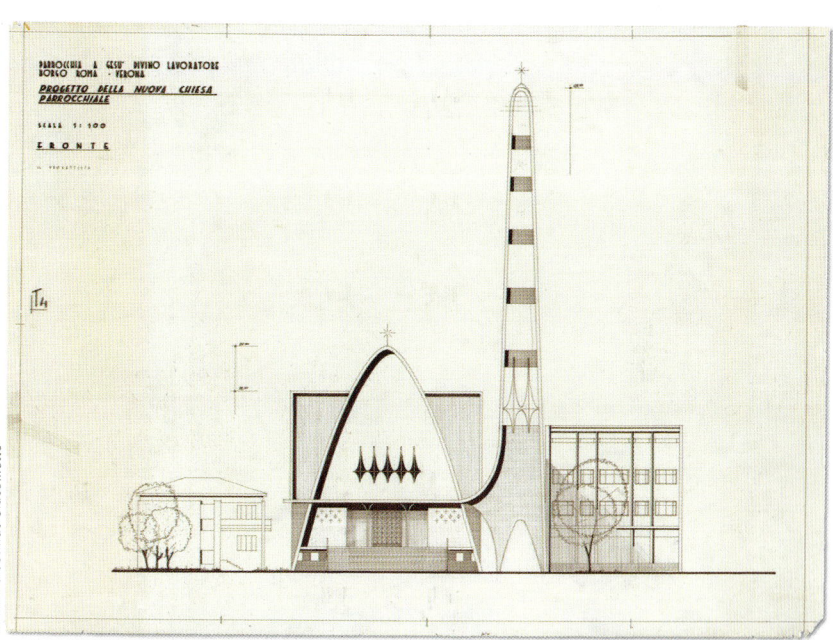

Archivio Gelindo Giacomello

Sergey Nikitin-Rimsky

Sergey Nikitin-Rimsky

Church of Christ the Divine Worker and Borgo Roma

E

Fabrizio Mauro

Tower of the Paper Fabric »

Via Dott. F. Garofoli 208,
San Giovanni Lupatoto
1930s

133 E

Sergey Nikitin-Rimsky

Here lies an empty battlefield; a scrap of vacant land in the heart of San Giovanni Lupatoto, where it was once hoped to build something new, and now plans are in place for a car park with offices and housing. This was a vast modernist complex of the paper fabric company Saifecs just 10 years ago. Built strictly in concrete with a portico of five pilasters, it provided jobs to thousands of people in the area. Developers and bureaucrats have since spared only the street's name, Via Della Cartiera, and an electrical unit with its protruding roof, which looks a bit like a teenager in a baseball cap. Verona's industrial age began relatively late and was short-lived; soon, there will be no remains of it at all.

Archivio Cristian J Folchi

Grandi Magazzini and Central Refrigerator Rotunda ⌃ »

Via Santa Teresa, 2 ,
Giuseppe Tromba, Pio Beccherle
1925–1930s

134 E

This colossal complex, surrounded by the railway, was developed in 1924 to store foreign and local goods, including grain, meat, fruit, and vegetables. What was once military territory next to the Porta Nuova station was quickly built with storage and facilities for various services and offices. The new refrigeration station by engineer Giuseppe Tromba already proved insufficient a year after the opening. Thus, they decided to build a giant refrigerator – with a dome. Engineer Pio Beccherle designed the Central Refrigerator in the spirit of the automation and rationalisation that was ruling over Europe in the wake of Henry Ford's success. The aim was to preserve food materials in the period between their arrival in Verona and their shipment, as well as to sort and package goods. The rotunda, directly served by the railway, developed around the massive rotating platform (with a diameter of 18 metres) under the dome. This platform sorted wagons loaded with goods into the seven refrigeration tunnels and eight cells for fruit and vegetables. The complex ceased operations in the 1980s. The municipality bought it, but didn't know what to do with it. Thankfully, music saved it: the Interzona Cultural Association was founded in 1992, beginning a 10-year marathon of raves and concerts inspired by post-Wall Berlin, the British underground, and Tarkovsky's cult film, *Stalker*. The Ministry of Cultural Heritage approved of the value of industrial archaeology. Businesses gained momentum here, followed by the state archive. In the 1990s, the complex seemed like a massive inspirational resource for the city, which could at last change Verona's destiny to be recognised as a prominent, new creative hub. However, in all these years, there has yet to be a single competition for individual projects nor a general concept. 'After thirty years the vision of the Magazzini Generali as a public space is still missing – owners think about real estate income but not about the urban situation,' said Alberto Vignolo, editor-in-chief of the magazine *Architetti Verona*. Mario Botta built offices for the Unicredit, who owns the territory through its philanthropic Cariverona foundation. Botta also curated the reconstruction of the Central Fridge (2009) for the Eataly restaurant, which is slowly progressing. Yet the project is clearly stalling without a vision; there is an urgent need for an international competition for the development of Magazzini and the adjacent areas.

E

Archivio Cristiano Folchi

Archivio Cristiano Folchi

Sergey Nikitin-Rimsky

Apartment Building ⌃
Via Santa Teresa 53,
Verona
1980s–1990s

135 E

Via Scuderlando Houses ⌄ »
Via Scuderlando 170–193,
Verona
19th–20th centuries

136 E

This self-confident Balnear façade looks a bit out of the place here. Though, from its balconies one may admire the development of the Magazzini Generali. The courtyard recalls a slightly ajar linen closet. From this spot, one can visit Via Tombetta, which embraces the condominium from the east with its low-storeyed urban fabric and modest 1920s Gothic and Liberty façades.

Timid art nouveau, rationalism, and even post-rationalism: Via Scuderlando and its many two-storey buildings has got it all. Step into the side lanes to experience their unique atmospheres. Twenty years ago, the Borgo Roma had an infamous reputation; today, however, the neighbourhood is comfortable and well-groomed.

Edilizia Popolare Novecentesca

E

Sergey Nikitin-Rimsky

Sergey Nikitin-Rimsky

Bauli Cakes Headquarters and Bar

Via Del Perlar 2, Verona
Rosario Firullo (addition)
1954, 1973–1977

137 E

In the 1980s it was fashionable to drop by for breakfast here on the outskirts; the bar of this famous confectionery factory had the most modern interior in town. Initially, it was a two-storey piece of ascetic modernism. Twenty years later, the owners wanted to refresh the interior, but architect Firullo suggested adding some floors instead. They could have gone even higher, but the regulations prohibited them from exceeding 30 metres. Thus, a spectacular pile of popular construction techniques is surmounted over the original two-storey cafe. In an unexpected turn of events, the supporting frame broke out of the concrete box. The house immediately became a symbol of the fast-growing company and the area as a whole, extending beyond Fiera di Verona.

Fabrizio Mauro

Fabrizio Mauro

E

Fabrizio Mauro

Sergey Nikitin–Rimsky

Santa Lucia II
Residential District

138 E

Via Valeggio, Via Monzambano
Maurizio Sacripanti, G. Bisoffi,
E. D'Andrea, N. Di Cagno,
G. Malatesta, P. Moroni
1956–1958

You'll want to visit this district with a soundtrack from the swinging 1960s, perhaps Mina and Celentano – or at least listen to the conversations at the open-air Club of the Elderly, which was once the railway depot. Verona did not ultimately choose prefabricated housing, but it did indeed flirt with the style. There is a fleeting feeling of Eastern Europe in Santa Lucia II. The silhouette of Monzambano 19, with its broken pediment, resembles a series 1510 – one of the first *Khrushchevkas* that provided free apartments to hundreds of thousands of people in Moscow and across the USSR. Of course, the 10 houses of Santa Lucia, each of which are three or four storeys, offered lots of space for refinement and idealistic experimentations. Maurizio Sacripanti, a beton lyricist from Rome and friend of the critic Bruno Zevi, landed in Verona just before he had designed a head-scratcher of a building for Peugeot in Buenos Aires. It is convenient to visit the parish church of San Giovanni Evangelista from here.

Sergey Nikitin–Rimsky

Sergey Nikitin–Rimsky

Fabrizio Mauro

Stadio Bentegodi

Piazzale Olimpia, Verona
Leopoldo Baruchello
1963

 139 E

E

The engineer Leopoldo Baruchello superimposed three rings, one over another, to create enough space for almost 40,000 spectators. The tribunes were covered for the 1990 World Cup. The stadium is now at risk of being demolished or reconstructed, so that it might host commercial spaces in the future.

When the Second World War ended, the men of Verona turned to football and never looked back. It became a focal attraction, a defining cultural code of the city: Verona would not be Verona without its team. In the 1985 season, Hellas Verona FC won the Italian championship. The Serie B team Chievo also plays here. Bentegodi Stadium was built in 11 months – a fruit of the same *il boom economico* period when Verona also launched its university and reconstructed Castelvecchio with Scarpa.

Sergey Nikitin–Rimsky

Sergey Nikitin–Rimsky

Sergey Nikitin–Rimsky

Palladio Condominium

Viale Andrea Palladio 26, Verona
Luciano Cenna
1979–1982

140 E

This heroic concrete condo raised on the property of the ice cream king Teo Sanson is happy to have a tight-knit community. With its 400 apartments, Palladio could be considered a small town in and of itself. In fact, its corners are protected by four towers. Cenna has conceived 40 different functional and dimensional types, among which are duplexes with a day level, a night level, and a roof garden on the flat terrace. The municipal administration demanded 30 apartments to rent to people in need, which turned out to be a bit of a miscalculation, as these tenants were unable to pay the high condominium expenses – in part due to the costs of central heating. As a result, there were serious deficits in the budget. Nevertheless, Palladio is still thriving. A large and well-kept garden is fed by the rainwater that is collected in the recently installed underground cistern.

Sergey Nikitin–Rimsky

Sergey Nikitin–Rimsky

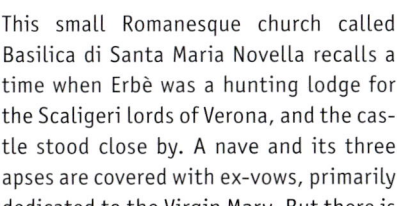

Sergey Nikitin-Rimsky

E

Basilica di Santa Maria Novella and the Starfighter in the Park

141 E

Viale G. Basilicà, Erbè
11th–12th centuries

This small Romanesque church called Basilica di Santa Maria Novella recalls a time when Erbè was a hunting lodge for the Scaligeri lords of Verona, and the castle stood close by. A nave and its three apses are covered with ex-vows, primarily dedicated to the Virgin Mary. But there is also a curious scene depicting the life of San Giuliano, in which two spouses rest in bed while a third person pounces on them with a dagger. Some locals have been trying to raise awareness about the monument since the 1980s. A nice park by the Tione River surrounds the church. There is an airplane in the trees – a monument to the curious speed duel that took place in Veneto in 1981 between the F-104 ASA-M Starfighter and F1 cars – Ferrari, Alfa Romeo, and Brabham. This was installed by the local Club Ferrari Erbè in 2006.

Sergey Nikitin-Rimsky

Sergey Nikitin–Rimsky

Palazzo del Diavolo
Via Roma 7, Sorgà
16th century

142 E

Called Palazzo del Diavolo, this finely designed volume stands alone at the outskirts of Sorgà. Locals say a magician – De Bursis of the Gonzaga Court – commissioned the villa and that he used it for diplomatic meetings, parties, and, above all, esoteric meetings. It was thanks to this client that the villa received its nickname. There is another palace of Diavolo just 29 kilometres away. Curiously, these marshy lands of Bassa Veronese also gave rise to other occult-inclined locals, such as the controversial Satanic death metal groups of the 1990s.

Sergey Nikitin–Rimsky

Sergey Nikitin-Rimsky

Villa Curtoni Tretti detta "Cortalta" (Erbè)

Via Cort'Alta, Trevenzuolo
16th century,
19th century (main house),
1832 (wings with porticoes)

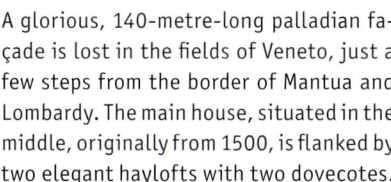

143 E

E

A glorious, 140-metre-long palladian façade is lost in the fields of Veneto, just a few steps from the border of Mantua and Lombardy. The main house, situated in the middle, originally from 1500, is flanked by two elegant haylofts with two dovecotes.

These extensions with tuff arcades were built for drying and storing grains in 1832 when the Venetian Grimani family were its owners. The façade still preserves some traces of its nineteenth century geometric ornamental paintings. There are other outbuildings, too, such as stables, the mill, and the blacksmith's and carpenter's shops. Inside, there are machines and other belongings that have accumulated over the centuries. Ninety people lived and worked here in the 1960, but there's no one to be found here now.

Sergey Nikitin-Rimsky

Villa Vecelli Cavriani

144 E

Via Caterina Bon Brenzoni 1,
Mozzecane
Adriano Cristofali
16th century

This graceful villa was falling into ruin until 20 years ago. Once an aristocrat dimora or 'dwelling' in the nineteenth century, the building was transformed into a hospital. It was then turned into a wool factory, only to later be abandoned. In the late 1990s, however, local cloth producer Italo Martinelli purchased the building. Now, after careful restoration, the building's lofty spaces have finally been brought back to life. It is often rented out for banquets and ceremonies. A restaurant, hotel, and school are also situated on the grounds of the villa. Designed by the Veronese Adriano Cristofali, author of Mosconi Bertani Villa in the Valpolicella, the villa's lovely interiors are adorned with playful trompe-l'œil frescoes painted by Francesco Lorenzi.

Sergey Nikitin-Rimsky

Sergey Nikitin-Rimsky

Sergey Nikitin–Rimsky

E

Macelleria Franchini ⌃
Via Caterina Bon Brenzoni 30,
Mozzecane
Fabrizio Boschini
1995

145 E

Former Fruit Market ⌄
Piazza della Repubblica/
Via Ragazzi del '99,
Valeggio sul Mincio
1920–1930

146 E

There is an unusual postmodern butcher shop across the street from Villa Vecelli Cavriani. The building looks a bit like a red velvet cake and features contrasting elements: various window forms, local red and white marble, and exposed metal structures. From the back courtyard, there are even more beautiful contrasts, which combine high-tech and brutalist elements.

It's a pleasure to meet this 1930s rationalist style building, featuring a characteristic stucco and brick façade, in the small provincial town of Valeggio sul Mincio. One might take the man relaxing with a cornucopia at the entrance to be a sign of baths or a brothel. In fact, this was once a fruit market, but it was abandoned decades ago.

Sergey Nikitin–Rimsky

Ladiras (iStock)

Borghetto sul Mincio
Valeggio sul Mincio
Ottorino Tognetti (restoration)
1975

147 E

While the nearby Parco Giardino Sigurtà may leave one with a strong botanical impression, the village of Borghetto sul Mincio, which lies just down the hill, is ideal for those who love to explore urban organisms. A charming mass of about a dozen houses and some mills, this borghetto was growing in the Middle Ages as a fief of the Abbey of San Zeno thanks to the toll money collected from the bridge. Later, this small village actually became a part of the fortified bridge. San Marco church still presides over the area with its medieval bell tower dating to the times of the La Scala family. The borghetto was just a village until the 1980s when it became a favourite lunch spot. A preservation plan was carried out by Ottorino Tognetti, a long-time collaborator of the famous restorer Piero Gazzola.

icenando (iStock)

Silvia Cozzi (iStock)

Visconti Bridge-Dam

Borghetto sul Mincio

Domenico dei Benintendi

1393–1395

148 E

Struck by a strong, megalithic feeling and captured by its huge rocks made of brick and stone, you may not be surprised to learn that this wide bridge was conceived as a hydraulic weapon. Gian Galeazzo Visconti, Duke of Milan and known for driving out the Scaligeri, took Verona and wanted to conquest Mantua. By constructing this bridge-dam, he hoped to block and divert the waters of the Mincio River from its regular route, leaving the town to die of thirst. Ultimately, his plan didn't work. Once connected by two walls to the dominating Scaliger Castle, this structure is 650 metres long and 25 metres wide. Visconti integrated the bridge into the fortified complex of Serraglio, an ambitious construction project started by the Scaligeri family with which they dreamed of protecting their lands from their neighbours and enemies. A 13-kilometre-long wall stretched from Valeggio sul Mincio to the swamps of Grezzano. Its ruins can be seen in the fields near Villafranca.

E

Sergey Nikitin-Rimsky

Sergey Nikitin-Rimsky

Villa Bertoldi and its aqueduct 149 E

Via Antonio Bertoldi 13,
Settimo di Pescantina
Arteco srl (renovation)
18th century, 2004–2008

E

This is a typical Venetian villa with large outbuildings and a vast garden. Concerts are organised here, but its most intriguing element is the aqueduct, which can be enjoyed simply by walking along the shore of the Adige River. This archaic structure is attributed to the Roman period but it's much younger.

Fabrizio Mauro

Fabrizio Mauro

Byblos Art Hotel Villa Amistà `150` `E`
Via Cedrare 78, Valpolicella
Ignazio Pellegrini 18th century,
Alessandro Mendini 2005

They say that Michele Sanmicheli was building something here at one point, in his typical unhurried manner. Two centuries later, the architect and aristocrat Ignazio Pellegrini built the current house. Byblos has recently converted the villa into a luxury hotel with a paradoxical art collection featuring works by Ettore Sottsass, Damien Hirst, Philippe Starck, and Eero Saarinen. The modern interior was created by Alessandro Mendini, a classic architect of Milanese design, co-founder of Studio Alchimia, and editor of *Domus*. Bright, vivid colours continue from the lobby to the rooms and finally to the spa, where you'll also find frescoes inspired by the Romans. A beautiful park is also on the premises.

Byblos Art Hotel

Byblos Art Hotel

E

Roberto Bianconi

Villa Serego in Santa Sofia

Via S. Sofia 1, Pedemonte,
San Pietro in Cariano
Andrea Palladio 1565,
Luigi Trezza 19th century

151 E

This is one of the last villas designed by Palladio, and the only known one in Veronese territory. It was named a UNESCO heritage site in 1996. Unlike his other creations, Palladio's space here revolves around the large colonnaded courtyard, which was modelled after the peristyle of the Roman villas. Only a small part was completed compared to the large extension in the *Four Books* by Palladio. At the beginning of the nineteenth century, architect Luigi Trezza added new habitable rooms along the western side of the building and completed the entablature and balustrade in the courtyard. The gigantic size of the iconic columns gives a grotesque impression, recalling tectonic visions of Giulio Romano in the nearby town of Mantua. The pillars are laid with blocks of limestone from the local quarries of Serego. Palladio's patron, Marcantonio Serego, married Ginevra Alighieri, one of the last descendants of Dante Alighieri, which gave rise to the still-existing Serego Alighieri family. Villa Serego Alighieri in Gargagnago now hosts the headquarters of Sandro Boscaini's wine empire, MASI.

Hans A. Rosbach

Sergey Nikitin-Rimsky

E

Villa Mosconi Bertani

152 E

Via Novare 2, Arbizzano
Adriano Cristofali
18th century

Negrar has just changed its name to Negrar di Valpolicella to highlight its leading position in the production of Valpolicella wine. Villas in this region developed in close relationship with the cultivation of wine, among other local delicacies. Adriano Cristofali built this imposing manor with two wings and a church, enclosed with a railing with obelisks. The palace is lavishly adorned. Its central hall of muses occupies two floors and was decorated by Prospero Pesci and Giuseppe Valliani with allegories of the arts and four seasons. The villa was one of the nests of the Romantic epoch in Italy: poet and aesthete Ippolito Pindemonte spent ten years here as a guest of countess Elisabetta Mosconi. It was he who suggested developing the park in the English style. From his journey to France, Pindemonte, who was a friend of Jean-Jacques Rousseau, suggested the idea of a rural chalet, which still stands on the lake. The villa, wine cellars, and splendid park are open for visits, tastings, and weddings. In 1888, they discovered the nearby Roman aqueduct that brought water from Garda to Verona. While in Negrar, you might like to visit the Romanesque church of San Pietro and the caves of Prun. Stone from the caves used to be removed and used for Verona's monuments and pavements. For visits, contact La Malga Association in advance. Villa Bertoldi, now Stefani, is another charming villa located nearby in the village of Palazzo. Large warehouses flank its elegant façade with Venetian Gothic loggias.

Chiesa di San Floriano »
Via Don Cesare Biasi,
San Pietro in Cariano
12th century, 1743

153 E

This mighty roadside volume temple was built on the site of a pagan cemetery. Quite stunningly, two Roman sepulchral stones serve as bases for buttresses that divide the main façade. In the deserted interior of the rural Church of San Floriano, the styles flow from Romanesque to baroque. The foundation of the bell tower is made of stone, while the barrel continues in alternating rows of tuff blocks and bricks. A charming cloister smoothly turns into the ancient Borgo.

Sergey Nikitin-Rimsky

Zýmē Azienda Shop
Via Cà del Pipa 1,
San Pietro in Cariano
Moreno Zurlo
2015

154 E

Sergey Nikitin-Rimsky

Celestino Gaspari is a romantic. Inspired by the high-tech distilleries of Scotch whisky, he created this temple for Valpolicella wine. Zýmē, meaning 'yeast' in Greek, is a three-level structure, with two levels underground, including the fifteenth century cave. The building totals 3,300 square metres in size and cost six million euros. In classic Italian fashion, the interiors synthesise a nonchalant attitude of archaeological self-awareness and a bit of a nightclub feel. A highlight is the roaring spring, which flows from a fractured rock and was discovered during construction.

E

Sergey Nikitin-Rimsky

Villa Della Torre Allegrini
Via della Torre 25, Fumane
16th century

155 **E**

Valpolicella's highlight is this fabulous villa of the sixteenth century, with its joyous and cosy peristyle and mute fountain. The villa was built by Giulio Della Torre, erudite and moralist, and his three sons, all Veronese religious authorities. The family had a famous salon in Verona frequented by the likes of Michele Sanmicheli and Matteo Bandello, the author of the original *Romeo and Juliet*. Who was the architect? The portico in the courtyard and the playful tone of the fireplaces with images of Satan and unicorns are thought to be the work of the cheerful genius of Giulio Romano. And they very well may be. But it is likely that the illustrious commissioner was the one to develop the programme. A bit later, Giulio's grandson, Marcantonio della Torre, added the towers to the main volume, thereby doing justice to their surname, which translates to 'tower'. In those days, the legendary Venetian courtesan and poetess Veronica Franco wrote poetry celebrating the 'candid beds' of the Della Torre family. The octagonal church originally featured an altar in the centre, by Michele Sanmicheli. Decades of abandonment were followed by decades of restoration, until the villa was finally bought by the wine company Allegrini. It is now open for visitors who want to order great wines or even stay the night.

Sergey Nikitin–Rimsky

Sergey Nikitin-Rimsky

Sergey Nikitin-Rimsky

E

Sergey Nikitin-Rimsky

San Giorgio di Valpolicella

Piazza della Pieve,
San Giorgio di Valpolicella
7th – 11th century

Strolling uphill, Garda and its vineyards provide nothing short of breath-taking views. The church, which is still the biggest in town, is based on the sanctuary of the seventh century. The church was not initially Christian though: on this site, archaeologists have found ex-votos dedicated to Luna, Fortuna, Vesta, and Sol, some of which are on display in the small museum attached to the church. Indeed, the Lombards who lived here converted to Christianity only towards the end of the seventh century CE. The three-naved basilica has apses both from Western and Eastern façades, like the Basilica Ulpia in Rome. Here in Garda, it is believed that the original altar was originally at the site of the current entrance, like in the earliest Christian temples. Today, ornaments and saints cover the church's walls and vaults. There is a ciborium from the period of the Lombard King Liutprand (eighth century) at the altar. The magnificent bell tower is a contemporary of the main building, while the cloister dates back to the seventh century.

Sergey Nikitin-Rimsky

A. berto Masnovo (iStock)

Alberto Masnovo (iStock)

Villa Nichesola-Conforti

157 E

Via Domegliara 5, Ponton di
Sant'Ambrogio di Valpolicella
Paolo Farinati
1580–1590

This villa is a purely theatrical forest of obelisks. Here, as in other famous villas of the area, its makers played with rustication following Giulio Romano's recipes in Palazzo Te. The Veronese law expert Fabio Nichesola invited Paolo Farinati, a leading Veronese painter, to embellish his villa. Or, more likely, since Farinati's frescoes once covered the exterior of the building, the artist played as architect as well. The entrance pillars greet visitors in Greek: 'Hello – I, the Lethe, welcome you'. Nichesola was one of the founders of the Accademia Filarmonica in Verona, and his son, Cesare, a canon of the cathedral, created a botanical garden and an antique collection here. After suffering during the Second World War and years of abandonment, the villa was recently restored. The idea of a villa-museum is dear to the heart of the current owner, a professor of the history of arts, Giuseppe Conforti. Here, he displays his collection of old prints, as well as a gallery of plasters from the classical and Renaissance ages.

Sergey Nikitin-Rimsky

Sergey Nikitin-Rimsky

E

Sergey Nikitin-Rimsky

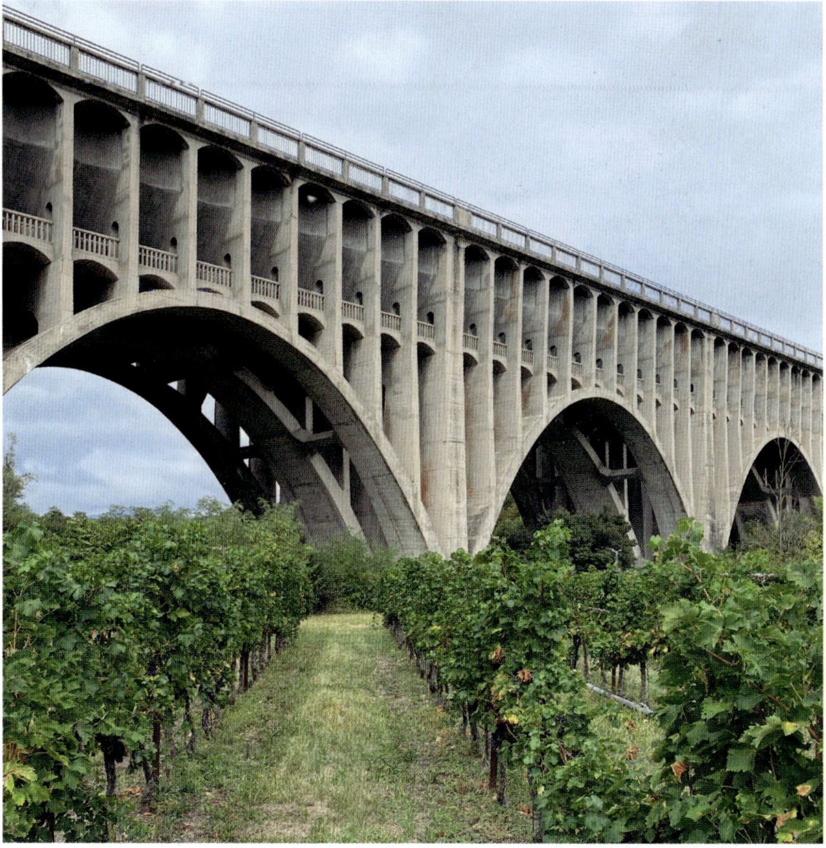

Fabrizio Mauro

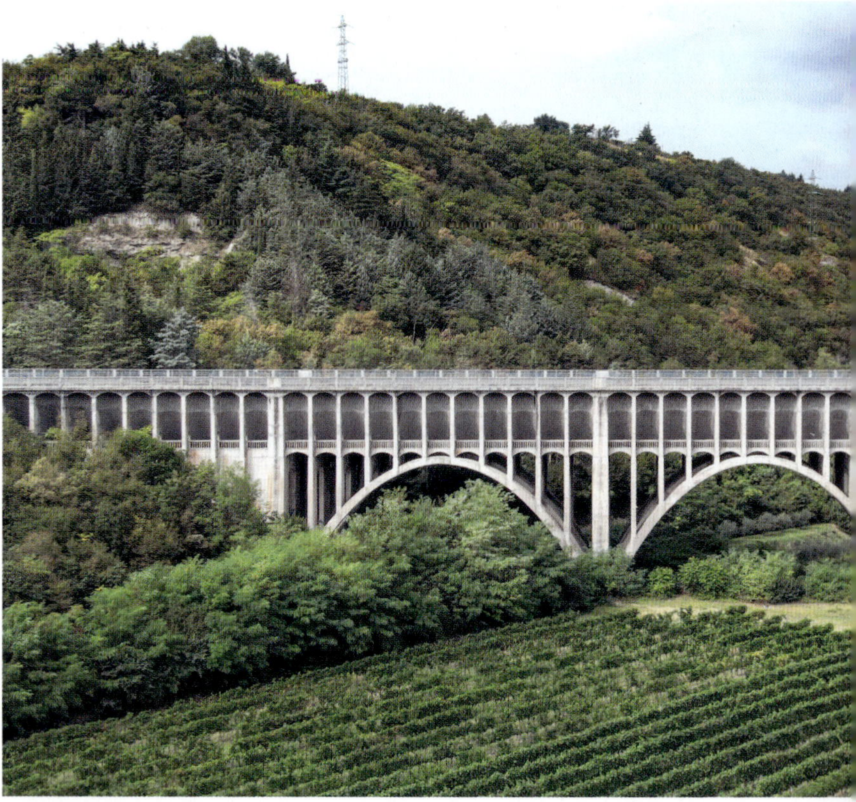

Progetto Dighe

Progetto Dighe

Acquedotto del Canale Biffis 158 E

Via Progno/Strada Provinciale 11,
Sega di Cavaion
Ferdinando Biffis
1943

This heroic aqueduct over Tasso Creek is the centrepiece of the 47-kilometre-long channel, finished in 1943. A 20-year-old ETH graduate named Ferdinando Biffis proposed building it in 1913, but it took a personal telegram from Mussolini in 1928 to halt provincial doubts and discussions and cause the Veronese to begin excavating and drilling tunnels. The aqueduct takes water from the Adige River in the village of Ala di Pilcante and returns it to the river near Verona. In the meantime, water is brought to the province's northern, more fertile areas. Construction was carried out mostly by hand, with rare use of some mechanical excavators. During the Second World War, prisoners of war from Yugoslavia, England, New Zealand, and Australia were forced to operate the aqueduct, right in time for Mussolini's arrest. Today, there is a bicycle path along the canal that leads from Verona to Rivoli.

E

Fabrizio Mauro

F

F

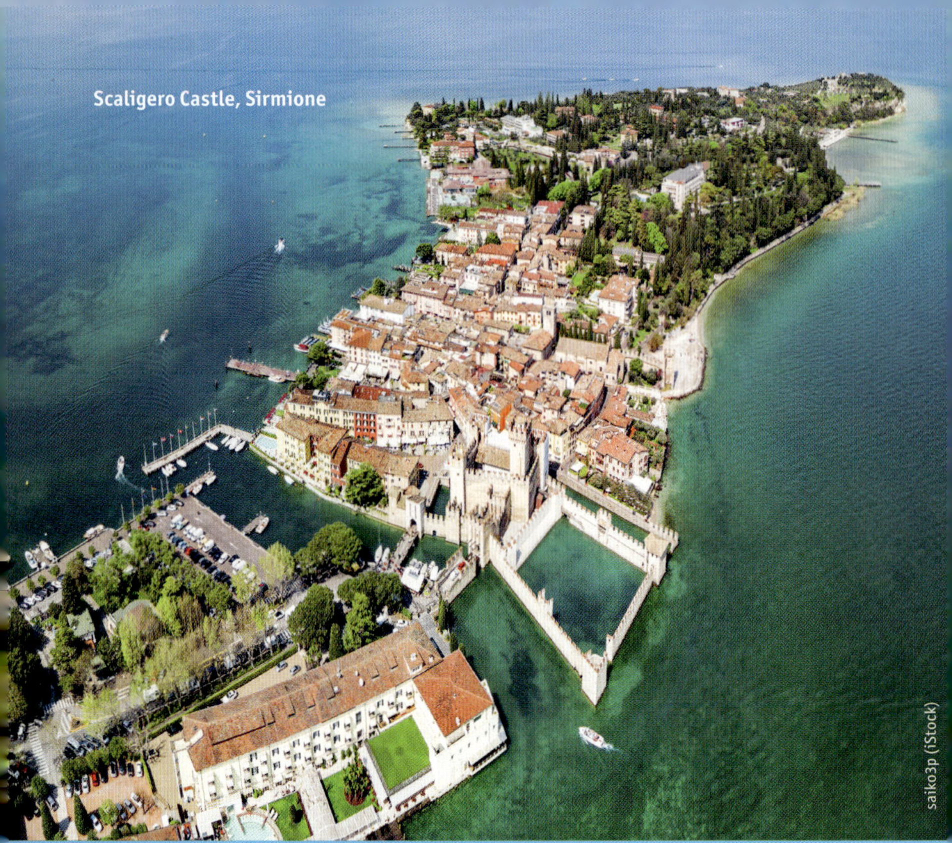
Scaligero Castle, Sirmione

saiko3p (iStock)

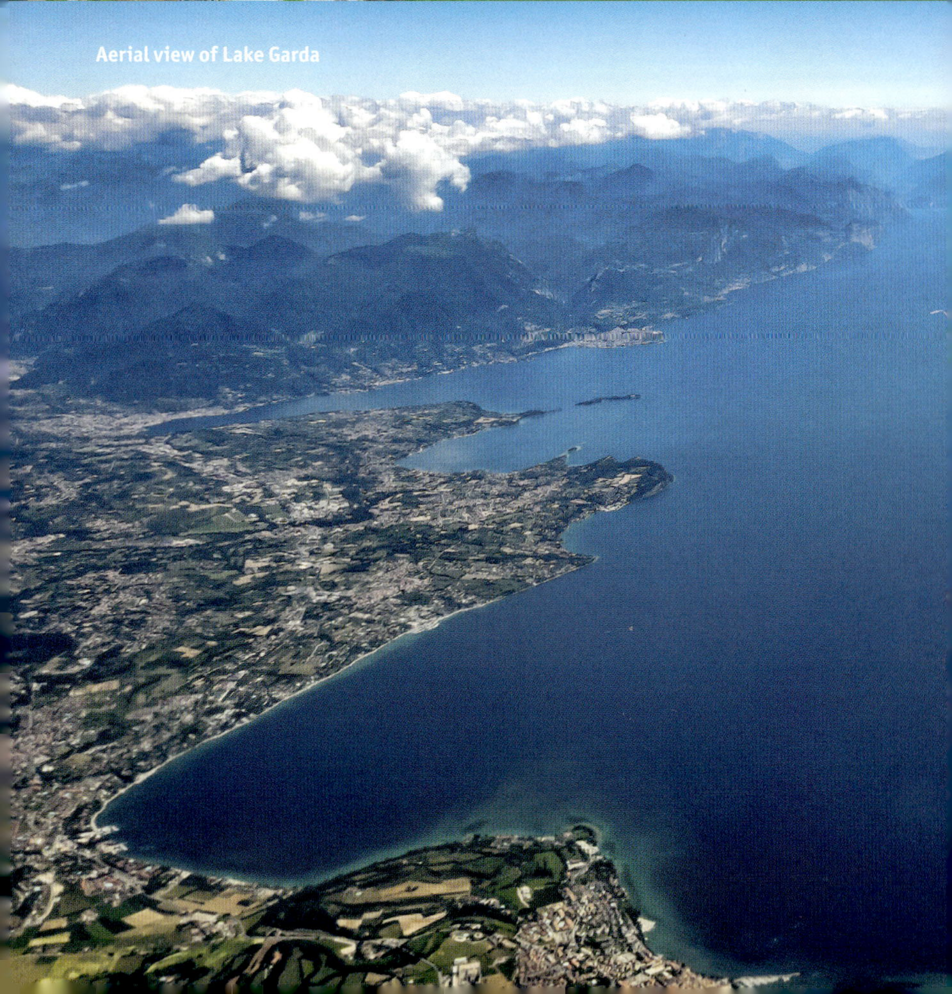
Aerial view of Lake Garda

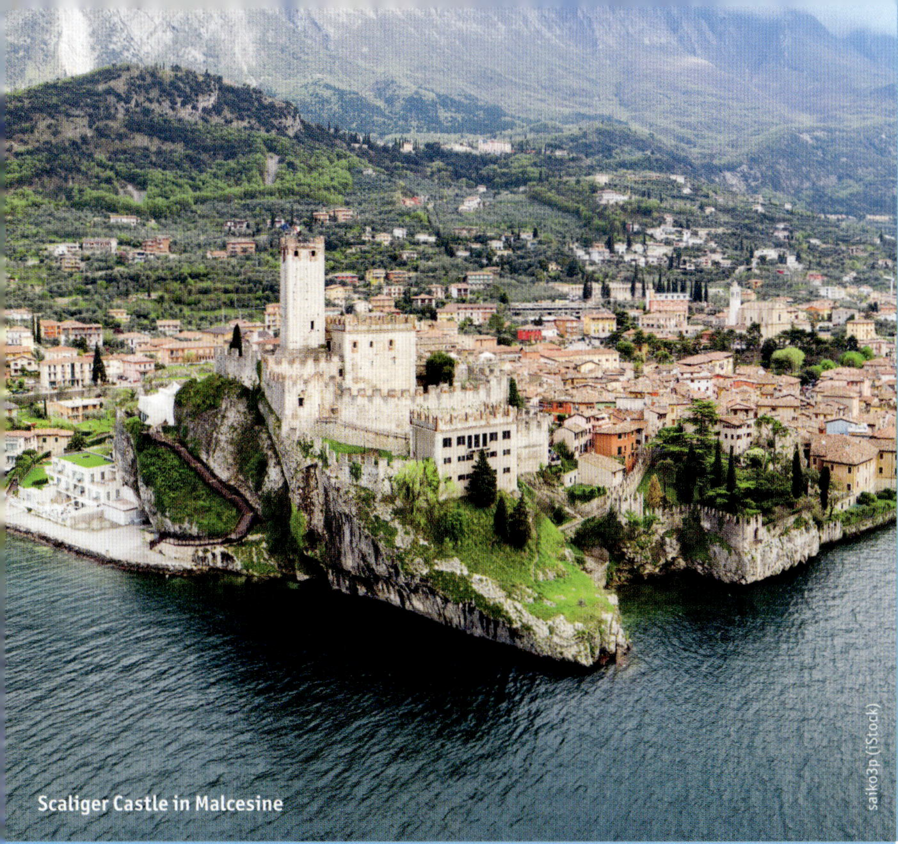

Scaliger Castle in Malcesine

saiko3p (iStock)

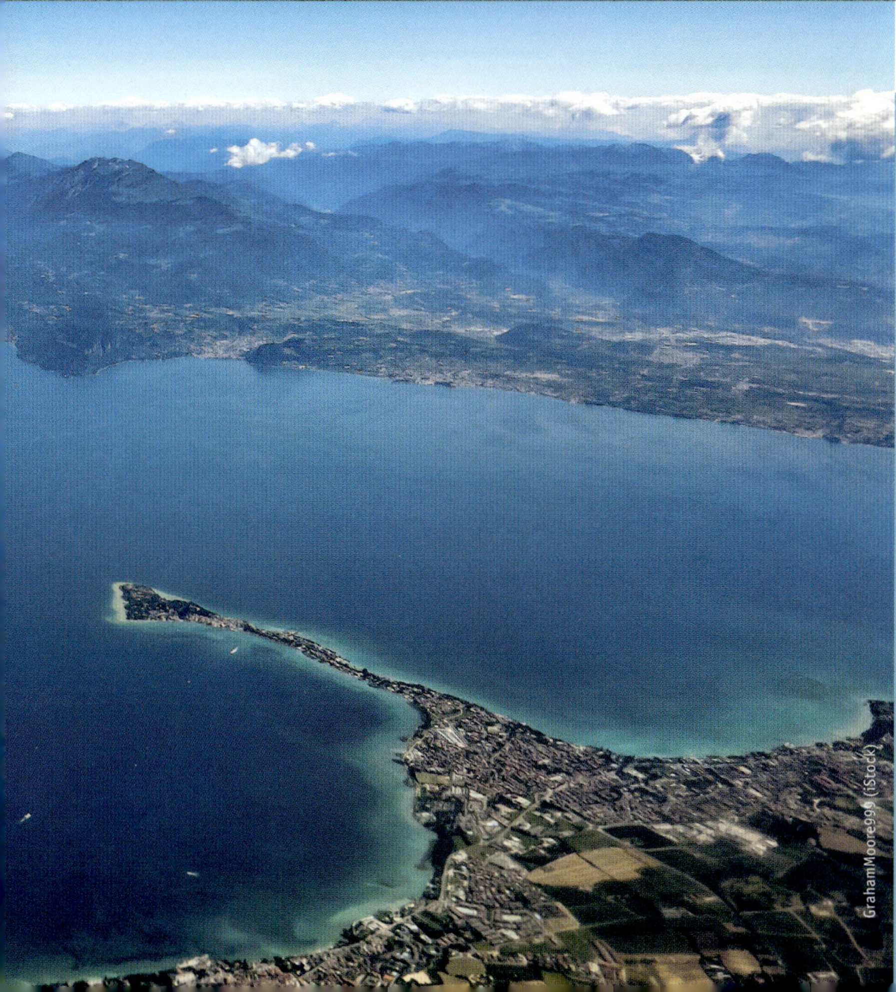

GrahamMoore999 (iStock)

Pieve antica di Santa Maria
Corso Italia 10, Garda

159 F

Garda town, whose name originates from the Germanic 'Warda' – a place of the guard – gave its name the lake that the town rests beside. The town was an important located in the Middle Ages. Its fortress once dominated the lake until Emperor Ottone destroyed it for an unknown reason. It's possible that his wife Adelaide requested its destruction, having been imprisoned there for some time. The church foundations are from the eighth century. Verona's bishop ordered the construction of the current temple in 1530, but due to a lack of financial resources, it took 235 years for the work to be completed.

Inside, there are precious remains of frescoes and stone reliefs from the pre-existent structure, as well as art nouveau-inspired paintings. The basilica gives the impression of a German church, rather than an Italian one, even though the territory was not yet part of the Austrian empire at the time of its construction. In Garda town, you may also see Palazzo Fregoso, which was built on the city wall. The Venetian general Cesare Fregoso lived here with his secretary and friend Matteo Bandello, the author of the novella *Giulietta e Romeo*. The Bard of Avon, a fellow known as William Shakespeare, would later transform this story into his celebrated play. Three kilometres away from the centre, hiding under cypress trees, there is a restaurant called Locanda San Vigilio, justly famous as the perfect place to enjoy sunsets over Garda.

Jarretera (dreamstime)

Camaldolese Hermitage of S. Giorgio

Località Eremo, Contrada
la Rocca 1, Bardolino
1704

160 F

Construction work on the building was finally completed in 1704. Following the Napoleonic suppression of 1810, the Hermitage was abandoned and the complex was inhabited by peasants until 1885, when the monks returned to the monastery.

The Camaldolese Hermitage of S. Giorgio is a peaceful place with a fantastic view over Garda. Situated amid nature, the pilgrimage site offers a wonderful view over Lake Garda. Visitors have the opportunity to take part in various masses or seminars. In addition, the monastery offers ten sleeping places for those guests who wish to experience monastic life and further their spiritual education. All visitors are asked to observe the rules of silence and meditation. You can reach it from Bardolino – about 4.5 kilometres away – and explore a convent from 1663.

Padre Giovanni Dalpiaz

F

Fabrizio Mauro

Villa Carlo Ottolenghi ⩢ »

Str. Scanelli 5, Bardolino
Carlo Scarpa, Giuseppe Tommasi,
Guido Pietropoli
1974–1978

It may come as a shock at first – one hardly notices anything behind the villa's fence amid the uncultivated vineyard. Then, you see the blocks and a pit between them. Is it an underground shelter? Nope. That is the house of Carlo Ottolenghi, the famous Venetian lawyer, philanthropist, and director of the Querini Stampalia Foundation. Strict zoning regulations required that the villa could only have one floor, so the builders dug it into the slope next to the entrance, leaving the rest of the plot to be used as vineyards, given that the location is in the heart of the precious Bardolino wine region. The long and narrow gorge leads to a compact one-bedroom house organised around a body of water. It is not open to the public yet, but hopefully it will be soon. Simply examining photographs gives you a thrill for this building's mix of sensitivity and playfulness. The surfaces range from a sterile, mirror-like polish to whimsical, cake-like appearances. Various themes sweep before our eyes. 'I wish for it to look like a ruined castle,' Ottolenghi cited Scarpa as saying, but the piece offers additional interpretations. The broken volumetric of the villa echoes Venetian calli, or narrow streets. It also reflects the tragic experiences of the twentieth century, including the Auschwitz concentration camp where Ottolenghi's father – the rabbi of Venice – died in 1944. Paradoxically, Scarpa's work came close to the ironic experimentation of Milanese conceptual design created by Ettore Sottsass and his Memphis Group.

Åke Eson Lindman

San Severo »

Via S. Severo 5, Bardolino
11th–12th centuries,
1932 (restoration)

162 F

Sergey Nikitin-Rimsky

F

This classical Romanesque basilica with a bell tower is situated at the entrance to Bardolino. Surrounded by olive trees, it once served as a guardian from the severe medieval times. It was built on top of a previous church from the ninth century. Visit the nearby San Zeno to feel the difference! During its lifetime, it has functioned as a warehouse, theatre, cinema, soldiers' barracks, music school, and horse stables. And yet, it still maintains the original interior and atmosphere. The calm, rustic, and well-measured interior contains three naves and a wooden roof. Tuff columns are decorated with lines of bricks – a common feature during that period throughout Europe. Frescoes cover the walls of the central nave, narrating the Apocalypse and the legend of the discovery of the True Cross. The main apse is a historical reconstruction from 1932, rather than the original, late-medieval apse. These restoration works were carried out by Piero Gazzola who would later be one of the authors of the Venice Charter.

San Zeno

Via S. Zeno 7, Bardolino
9th century

163 F

Tucked away within agricultural companies and a quiet suburban atmosphere, this church rather resembles a farm building. Dedicated to the holy patron of Verona, San Zeno, it is a rare piece from the Carolingian Renaissance that survived the 1117 earthquake. The floor plan is arranged as the Latin cross, with barrel vaults on the side arms and a cross on the lantern. Its columns are borrowed from the Roman villas that were once abundant in the area.

Sergey Nikitin-Rimsky

Villa Pederzoli
Via Monte Noal e Pigno/
Strada del Barum, Bardolino
Angelo Mangiarotti
1971

It's not often that you meet a graduate of the Milan Politecnico in Veneto and it's even less likely that this graduate is the ever-busy luminary of Italian design, Angelo Mangiarotti. Yet Verona's Fiat dealer Giancarlo Pederzoli found him to be an easy-going person with a reasonable fee. Thus, Mangiarotti built him a selling point, followed by Villa Pederzoli. The villa is located in a luxurious setting just above the lake. Pederzoli initially had a different plot, but a road crossed through it, so he sold it to Ottolenghi (see 161: Villa Carlo Ottolenghi). A dream of the 1960s, the villa consists of a few horizontal concrete plates around a central fireplace. The walls are windows, providing residents a full view of the magnificent garden outside. Pederzoli originally thought he would prefer something more modest, like Farnsworth House by Mies, but was charmed by Mangiarotti's fashionable style. The villa was only lived in for two years and then abandoned for decades. The new owner, Jürgen R. Koffle, has restored the house and garden, and continues to fill it with objects by Mangiarotti. Around the same time that the villa was being constructed, Pederzoli and Mangiarotti were building another ensemble: Sixty-two single-family holiday houses just five kilometres from Bardolino, where you can rent a tiny Mangiarotti for one night (Villetta Parco Murlongo).

Sergey Nikitin-Rimsky

Sergey Nikitin-Rimsky

Archivo Angelo Mangiarotti

F

Fabrizio Mauro

Peschiera del Garda

Peschiera Fortress and
Ponte dei Voltoni
Michele Sanmicheli,
Guidobaldo Della Rovere (designer)
1550s

165 F

Peschiera del Garda may look like a charming resort town with all its cafes and cypresses, yet for the Venetian and Austro-Hungarian administrations, its primary function was related to defence and security. The Peschiera fortress, a UNESCO World Heritage site, features two gates, bastions, and fortified canals. The ensemble was designed by Guidobaldo Della Rovere and carried out by Michele Sanmicheli. The fancy Ponte Dei Voltoni bridge's lowered arches mark where the Mincio River flows into Lake Garda. The Austrians are credited with strengthening Peschiera del Garda, making it one of their four main strongholds in Italy.

Sergey Nikitin–Rimsky

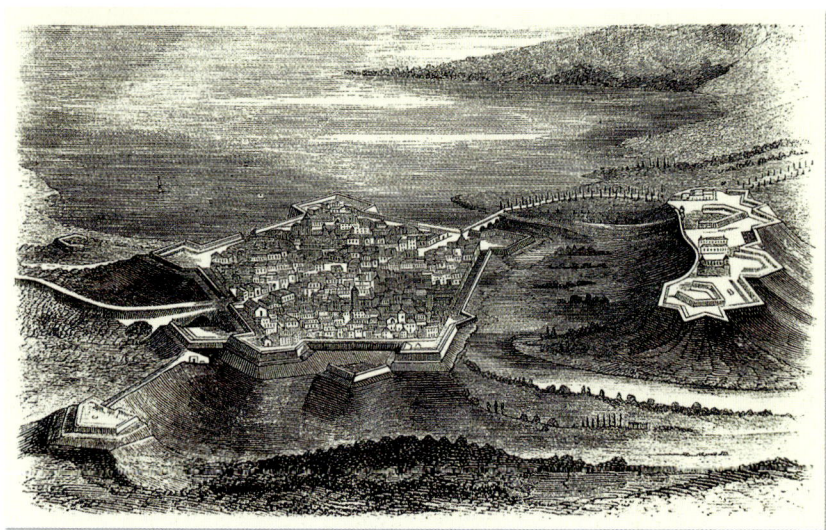

Illustration of Peschiera del Garda (19th century)

Porta Verona by Sanmicheli, reminiscent of his monumental gates of Verona

Caserma XXX Maggio and Palazzina del Comando

Via XXX Maggio,
Peschiera del Garda
Piazza della Serenissima,
Peschiera del Garda

166 F

Sergey Nikitin-Rimsky

Between 1815 and 1866, the Austrians were busy creating the Quadrilatero, a defensive system between the fortresses of Peschiera del Garda, Mantua, Legnago, and Verona. Difficult to circumvent, it hindered the movement of enemy troops in the Po Valley. The town centre is still dominated by spectacular structures from the 1850s when Austrian General Josef Radetzky led and reformed the military forces. With its neoclassical front, complemented by a clock, cypresses, and cedars, the Caserma XXV Aprile could be used as a town hall or a big villa. It is, in fact, looking for a new owner. The Palazzina del Comando (Parco Catullo 1), which is now a museum, is on the same Piazza Serenissima. The neoclassical San Martino church was also converted for military use during Napoleon's times. Next door, the Austrians built a military hospital in the Rundbogenstil style, known for its round arches. Most recently referred to as Caserma XXX Maggio, it then served as a barracks and military prison before being closed. The Austrian Arsenal, called 'Port Verona Artillery Barracks', was recently opened to the public to host various business and cultural events.

F

Fabio Michele Capelli (iStock)

precinbe (iStock)

Torre monumentale di San Martino della Battaglia

167 F

Via Torre 2, San Martino della Battaglia
Giacomo Frizzoni, Luigi Fattori (engineer)
1880–1893

Natalia Shantsevalova

The Battle of Saint Martin in 1859, called the Solferino, was the final battle of the second war for the unification of Italy (Risorgimento). Tens of thousands of French and Italian troops – though at this time Italy was officially called the Kingdom of Sardinia – fought against equal numbers representing the Austro-Hungarian empire. The resulting peace agreement gave Italy not only Lombardy, but the chance to annex the Central Italian duchies. Yet the battle also had global significance: Swiss businessman Jean-Henri Dunant toured the field the day after and was bewildered by the sight of thousands of wounded soldiers left dying. He convinced the locals to care for the wounded regardless of side and convinced the French to release captured Austrian doctors. He went on to co-found the International Red Cross and prepare the Geneva Convention. Dunant was the first to receive the Nobel Peace Prize in 1901. It took 10 years to collect money from all over Italy to celebrate the battle with a worthy memorial. Frizzoni designed a tower in the rustic Gothic style – a strange choice, since the style was associated with Austrian military architecture in those days. The tower's first hall has a bronze statue of Vittorio Emanuele II, the Sardinian king that unified Italy together with Garibaldi, sculpted by Antonio Dal Zotto. The interiors are frescoed with war episodes and a belvedere is found at the top. Learn more about this and other battles in the area by visiting the national museum next door.

Castello Scaligero a Sirmione »

168 F

Piazza Castello 34, Sirmione
13th century

Verona's most successful feudal lords, the Scala family or Scaligeri, were afraid of a surprise attack and built castles at nodal points. This castle in Sirmione is a medieval port fortification at a strategic place on the peninsula, started by Mastino Della Scala in 1277. With its Ghibelline swallowtail merlons and picturesque composition, it is one of the most popular attractions on the lake. The castle walls are built with lake pebble and bricks. Still surrounded by a moat, it can only be entered by two drawbridges. Inside, there is a small museum with archaeological discoveries. Other Sirmione landmarks include the church of San Pietro in Mavino, which features remarkable frescoes from the fourteenth century.

Fabrizio Mauro

Fabrizio Mauro

F

Fabrizio Mauro

Villa Cortine Palace Hotel

Villa Cortine Palace Hotel
Viale Gennari 2, Sirmione
1890–1899

169 **F**

The neoclassical villa was built at the end of the nineteenth century for conservative politician Kurt von Koseritz from Dessau, Germany. Occupying five hectares of the petite Sirmione peninsula, the villa's picturesque park, terraces, and thematic fountains are undoubtedly one of the town's greatest highlights. In the 1950s, it was converted into a hotel with lavishly decorated interiors inspired by the visions of Ancient Rome and Andrea Palladio.

F

Villa Cortine Palace Hotel

Grotte di Catullo
Piazza Orti Manara 4, Sirmione
BCE/CE

170 F

Just by looking at these grandiose ruins from the water, one can imagine the luxurious villa that was built here at about the time when BCE was turning into CE. In addition to the residential areas and long arcades with breath-taking views, the ensemble featured thermae baths, which Sirmione is still famous for, and a 43-metre-long underground cistern that once collected water for the house and garden. The historic olive grove was recently restored. The villa at the northernmost end of the Sirmione peninsula, covering an area of about two hectares, has still only partially been brought to light by archaeologists. But who was the owner? In the Quattrocento, Italian humanists rediscovered Roman poet Gaius Valerius Catullus. In Carmina 31, the poet describes his return to his family's house in Sirmione, causing intellectuals to think that the Grottoes was his place. Today, however, it is considered unlikely that Catullus had anything to do with the villa. It appears to have been built after his death, but his great name made the place famous, appealing to artists and elites. Palladio, for instance, came here to study Roman architecture. Plus, one of the scenes of the popular contemporary film *Call Me By Your Name* was shot here.

Nicoleta Stella

Nicoleta Stella

F

Stazione di Desenzano e Sirmione

171 F

Piazza Einaudi 10,
Desenzano del Garda
1854

The station is one of the rarest preserved parts of the Imperial-Regia Privilegiata Strada Ferrata Ferdinandea Lombardo-Veneta: a railway between Venice and Milano. It was built when Veneto and Lombardy were part of the Austro-Hungarian empire to facilitate military control and commercial connections in the empire's southern areas. The station's main façade looks like a villa with its neoclassical pavilions. The pavilions are crowned with proto-Secession chandeliers reminding us we are at a resort, while the main body and clock indicates precision. The charming original iron shed with Greek ornamentation over the entrance and the platform has been preserved thanks to the locals. The piazza in front of the station is adorned with olive trees and chestnuts. There are villas from the past century behind the smiling post-war brick-and-concrete condominiums. It's an ideal starting point to explore the town. The station opened on 12 April 1854, together with the unfortunate Desenzano Viaduct, a pharaonic neo-Gothic construction of 17 pointed arches around 30 metres tall. The viaduct proved to be so shaky that people were afraid to remove the wooden scaffolding for some time after its completion! After decades of improvements, it was destroyed by bombs during the Second World War and rebuilt in a plain modernist style.

Sergey Nikitin-Rimsky

Sergey Nikitin-Rimsky

Porto Vecchio di Desenzano

Piazza Malvezzi, Desenzano
Giulio Todeschini

172 F

The charming old port of Desenzano was first built between the thirteenth and fifteenth centuries. At that time, it was simply a lake bank with some warehouses, but merchants needed a protected bay to load and unload their boats. Two distinctive strips of land that enclose the rectangular bay were filled in the lake in the fifteenth century. It was further developed to serve the flourishing grain market in the times of the Venetian Republic. Architect Giulio Todeschini designed arcades of the municipal house at the end of the sixteenth century, still known as Palazzo Todeschini in his honour. This building formed the well-known scenic backdrop to the port. Next to the last arch of the port of Todeschini is the stone of the unemployed: the jobless and bankrupt had to declare themselves by climbing over it. To the right of the Todeschini, windows of various colours and shapes are reminiscent of the Venetian period. It took almost a century to build a gorgeous lighthouse, and the Venetian-style bridge appeared in the 1930s. Façades from neoclassicism to Liberty (art nouveau) decorate the streets nearby. Todeschini also contributed to two sections of Palazzo del Provveditore, presumably unfinished (Piazza Mazzini 13). Mayer and Splendid is the oldest working hotel, owned by the Mayer family since the nineteenth century (Piazza Ulisse Papa 10). Among its guests were Lord Byron, composer Puccini, King Victor Emmanuel II of Italy, Napoleon III, and poet and Nobel prize winner Carducci.

F

Sergey Nikitin–Rimsky

Duomo di Desenzano

173 **F**

Via Roma 5, Desenzano del Garda
Giulio Todeschini
1586–1611

The Cathedral of Desenzano dedicated to Santa Maria Maddalena was built from 1586 to 1611 by the Brescian architect and passionate researcher of antiquity, Giulio Todeschini. The result is an original neoclassical basilica with two lines of Tuscan order arcades that divide the naves. A well-tempered baroque façade is embellished by statues by Lorenzo Muttoni and Santo Calegari the Younger.

Denis Vostrikov (dreamstime)

Antanovich1985 (dreamstime)

Antanovich1985 (dreamstime)

Chiesa di Santa Maria

Strada Provinciale 39,
Manerba del Garda
14th century

174 F

Prepare to be embraced by this church's squatty Romanesque entrance. Initially built on the remains of the large, fifth century Roman villa, it was rebuilt and extended many times, achieving its original three-nave plan from the fourteenth century. Go inside to see the frescoes depicting the martyrdom of Sant'Orsola and the Madonna enthroned with Saints Rocco and Sivino. The altar's elements are highlighted in red – a glimpse of the good old rustic Middle ages. In Manerba, there is another Romanesque church, Chiesetta di Santa Lucia, which contains an interesting collection of frescoes from different time periods.

F

Cinzia Vivenzi

Harry Fabel

Sergey Nikitin-Rimsky

Villa Borghese-Cavazza
Isola del Garda
Luigi Rovelli
1894–1901

175 F

During a spiritualist seance, 18-year-old Maria Annenkova (in English: Annenkoff) met French queen Marie Antoinette, who called her grandniece. In those days, Maria was the maid of honour of the Grand Duchess Alexandra Iosifovna of Russia, and the seance happened in the gracious Marble palace of St. Petersburg. This story confused the royal life, and young Annenkova was sent to Europe for health treatment. A decade later, she met Duke Gaetano De Ferrari of Genoa with whom she conceived the design of this fantastic villa in the neo-Venetian style. Luigi Rovelli, also Genoese, was invited to transform their dreams into stone, naturally creating a variation of the Palazzo Ducale, complete with lancet arches, flowered decorations, and a wonderful garden full of rare and exotic plants. De Ferraris's daughter Anna Maria – a photographer and passionate traveller – married the prince and racing driver Scipione Borghese. Their descendants still own and live on the land.

Ville in Italia

Sergey Nikitin-Rimsky

F

Parking Martiri della Libertà »   176 E
Salò
Mauro Salvadori, Ermes Barba,
Chiara Odolini,
Mauro Medolago Poli
2006

Sergey Nikitin-Rimsky

There is still a certain nostalgia felt around Salò. Some parts of the city are decorated with surviving posters proposing an exploration of the sights of the Italian Social Republic (RSI), an ephemeral institution presided over by Mussolini and backed by the Nazis. Just like the Berlin wall, death sells. What's more is that it also dictates architecture. A few years ago, a car park on a former industrial site was reorganised into a 544-slot space with monumental arched gates. The space is reminiscent of the metaphysical experimentation taken on by Italian architects during the Mussolini period, including the Vittoriale of D'Annunzio.

Torre dell'orologio »   177 F
Piazza Vittorio Emanuele II,
Salò
15th–18th centuries

Garda FeWo

As part of the Venetian Republic, Salò's clock tower may be reminiscent of the one at Piazza San Marco, or even more so of the one built in the nearby Brescia, which was also part of Venice. With a bell installed at the top, this belvedere allows visitors to enjoy a panorama of the city as they peer over a huge lion of St. Mark, the holy patron of Venice. Beginning in the thirteenth century, this bell tower was one of the entrance gates in the fortification of Salò. At that time, there was a drawbridge below, which traversed a deep pit filled with lake water. A public clock was placed on the structure in 1766. It was large and easily visible to citizens. Bortolo Antonio Bertolla, a watchmaker from the Val di Non, made the clock and it ticks to this day. Using the same elements as in Brescia, the leaders of Salò styled the tower as a baroque triumphal arch. Its functional feature – the bell – is shyly hidden behind the baroque tympanum. The tower marks the start of Salò's main street, Via San Carlo, with its many lovely buildings.

Sergey Nikitin-Rimsky

Promenade di Salò

Lungolago Giuseppe Zanardelli
Vittoriano Viganò,
Demetrio Costantino
1906, 1986–2011

178 F

An earthquake destroyed the private villas at the waterfront of Salò in 1901. However, the wreckage provided an opportunity to build a promenade to line up with the lake's hotels and cafés, just as had been done in nearby Gardone. As time passed, cars became increasingly popular among the Italian middle class, and pedestrians had to concede more and more space for traffic. It took brutalist architect Vittoriano Viganò in the 1980s to persuade city hall to renew Salò and give it a new identity. Viganò advocated for a shift away from the car in a 1991 article for *Domus* magazine. He thought that slowing down would help citizens and tourists rediscover the urban texture and nature of the city. To this day, locals are immensely proud of their promenade. The project required historic tracks to be repaved, and car traffic eliminated completely on the lakefront. One landmark in particular is the 'Viganò', a neo-futurist pedestrian bridge made of steel. The promenade culminates with a cosy town piazza built around the 1400s: The Palazzo della Magnifica Patria (Lungolago Zanardelli 55) is known for its frescoed portico and various memorial plaques.

Museo di Salò (formerly Chiesa di Santa Giustina)

Via Brunati 9, Salò
Giovanni Tortelli (conversion)
1587, 2015

179 F

This former church was converted into a museum featuring evocative collections to celebrate and showcase the winding history of Salò. It was during Venetian rule when Salò became the capital of the 'Magnifica Patria', a union of Riviera towns giving life to urban and educational renewal. The town became known globally during the Italian civil war of 1943 to 1945 when it became a capital of Mussolini's Republic of Salò. There are special rooms for collections of drawings and music in Salò. For example, the inventor of the violin, Gasparo da Salò, was born here. Giovanni Tortelli, an architect from Brescia, curated the installation of the new museum.

F

Rubner Holzbau

Museo di Salò

Duomo di Santa Maria Annunziata

Piazza del Duomo, Salò
Filippo delle Vacche
1453–1503

180 F

You may not entirely understand the grandeur and significance that the city of Salò once held before entering this modest-looking unfinished façade. Although it was devastated by Napoleon's troops in 1797, this duomo or cathedral, is still replete with paintings, stuccos, and carvings. Construction of the Cathedral of Santa Maria Annunziata started in 1453 by Filippo delle Vacche, an architect from the village of Caravaggio. It is divided into three naves by grey stone columns, following the design of the Sant'Anastasia Basilica in Verona, as requested by the commissioners. The style interestingly straddles late Gothic and Renaissance architecture. Consider the façade: the central portal with a sculpture in white marble is clearly Renaissance, while the two side doors have a Gothic touch. Note the unassuming, contemplative expression of the saints, which were created by two leading sculptors of Renaissance style in the area: Gasparo Cairano and Antonio Mangiacavalli. The highly expressive crucifix by Giovanni Teutonico soars high above in the interior. Carved in applewood with translucent drops of resin representing blood, it was the first and only decoration of the church for some time. The church has preserved a collection of marvellous paintings by provincial artists, including Moretto da Brescia, Zenone Veronese, and Paolo Veneziano. In the chapel of Sacramento, there is a spectacular vault with whirling golden columns painted by Giovan Battista Trotti. The wooden group of lamentation over Christ's body is by Pietro Bussolo. The lower layers of the bell tower are from the eleventh century, and its final tier – designed as a domed gazebo and evocative of medieval manuscripts – is from the fifteenth century. Outside lies the Piazza del Duomo, which offers the best gelato in town and hosts music events in summer. The promenade behind the church offers one of the most magnificent views of the lake.

bwzenith (iStock)

Hotel Salò du Parc Luogo »

Via Cure del Lino 1, Salò
*Vittoriano Viganò,
Demetrio Costantino*
1983–1990

 181 F

As if D'Annunzio's decorative warships were not unusual enough, a white submarine (or bathyscaphe) floats along the main road of Salò. Surprisingly, it is a luxury hotel. A peaceful bike stand invites you to swap vehicles and take a promenade along the lake, which Viganò, an architect who was madly in love with Garda, has been designing for the past 15 years of his career. The front façade is a slab of white with a narrow line of windows and loggias. It is only when you look at it from the lake you realise that behind the white wall there are actually two blocks, each five floors high. These were the golden days when architects could persuade developers to consent to more daring styles.

Sergey Nikitin-Rimsky

F

Sergey Nikitin-Rimsky

Autosilo Salò du Parc »

Via Cure del Lino 1, Salò
Vittoriano Viganò
1995

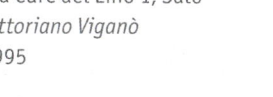 182 E

Leave the car behind to explore Salò. As the name implies, this car park is part of the Hotel Salò du Parc across the road.

It was the final gesture of architect Vittoriano Viganò, often called the leader of brutalism in Italy: a façade of piled up concrete blocks in the form of sticks and beams. Here, he returns to his most famous project, Casa La Scala, also on Garda, constructed for French critic André Bloc, founder of *Architecture d'Aujourd'hui*.

Grand Hotel Gardone

Corso Zanardelli 84,
Gardone Riviera
Angelo Fuchs 1884,
Hermann Billing (restoration),
Wilhelm Vittali (restoration)
1897, 1904

183 F

This temple of eclecticism, epicentre of the tourist industry, and Garda's Belle Epoque was started by a couple of the Austrians who chose to remain in Italy after its war with Austria in 1866 – Luigi Wimmer and his wife, Emilia. Ex-Garibaldi fighter, Luigi had settled down in the area, living in what later became the estate of writer Gabriele D'Annunzio. Soon enough, he would become the mayor of Gardone Riviera. Around the same time, he opened a modest hotel on the lakeshore, a business that his wife and their friend Angelo Fuchs continued after Wimmer's premature death. The great success of the Grand Hotel and Gardone itself can be attributed to the popular German physiotherapist Ludwig Rohden, who recommended this particular part of the lake to his customers for its mild climate. It was the first modern hotel on Lake Garda to open its doors, finally taking shape in 1904 with 300 rooms. A somewhat Moorish watchtower was added, which also functioned as a water reservoir. This was probably the first big project by Hermann Billing and Wilhelm Vittali, whose partnership would go on to dominate hotel architecture in southern Germany before the First World War. The Grand Hotel preceded the fabulous institutions of Les Bains and Excelsior on Lido in Venice. The hotel's first real encounter with international fame took place when King George of Saxony stayed here in 1905 with his family and court. Gardone was loved for its 'mitteleuropean' atmosphere, which was considered chic at the time. The list of famous guests includes Sir Winston Churchill, novelists William Somerset Maugham, Stefan Zweig, as well as Vladimir Nabokov, and of course, Gabriele D'Annunzio as he waited for his Vittoriale memorial villa to be completed. Paul Heyse, German poet and Nobel Prize Laureate in Literature, set his novella *Eine venezianische Nacht* ('A Venetian Night') here. However, everything changed after the First World War. German and Austrian citizens – now seen as former adversaries – lost almost all of their property in Italy, including their means to travel to the lake. Vacationing itself radically changed. When the Grand Hotel was built, it was meant for winter visitors. In the 1920s, it opened its doors to the Italian middle class, who sought the cool air during hot summer days. You'll find original, well-preserved interiors in the lobby; in fact, only the chandeliers were replaced here in the 1960s. The town-facing façade is nothing, since visitors almost always arrived by boats. Instead, lake façades are a flight of fantasy, exuberant and rich, spanning from geometric art nouveau to pastry Renaissance. Golden mosaics meet violent colour schemes. Don't miss the capitals of the southern porch painted in turquoise! Various designs grace the balconies' plat bands and railings. On vacation, everything is possible.

F

Sergey Nikitin-Rimsky

Torre San Marco
(formerly Torre Ruhland)

Corso Zanardelli 142,
Gardone Riviera
Heinrich Schäfer 1900,
Giancarlo Maroni 1925

184 F

A romantic landmark on the western shore of Lake Garda, this tower is also a reminder of Garda's Italianisation after the First World War. German industrialist Richard Langensiepen built this house with an observatory for his son in the neo-Gothic style, but 20 years later, it was refaced to look like the Venetian castle and became San Marco Tower. It was the poet and public figure Gabriele D'Annunzio who bought the structure in 1925, making it part of his Vittoriale ensemble (see 187: Vittoriale degli Italiani). For many years D'Annunzio's MAS ship was anchored at the dock of the tower before being re-housed inside the Vittoriale. The actual owners proudly announce that the tower was once a meeting place for Benito Mussolini and his lifelong lover, Claretta Petacci, between 1943 and 1945.

Brenda Kean (dreamstime)

Sergey Nikitin-Rimsky

Giovanni Del Curto (dreamstime)

Villa Alba (Villa Ruhland)
Corso Zanardelli 153,
Gardone Riviera
Heinrich Schäfer
1901–1910

185 F

Even after losing Northern Italy, the Austrian emperor thought about the Garda shores. They say Franz Joseph I planned to visit Villa Ruhland, but he never had the opportunity due to the First World War. It's possible that Ruhland originates from the old spelling of the legendary Roland. In exquisite neoclassical style, with ionic columns, this structure resembles the monuments of the Acropolis in Athens. The splendid sculptures on the pediment crowning the façade are copied from the Parthenon. In contrast, another façade with the caryatids bears a resemblance to the Erechtheum – another temple from the Acropolis. The commissioner was the German entrepreneur Richard Langensiepen, owner of the huge machine factories and foundries in the German and Russian empires. Inside the palace, some interiors are adapted for modern usage, such as luxury weddings or parties. You can walk and, rather unexpectedly, drive your car through a charming little park, which was a little bit overrun by the housing estates in the swinging 1960s. The adjacent San Marco tower was once a part of the estate, connected to the villa by the viaduct.

F

Chiesa Luterana
Via Vittoriale 4/A, Gard. Riviera
Aage von Kauffmann
1897

186 F

Before war broke out in 1914, tourists in Garda spoke German and the town itself had a second German name: Hildebrandsburg, the town of *Hildebrand*. According to the *Song of the Nibelungs*, he is the armourer, brother-in-arms of Dietrich von Bern. While the Grand Hotel had a special room for protestant celebrations, there were too many visitors from northern Germany during the winter to host them all. The local *club per il culto evangelico*, 'Evangelical cult club', commissioned the design to Danish-born Aage von Kauffmann, who was a successful architect of villas and churches in the Rhine-Main area.

Sergey Nikitin-Rimsky

Vittoriale degli Italiani

Via al Vittoriale 12,
Gardone Riviera
Giancarlo Maroni,
Gabriele D'Annunzio
1921–1938

What if you want a villa in a pristine location and a national monument in honour of yourself built during your lifetime, but you didn't want to pay for it? Follow the example set by Gabriele D'Annunzio, the Italian poet and novelist! After Italy won the First World War, it took the long-desired cities of Trento and Trieste. Yet the country was in an economic and moral downturn. The Italians had to leave their nests in the Dalmatia region (present-day Croatia, which was then part of the Austro-Hungarian Empire): Fiume, Zara, Gorizia, Capodistria, and other towns where they had been living since Venetian times. D'Annunzio came on the scene at this time, and with the help of war veterans, occupied Fiume, a major city with a population of 65,000 people. They stayed there for one year, writing a constitution and coining their own money, until international authorities forced Italy to drive out their veterans and hand the city over to Yugoslavia. Upon returning to Italy, D'Annunzio found his peace on the shores of Lake Garda, where he conceived his most voluminous and expensive work: the villa that would celebrate everything he had done for his homeland, the patria. He called it *Vittoriale*, meaning 'victorious', and bequeathed it to Italy, along with the enormous debts that were needed to bring his idea to fruition. In one instance, D'Annunzio dragged the bow of the Italian cruiser Puglia up the hill. He also brought an anti-submarine MAS ship and even the airplane SVA that D'Annunzio himself used to fly to scatter proclamations over Vienna in 1918. He managed to do it all, and finally, after his death, a mausoleum was erected in honour of him and his army friends – a mistical white-marble rotunda surrounded by cenotaphs. Every element here is an intricate pastiche of sounds and voids; everything is so full of meaning that one could never manage to mentally reconstruct the ideas, apart from D'Annunzio himself. Its theatrical exaltation is reminiscent of Dalí's Theatre-Museum in Figueres, another ego-centric project. The only difference is that here, on Garda, no irony is admitted. The Nike statue over the huge Pillar of Piave at the entrance of the ensemble is called 'Victory with Tied Feet'. Take a look inside the poet's house, la Prioria, and you'll sneak up on the suffocating and pictur-esque eclectics of his Belle Epoque taste. Architect Francesco Amendolagine just-ly diagnosed it as a *horror vacui*, meaning 'fear of vacuum'. The door of the poet's study is made precisely for the height of D'Annunzio, who was 1.6 metres tall. It is said that he loved taller people to bow down before him. Giancarlo Maroni, grad-uate of the Accademia di Brera and a First World War veteran, is the architect of the complex. By 1925, Maroni had already de-signed the hydroelectric plant in Riva del Garda. His taste was pleasingly balanced between mannerism, neoclassicism, and deco. Undoubtedly, Vittoriale, with its fantastic terrain, immersed in olives and cypresses, is a place to explore and enjoy from various angles. Consider attending one of its open-air concerts in the amphi-theatre during the summer.

Dudlajzov (dreamstime)

Grand Hotel Fasano
Corso Zanardelli 190,
Gardone Riviera
1888, 1903

188 F

It is hard to find well-preserved interiors of Belle Epoque in Italy. Visiting the lobbies and bars of the Grand Hotel in Fasano offers a glimpse into a fairytale play of *chiaroscuro*: bold contrasts of light and dark. From granny-dark cupboards and chandeliers, to detailing in granite and grey stone, the hotel's preservation over the last 100 years is apparent. What makes it all the more unique is that it is one of the finest examples of the *Gründerzeit* style in Italy: an interesting mix of Renaissance and medieval heritage that was in vogue in German-speaking countries at the turn of the XX century. Sadly, the architect remains unknown; we know only the name of the owner: Boem. One of the first modern tourist attractions on the lake, this hotel on the shore of Lake Garda was founded in 1888 as a hunting lodge of the Austrian royal family, though princes and princesses never visited. Among its early comforts were central heating and hot water, which was important because tourists preferred to

visit Garda during winter months back then. In 1903, the hotel was enhanced and rebuilt into its present state, a curious multi-volume ensemble decorated with idyllic grisaille painting. Thanks in part to the 12,000-square-metre landscape park, filled with palms and banana trees, the hotel has attracted guests like writer Paul Heyse, artist Gustav Klimt, film director Federico Fellini, and actor Marcello Mastroianni. The Mayr family reconstructed this magnificent building after it was damaged during the Second World War and still runs it to this day.

Sergey Nikitin-Rimsky

Sergey Nikitin-Rimsky

Hotel Golfo (formerly Villa Bianchi)

Via Aquilani 1,
Toscolano Maderno
20th century

189 F

This palace has shined for almost one hundred years in the most prestigious location of Toscolano along the lake promenade. Unfortunately, it has been abandoned for more than a decade; no one wants to buy it since the new owner will have to spend millions on restoration. Severe monument protection laws have scared businesses away and a memorial is not possible. The good news is that the hotel is richly decorated on the outside with sgraffito and cast-iron. On the lake side, looking into the veranda and through the broken glass, it becomes clear that the Liberty era is still alive and well in this building. The Garda painter-vagabond Angelo Landi (1879–1944) decorated the walls of the staircase with atmospheric murals, which still exist today, as well as the veranda ceiling. The frescoes depict the legend of Engardina, the mythical queen of the dwarves who gave the blue colours to the waters of the lake after Neptune kidnapped her. As soon as Landi completed the murals, the Republic of Salò seized the building, thereafter housing the Seat of the Republican Fascist Party and the Command of the Black Brigades. Mussolini's main propagandist, Alessandro Pavolini, worked there until April 1945 when he was captured and executed by partisans. In front of the Golfo, there is a public square developed around the shining marble monument 'Bella Italia', which was dedicated to Prime Minister Giuseppe Zanardelli who used to live nearby. The monument depicts Italy as a glamorous young lady desperately looking in the direction of the city of Trieste, which was still Austrian in those days. The stone girl is now surrounded by cacti.

Sergey Nikitin-Rimsky

F

Sergey Nikitin-Rimsky

Sergey Nikitin-Rimsky

Chiesa di Sant'Andrea

Piazza San Marco 16,
Toscolano Maderno
11th–12th centuries

190 F

A small jewel of Romanesque style along the lake promenade in the very centre of the town, this church was built in the twelfth century on top of the ruins of an ancient Lombard church. The materials included marble and recycled Roman tombs. Some small improvements began on the little church in the baroque era.

Fortunately, the changes didn't reach very far; inside, on the intricate carvings, some paint is still visible, allowing the viewer to imagine how the temple shone in the Middle Ages when it was surrounded by a village of fishermen. The dome of the altar is uniquely grafted between the columns and the roof. The bell tower dates back to 1469. Saint Ercolano, once bishop of Brescia, was buried in the church at the time of his death, but he was later transferred to the Monumental Church of Maderno.

Sergey Nikitin-Rimsky

Sergey Nikitin-Rimsky

Café Centrale

191 F

Piazza San Marco, 17,
Toscolano Maderno
1970s

It's not easy to find an interior from the 1970s, so be sure to take a look into this café to enjoy Italian Balneal postmodernism with azure accents. It also features a gallery of famous people from the area – a simplified version of the Florian at San Marco in Venice.

Sergey Nikitin-Rimsky

Casa della torta bakery

192 F

Via Benamati 58,
Toscolano Maderno

Mass tourism drastically changed Garda towns, but there are still lovely angles where you can feel the good old Italy with its family businesses. For instance, at this bakery in operation since 1850. Thirty years ago, a Milanese artist came to spend a summer in Toscolano. He was a frequent customer and the patron Giuseppe eventually asked him to paint the outer walls. His naïve and jocular manner worked well. The artist, Enzo Cavallari, came back to refresh the paintings later on. While observing the canvases inside that were painted in the 1990s, you might wonder if the patrons paid for these works with their cakes.

F

Sergey Nikitin-Rimsky

Villa Lucia

Via Benamati 58,
Toscolano Maderno
18th century

 193 F

Referred to as Rizzardi, Brunati, and Bulgheroni, after the former patrons of this villa, Villa Lucia was not only a delightfully pleasant place, but also the site of a hardworking industry. Behind stone wall with a turret, there is a garden with statues and balustrades. The main attraction, however, is the lemon grove that triumphantly climbs the hill; a symbol of the flourishing economy on this shore of Lake Garda. From the seventeenth century onward, Villa Lucia served as a guesthouse for the Gonzaga family whose palace is nearby.

Sergey Nikitin-Rimsky

Palazzo Benamati

Via Benamati,
Toscolano Maderno
1750–1800

 194 F

A province sometimes becomes a place for unexpected innovation. Behind the ordinary façade of this palace, there is a fantastic golden ceiling in the baroque-proto Liberty design, peppered with blue dots that create a surrealist atmosphere. It was once the estate of the Benamati, an influential family in Maderno. Its final owner, priest Don Cristoforo Benamati, chose to give the palace to the municipality in 1799, leaving an endowment for a school. Locals say the magic vault is from the late nineteenth century, but would someone have painted such a thing for a school? There is another remarkable tresco illustrating the fire of Maderno from the eighteenth century.

Sergey Nikitin-Rimsky

Museo della Carta

Via Valle delle Cartiere,
Toscolano Maderno
14th century

195 F

Giorgio Cavallera

Toscolano River Valley was one of the first and most important places in Europe for the paper industry. The stretch of the valley called Valle delle Cartiere was already included in a document from 1381 that defined the rules for water use. The business started to decline after the fall of the Venice Republic. Fifteen years ago, local enthusiasts began to create a museum collecting old machines, techniques, and stories in one of the biggest mills called Maina Inferiore. There is still a working paper factory on the shore of the lake, housed in a modernist building right next to the city beach and the old port.

F

Giorgio Cavallera

Giorgio Cavallera

Yulia Semenova

Villa Bettoni in Bogliacco (now part of Gargnano)

Via della Libertà, Gargnano
Adriano Cristofali,
Antonio Marchetti
1750s–1760s

196 F

Viennese restraint outside and exuberant rococo inside – looking at this palace from the lake reminds one of Schönbrunn, the heart of the Austrian monarchy. The Schönbrunn influence can even be seen in the building's colours: green for the window shutters, mustard yellow for walls, and white for details. Yet the Habsburgs themselves never had a residence on the shores of Garda, so why is there such a resemblance? In 1752, Empress Maria Theresa granted the title of Counts to the Bettoni family for their services to the Austrian army. It was the signal to set up their new nest at the imperial scale. Leading Veronese architect Adriano Cristofali was called to design the villa on the site of an existing building from the 1600s. They quickly replaced Cristofali with the leading master from Brescia, Abbot Antonio Marchetti, who is now considered the building's principal author. The lakeside central block has colossal pilasters atop a rusticated stone base. The rooftop balustrade features statues of the gods: Bacchus, Ceres, Jove, Venus, Pluto, Tethys, Juno, and Mercury, sculpted by Giovanni Battista Locatelli. Connected to the villa by two overpasses is the garden with a large exedra and numerous statues.

An excellent example of a building-monument from the Enlightenment period, Villa Bettoni celebrates not only the success of its commissioners, but also their moral virtues. Sculptural groups in the garden depict Charity, Strength, Glory, Honour, Loyalty, and Prudence, which can be found near the cave. The grand staircase with several ramps is a bit smaller than that of the Hermitage in St. Petersburg, but it is decisively richer than the one in Vienna's Belvedere. Greek divinities are depicted on the frescoes, painted by artists Bernardino and Fabrizio Galliari. Images of Mercury and Minerva allude to the military vocations of the Bettoni, Ercole and Omphale refer instead to happy marital unions. The villa served as the seat of the Council of Ministers of the Republic of Salò at the end of the Second World War. The Bettoni family still owns the villa, and visits to the palace and gardens can be arranged through their website.

Yulia Semenova

Chiesa di San Francesco
Via Roma 47, Gargnano
13th–18th centuries

197 F

The bishop of Brescia invited Franciscans to Gargnano in the mid-thirteenth century. It was these friars who introduced lemon growing to the region, which would become the area's biggest business until the 1950s. They also built the Church of San Francesco, which underwent many changes, losing its original three-nave structure in the process while preserving the fine pictures by Giovanni Andrea Bertanza, Andrea Celesti, and other unknown masters of the Lombard school. A cosy cloister stands next with oriental ogee arches, giving an effect of raised curtains. Could it have been originally painted as a curtain? Each capital is different from the other: lemons, monks, lions, as well as birds and fish. Within this naive antiquity, you may be surprised to see an elegant Renaissance portal from the fifteenth century depicting the life of Jesus on the architrave. The centre of the cloister once had an ancient well that was later replaced by a cypress.

Sergey Nikitin–Rimsky

F

Sergey Nikitin–Rimsky

Sergey Nikitin–Rimsky

Palazzo Feltrinelli (now University of Milan) ⌄

Via Castello 3, Gargnano
Francesco Solmi
1898–1899

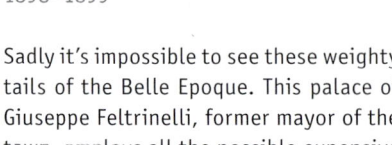

Sadly it's impossible to see these weighty tails of the Belle Epoque. This palace of Giuseppe Feltrinelli, former mayor of the town, employs all the possible expensive materials – bronze, stain-glass windows, and marble – to create a somewhat gloomy neo-Renaissance interior. The house went out of fashion almost immediately after it was completed and the Feltrinelli family soon gifted it to their native city. In 1943, like many imposing buildings in Salò province, it was requisitioned by the Fascist government of the Italian Social Republic, who converted it into Benito Mussolini's headquarters. It now functions as a branch of the university.

Sergey Tsvetkov (dreamstime)

Chiesa di San Martino »

Via Don Primo Adami 46,
Gargnano
Rodolfo Vantini
1722 (bell tower), 1837–1845

The Church of Saint Martin is a landmark in the centre of old, dense Gargnano. It all started in the eleventh century when the Benedictines built a large basilica. The city's residents decided they wanted something new in the nineteenth century. Rodolfo Vantini, already nationally famous for his Monumental Cemetery in Brescia, came to design the church. With his clear taste for symbolic neoclassicism à la' Étienne-Louis Boullée, Vantini created the elegant elliptical rotunda with a marvellous interior, culminating with a scenic altar. Pieces by Cignaroli, Celesti, and Bertanza grace the walls.

Roman Babakin (iStock)

Sergey Nikitin–Rimsky

Villa Feltrinelli

Via Rimembranza 38, Gargnano
Alberico Belgiojoso
1892–1899

200 F

Gargnano is the birthplace of the Feltrinelli family: successful lumber magnates, bankers, developers, and benefactors that are now mostly known through the publishing house started by Giangiacomo Feltrinelli in the 1950s. This villa was built as a lake retreat from Milan, where the family did business, but it is mostly associated with Benito Mussolini who spent here his last months as a leader of Italian Social Republic. The house is a lovely piece of eclecticism with a touch of Moorish Gothic, which was fashionable in Europe in those days. It was presumably erected by Alberico Belgiojoso, the father of Lodovico, a founding member of BBPR. The lake façade was once dominated by a hexagonal turret, but that was demolished by the Nazis for security reasons during Mussolini's residence. An exclusive hotel now, the villa was restored by San Francisco designers Babey Moulton Jue and Booth to reflect a solid residence of the Belle Epoque with stain glass, carpets, cast-iron grid, frescoes, stuccos, marble, and Mussolini's desk. Unfortunately, the villa, including its joyful gardens and antique lemon houses, is closed to public. The road that leads to it is called Via Rimembranza, recalling the dramatic events that were staged here.

F

Thomas Fluegge (iStock)

Sergey Nikitin-Rimsky

Chiesa di San Giacomo
Via della Rimembranza,
San Giacomo
12th century

201 F

Past Villa Feltrinelli, the cobbled street will lead you up to a tiny church with a bell tower, the oldest building in Gargnano. Charles Borromeo changed the fortune of this simple cubic structure during a visit to Gargnano. He ordered that bigger doors and windows be made to let some air and light inside. Until recently, the wooden statue of Saint James stood on the altar, but it was put in storage for fear of theft. There is a small room to the right from the apse, revealing a breath of archaic manner in the form of a fresco of the Crucifixion on a starry sky. The courtyard is a lakeshore area with a pier and small beach where people bathe during the summer. A rustic canopy is attached to the lake façade, with pillars laid of nearly untreated stone. These frescoes under the canopy once decorated the altar inside, but Saint Charles Borromeo didn't appreciate them. The fresco portrays Saint Christopher with his eyes wide open and a child on his shoulders; this saint is venerated by the fishers whose pleas were bountiful here. The old lemon groves around the church were recently converted into elegant housing.

Sergey Nikitin-Rimsky

Lemon groves turned into housing

View from the lake

Sergey Nikitin-Rimsky

Sergey Nikitin-Rimsky

Fresco on the lake side

Sergey Nikitin–Rimsky

Limonaia Prá de la Fam (Lemon Greenhouse Museum)

Strada Statale Gardesana Occidentale, Tignale
1754

202 F

In the 1950s, lorries defeated Garda lemons. It became cheaper to bring them in from Sicily than to source them locally. But before that, the fruit brought a lot of money to the lake. People ate them in Turin, Vienna, and Milan. The peasants did everything to protect their livelihoods, staying awake during the frosty winter nights to make bonfires so that the trees wouldn't freeze. Some of the lemon orangeries were transformed into residential buildings, while others still proudly stand on the Riviera. This one was converted into a museum and small production centre in 1984. Visitors can test and buy local limoncello and other sweets.

Sergey Nikitin–Rimsky

Strada Gardesana Occidentale (SS45bis)

203 F

Between Gargnano and
Riva del Garda
Arturo Cozzaglio (engineer)
1929–1931

From the fabulous hilly landscape immersed in lemon groves to the magnificent tunnels right through to the carefully interwoven cypresses, olives, and capers, this road embodies a narrative that most can only dream of. This is Gardesana Road between Gargnano and Riva del Garda, an outstanding monument of engineering aesthetics and romantic symbolism. The stone walls were not polished in the original 1930s tunnels, leaving heroic boulders, like the ones on the frescoes of the Giants Hall by Giulio Romano in Mantua. Among them, the Ciclopi and Vesta tunnels stand out today. Electric lighting is complemented by open breaks revealing the forever blue of the lake. Each tunnel here is unique with its own rhythm and shape, from round to parabolic to square and rectangular forms. It's hard to believe in our automobile age, but there was only water transport between towns on the Brescia shore of Garda until the 1920s. Cozzaglio prepared his project in 1922 and engineer Giulio Angelini was invited to curate the road's floral design. However, the economic situation in post-war Italy did not allow the construction to begin as planned. In fact, it was poet D'Annunzio who came to rescue. At that time, he was building a memorial complex in honour of his Fiume campaign. Thanks to his connections in the government, he helped to break through the implementation of the project at the end of 1931. He also named the road ever so poetically: *Meandro*, 'meander', after the famous Greek ornament. The name was inspired by the road's tortuosity and beauty. Intended for low traffic of a maximum of two lanes, old photos show how it was once travelled by people riding donkeys and locals walking. It was only when it was completed that the authorities realised that the road was essential for transport between the Alps and Italy. Subsequently, expansion took place and some of the walls were concreted since the soil has a tendency to move and cause landslides. I recommend driving along it at least once at the lowest speed possible to enjoy a sequence of galleries and glimpses over the lake and surrounding mountains, probably early in the morning in order to avoid traffic. If you have time, take the nearby Strada della Forra deviation (n. 204), one of the most beautiful in Europe.

F

Sergey Nikitin-Rimsky

Aerial view of Riva del Garda (left) and the Sarca River

Riva del Garda

zodebala (iStock)

zodebala (iStock)

Strada della Forra

204 F

Between Gargnano and Tremosine
Arturo Cozzaglio (engineer),
Giuliano Massarani, Lelio Franchi,
Tullio Massarani
1913

Forra means 'gorge' – and this is one gorgeous gorge. By car or by bike, you can access the Gardesana deviation from the village of Tremosine to Pieve – a must see for all who appreciate romantic landscapes and engineering. This work actually preceded the Gardesana by 20 years; it was finished just before the First World War collapsed Italy's economy. Yet, it set the scene for what was to come by leaving as much of the natural beauty of the landscape as possible. The road winds alongside the Brasa River. Carved out of a cliff, it offers stunning views over the lake and its valleys. The final phase is the *forra*: a natural tunnel culminating with a waterfall. Arturo Cozzaglio, a local geologist, was the mind behind the construction. He had a visionary idea to put the stream into the tube and use its bed for the spectacular road. A restaurant called La Forra can be found at the end of the most scenic part of the route. Believe it or not, the return trip is even more stunning; you can almost feel the tension between the rocks. There is a memorial plaque at the entrance of the tunnel in the return direction, which commemorates four workers who died during the road's construction. The inauguration ceremony was held in May 1913 and brought quite a lot of cars, quite surprisingly, since the Gardesana road didn't exist yet, so they had to be ferried over. The strada was mostly used by lorries to carry lumber and coal to the mountain villages until 1931. In a way, this piece of Gardesana, cut through beautiful nature, could be compared to the Via dei Fori Imperiali in Rome, which was cut right through the middle of the Roman Forums in the same period – to combine modernity and antiquity. Winston Churchill, who loved Garda, called it the eighth wonder of the world. 'Dangerously beautiful', as one blogger described it. But before driving a vehicle here, be sure to brush up on your driving skills and check exactly how full your tank is. A small car is better, don't forget to check the horn.

Sergey Nikitin–Rimsky

Port (u*o)s (wikimedia)

Centrale Idroelettrica di Riva 205 F
Via Giacomo Cis 13,
Riva del Garda
Giancarlo Maroni
1925–1929

Giancarlo Maroni was born in Arco, a gorgeous town just next to Lake Garda. After Maroni returned from the First World War, one of his first commissions was a hydroelectric plant that used the descending water from Lake Ledro, a mountain lake located 583 metres above the station. In those days, this was also home to the largest turbine in the world. Maroni had a delicate task: to transform the industrial structure into a front-row attraction on the lakeshore of the tourist town. By incorporating different heights and playing with the Roman legacy, he created a pleasant, slightly secluded face. The façade resembles ones by his Milanese colleague Giovanni Muzio and the metaphysical visions of De Chirico. The bas-relief, *Neptune is trying to escape the lighting*, is by Silvio Zaniboni. I also recommend visiting an electric plant in Cogolo, shaped as an Alpine house, with its mural-adorned halls and offices. The good news is that the Italian energy industry is aware of these buildings' beauty and will allow you to visit upon booking.

F

Schlenger86 (dreamstime)

Roberto Vuilleumier

Chiesa di S. Maria Inviolata
Viale Roma 50, Riva del Garda
1603–1630

206 F

Any other church on Lake Garda will appear bleak after seeing this one. What brings such a stunning interior in a parish church to a provincial town? Even Verona doesn't have baroque interiors of this quality! The Inviolata church in Riva del Garda was built from 1603 to 1639 by an unknown architect. A square-shaped plan from the outside and an octagonal plan inside, this church includes five altars, marble floors, carved wood accents, and altarpieces by Palma the Younger (Palma il Giovane) – not to mention the dome! The dome is completely covered with stuccos, gold and bronze lines, and oil paintings.

Polish-Italian master Martino Teofilo Polacco executed the fresco titled *The coronation of Mary in heaven* in the centre. A former captain of Riva, Giannangelo Gaudenzio Madruzzo and his wife Alfonsina Gonzaga commissioned it. In those days, the Madruzzo family was at the top of the Catholic world; Giannangelo was a nephew of Pope Pius IV, who presided over the Council of Trento. Among Giannangelo's other relatives were two cardinals. At the turn of the seventeenth century, the Catholic Church needed a few miracles to fight the Reformation, so Giannangelo Madruzzo decided to promote a miraculous image of the Virgin Mary with a child and Saints Sebastian and Rocco. This painting was found on a modest structure nearby and has been rehoused inside the main altar of the church.

Sergey Nikitin–Rimsky

Fabio Staropoli

F

Spiaggia degli Olivi

207 F

Via Giardini di Porta Orientale 5,
Riva del Garda
Giancarlo Maroni
1932

Show me your porticoes, and I'll say who you are. The Italy of the 1930s rediscovered its Roman legacy but at the same time took a deep interest in sports. After tourism on Lake Garda shifted from winter to summer, visitors began swimming in the lake. A magnificent public beach area celebrates this shift at the northern-most point of the lake. This beach offers everything: a theatre, a dance hall, a library, meeting rooms, and a cafe, of course. Set against the dramatic landscape of the lush mountains, a diving tower is topped by an elegant domed rotunda. For many years, Olive Beach was the symbol of the town. At one point, it was nearly abandoned, but thankfully was restored recently to the black-and-white glamour of the 1930s. The architect was Giancarlo Maroni – the same Maroni who spent his life designing the Vittoriale for writer Gabriele D'Annunzio. In Riva, he is also responsible for the hydroelectric plant, Sole Hotel, and Piazza San Rocco.

Sergey Nikitin-Rimsky

Chiesa della Santa Trinita
Viale Roma, Arco
Heinrich Fricke
1897–1900

 208 F

The rediscovery of Lake Garda and its mild winter climate in the Belle Epoque began with the town of Arco, perched just above the lake, while it was still part of Austria-Hungary territory. The local Lutheran Evangelical community built the Trinity Church. It was inaugurated in February 1900 but abandoned from the outbreak of the First World War until 1935. At this time, it was entrusted to the Catholic community, who dedicated it to Saint Teresa of the Child Jesus. It returned to the Evangelist community in 1972.

Romanticism and nationalism brought back Gothic style to the nineteenth century. Painter and architect Heinrich Fricke went a step further by creating an exalted fairytale fantasy with a touch of *Sezession* style. The roof is made with polychrome tiles. Red and grey stone is used for the masonry, mixing elements of northern Germany and Tyrol. The surrounding palms were planted in the 1930s when Mussolini hoped to capture North Africa. The temple's neo-Gothic style sparked political controversies at the time of its inauguration. Some locals thought it looked too 'Germanised' for an Italian city like Arco. A similar outcry occurred later with the Tower San Marco in Gardone (n. 184 in this book).

Collegiata dell'Assunta

Piazza III Novembre, Arco
Giovanni Maria Philippi (Filippi)
1613–1630

209 F

A lovely town is gathered around this powerful building. Giovanni Maria Filippi started building in 1613 on the remains of a previous structure of Romanesque origin. The monumental façade is supported by powerful double-order pilasters, both doric and ionic, reminiscent of the gorgeous Roman baroque style that Filippi had studied in Rome. The bell tower has a typical Tyrolean onion dome. A violent plague epidemic delayed the church's consecration for 40 years until 15 May 1671. By the end of the nineteenth century, Arco had become a fashionable Kurort town. The tourists themselves paid for the newer embellishments, including ornamental floors and the polychrome stained glasses. The coffered ceiling of the presbytery and the vaults of the side chapels were completed after the Second World War. Filippi is famous in Czechia since he was a Court architect of the Holy Roman Emperor Matthias, his name there is transliterated as Philippi.

F

Aerial view of Arco

F

Sergey Nikitin-Rimsky

Sergey Nikitin-Rimsky

Chiesa di San Apollinare
Via Legionari Cecoslovacchi,
Arco
8th–9th centuries

210 **F**

Sergey Nikitin-Rimsky

This tiny church is half-hidden in an olive grove on the left side of the long and beautiful Via Legionari Cecoslovacchi. City hall did great job restoring and re-opening it but forgot to assign a house number to the oldest structure in Arco. You'll have to look for Villa Santoni next door. This site is worth visiting for those who want to see an original interior from the fourteenth century. Frescoes cover the walls of the pronao and the nave, featuring curious details about local life such as the crayfish on the table of the Last Supper. Existing documents about the church are from the fourteenth century but based on its location outside the town walls and its architecture, scholars consider it to be an Aryan place of worship, dating back to the eighth and ninth centuries. The church was abandoned and became home for vagabonds for almost a century. In 1866, the archiepiscope of Trento even ordered its demolition in order to put an end to the unworthy use of the space. Fortunately, the demolition never proceeded and restoration work brought the frescoes covered with layers of time and stucco back to light in 1882. The church is open and beautifully illuminated during the summer.

Palazzo dei Capitani del Lago 211 F
Via Capitanato 4, Malcesine
13th–15th centuries

In order to rule the Eastern shore of Lake Garda, Venetians created the Gardesana dell'Acqua – a federation of 10 lake municipalities with broad autonomy, which lasted until the Napoleon era. The group's captain had an obligation to watch over and defend the Gardesana borders and carry out policing duties. Venice chose Malcesine as the residence of the captain since the town is located on the border with Tyrol and below Mount Baldo (by the way, there is a cableway to reach a viewpoint). They purchased an old Scaliger's palace next to the citadel and handed it to the captains. Interestingly, its Venetian-style façade appeared before it became a representation of the Venetian institution, simply because the Scaligers loved it. The palace stands in the garden on the lakeshore; Those days the lake was the best and the safest road. Inside, there's a frescoed hall with of captains' coat of arms. Now, the Malcesine Town Hall is based inside.

Sergey Nikitin-Rimsky

Sergey Nikitin-Rimsky

F

Porto di Cassone ⌃ 212 F
Cassone di Malcesine

Cassone, an idyllic fishermen's village between Brenzone and Malcesine, is known for having the world's shortest river. Starting under one of the houses on Via San Carlo, the Arli River is only 175 metres long. The river and a spring are crossed by four different bridges of various styles and periods. There is also a small waterfall nearby. Saints Benigno and Caro church, a single nave fifteenth century structure, features a painted coffering vault. The church has been immortalised thanks to Gustav Klimt's artwork from 1913. A few colourful houses resembling the Venetian Gothic style are gathered around the tiny marina. A former fish hatchery has been transformed into a museum about Lake Garda. The ancient tower with a small bell-turret guards the lake.

Aerial view of Malcesine

F

Appendix

Index of Architects

Listed by project number

Bibliography

The author consulted the works listed below while writing this book.
They are presented here as suggestions for further reading.

Fundamental regional volumes of Touring Club Italiano:
Colombini, Paola, *Touring Club Italiano: Veneto (esclusa Venezia)* (Milan: Touring Club Italiano, 2007).

Ferrari-Bravo, Anna, *Touring Club Italiano: Trentino Alto Adige* (Milan: Touring Club Italiano, 2007).

A guidebook full of insights and made by local experts:
Brownell, Penelope, and Curcio, Francesca, *Verona: Guida storico-artistica* (Verona: Cierre Edizioni, 2016).

Special historical periods are treated in the following volumes:
Arslan, Wart, *L'architettura romanica veronese* (Verona: Tip, 1939).

Brugnoli, Pierpaolo, and Sandrini, Arturo, *L'architettura a Verona nell'eta' della Serenissima* (Verona: Mondadori per Banca popolare di Verona, 1988), sec. XV–sec. XVIII.

Brugnoli, Pierpaolo, and Sandrini, Arturo, *L'architettura a Verona – Dal periodo Napoleonico all'eta' contemporanea* (Verona: Mondadori per Banca popolare di Verona, 1994).

Brugnoli, Pierpaolo, *Urbanistica a Verona (1880–1960)* (Verona: Ordine degli architetti della Provincia, 1996).

Cenni, Nino, Fiorenza Coppari, Maria, and Franzoni, Lanfranco, *I segni della Verona scaligera* (Verona: Cassa di Risparmio di Verona Vicenza Belluno e Ancona, 1988).

Cenni, Nino, Fiorenza Coppari, Maria, and Franzoni, Lanfranco, *I segni della Verona veneziana (il Seicento)* (Verona: Cassa di Risparmio di Verona Vicenza Belluno e Ancona, 1992).

Cenni, Nino, Fiorenza Coppari, Maria, and Franzoni, Lanfranco, *I segni della Verona veneziana (il Settecento)* (Verona: Cassa di Risparmio, 1993).

Cenni, Nino, Fiorenza Coppari, Maria, and Franzoni, Lanfranco, *I segni della Verona veneziana (1405–1487)* (Verona: Cassa di Risparmio di Verona Vicenza Belluno e Ancona, 1989).

Cenni, Nino, Fiorenza Coppari, Maria, and Franzoni, Lanfranco, *I segni della Verona ottocentesca (1405-1487)*. (Verona: Cassa di Risparmio di Verona Vicenza Belluno e Ancona, 1994).

Longhi, Davide, *Novecento. Architetture e città del Veneto* (Padua: Il Poligrafo, 2012).

Magagnato, Licisco, *Arte e Civilta A Verona* (Verona: Neri Pozza editore, 1991).

Marchi, Maria, and Cenni, Nino, *I segni della Verona romana* (Verona: 1986).

Varanini G. M., and Castagnetti, A, *Il Veneto nel medioevo* (Verona: Arnoldo Mondadori per Banca popolare di Verona, 1989).

Vecchiato, M., *Verona nel Novecento. Opere pubbliche, interventi urbanistici, architettura residenziale dall'inizio del secolo al ventennio (1900–1940)* (Verona: Editrice La Grafica, 1998).

Vecchiato, Maristella, *Verona: la guerra e la ricostruzione* (Verona: Editrice La Grafica, 2006).

Local historian Giovanni Luigi Lugoboni collected many interesting facts about the palaces in Verona:
Lugoboni, Giovanni Luigi, *Dimore, ville, palazzi veronesi. Conoscere Verona attraverso le prestigiose dimore, i palazzi pubblici e privati, le ville, i ponti storici, i monumenti, i progettisti e i committenti di tutte le epoche, dalla Verona romana ai nostri giorni* (Verona: Cierre Edizioni, 2017).

Specific topics:
Autonomous Province of Bozen, *Denkmalpflege in Südtirol: 2010 – Tutela dei beni culturali in Alto Adige: 2010* (Bolzano/Bozen: Tappeiner, 2012).

Basso, Maddalena, and Bertoni, Camilla, *Il cimitero monumentale di Verona (Italiano)* (Bologna: Scripta, 2019).

Bolla, Margherita, 'Gli interventi di Antonio Avena in ambito archeologico,' in Marini, Paulo (ed.), *Medioevo ideale e Medioevo reale nella cultura urbana: Antonio Avena e la Verona del primo Novecento* (Verona: Banco popolare di Verona, 2003), pp. 121–131.

Brogiolo, Gian Pietro, *Toscolano e Maderno. Paesaggi, comunità, imprenditori tra medioevo ed età moderna* (Mantova: SAP, Società archeologica, 2018).

Coden, Fabrio, and Franco, Tiziana, *San Zeno in Verona* (Verona: Cierre Edizioni, 2014).

Coden, Fabio, 'Santa Maria della Vittoria Vecchia (San Giorgio), committenza di Cangrande II nella Verona del XIV secolo,' in Brunelli, Daniela, and Franco, Tiziana (eds), *San Francesco di Paola a Verona: Storia e contesto di un convento diventato sede universitaria* (Verona: Cierre Edizioni, 2019) pp. 135–146.

Comune di Pescantina, Pescantina, *In Valpolicella, lungo l'Adige* (Verona: Intergrafica).

Conforti Calcagni, Annamaria, *Le mura di Verona* (Verona: Cierre Edizioni, 1999).

Fontanili, Francesca, *Casa di Giulietta, metamorfosi di una dimora storica: reale e ideale si uniscono nel presente* (Bologna: Museologia Archeologica, 2015).

Hemsoll, David, and Davies, Paul, *Sanmicheli and his patrons: planning for posterity* (Vicenza: Centro Internazionale di Studi di Architettura Andrea Palladio, 2000).

Marcorin, Francesco, 'Alcuni documenti inediti relativi alla facciata sanmicheliana di palazzo Bevilacqua a Verona,' *Annali di Architettura*, XXV (Venice: Marsilio, 2013).

Marini, Paola, and Campanella, Christian, *La Basilica di Santa Anastasia a Verona: Storia e restauro* (Verona: Banco Popolare, Gruppo Bancario, 2011).

Marini, Paolo, *Medioevo ideale e medioevo reale nella cultura urbana. Antonio Avena e la Verona del primo Novecento* (Verona: Cierre Edizioni, 2004).

Morgante, Michela, *Borgo Trento, un quartiere del Novecento tra memoria e future* (Verona: Fondazione Cattolica Assicurazioni, 2010).

Pisani, Anna, *I Magazzini Generali di Verona tra storia e progetto* (Milan: Politecnico di Milano, 2011).

To explore the contemporary local architecture scene its depth, I recommend:
Architetti Verona magazine edited by Alberto Vignola (in Italian). It is also available on *www.issuu.com* for free.

Ville of Valpolicella:
Brugnoli, Pierpaolo, *Villa Della Torre a Fumane di Valpolicella* (Treviso: Antiga Edizioni, 2014).

Conforti, Giuseppe. *Centootto Ville della Valpolicella. Foto di Lou Embo e Fulvio Roiter* (Pescantina: Damolgraf, 2016).

Luciolli, Mario, *Ville della Valpolicella* (Verona: Jago Edizioni, 2010).

Monographs about architects:
Beltramini, Guido, and Zannier, Italo, *Carlo Scarpa: Atlante delle architetture* (Venezia: Marsilio Editori, 2006).

Comune di Verona, *Rinaldo Olivieri architetto e scenografo – Dall'idea all'oggetto* (Verona: Studio La Città 1, 1991).

Davies, Paul, and Hemsoll, David, *Michele Sanmicheli* (Milan: Electa, 2004).

Fonatti, Franco, *Elemente des Bauens bei Carlo Scarpa* (Wien: Edition Tusch Buch- und Kunstverlag, 1984).

Gavazzi, Alberto, and Ghilotti, Marco, *Luigi Caccia Dominioni* (Milan: Solferino Edizioni, 2014).

Luzio, Claudio di, *Rinaldo Olivieri. Architettura come luogo della memoria* (Bari: Dedalo, 1983).

McCarter, Robert, *Carlo Scarpa* (New York City: Phaidon Press, 2013).

Mulazzani, Marco, *L'architettura di Massimo Caramassi* (Milano: Mondadori Electa, 2016).

Schultz, Anne-Catrin, *Carlo Scarpa. Layers* (Stuttgart: Edition Axel Menges, 2007).

Acknowledgements

I would like to thank:

- Stefano Aloe, Cristiano Folchi, and Marina Sorina, who were the first to show and explain Verona to me, and who helped me immensely as I compiled this book.
- Marina Avdonina, Luca Trevisan, Alberto Vignola, Giulio Zavatta, Vittorio Cecchini, Camillo Botticini, Camilla Bertoni, Luciano Cenna, Maurizio Cossato, Giuseppe Conforti, Francesca Briani, and Sergio Mazzanti for the hours of consultations and invaluable insights.
- Historians Pierpaolo Brugnoli and Gian Maria Varanini for their insights.
- Alexey Krupin, who added some incredible stories to this book.
- Christoph Schwarzkopf, Monika Lenhard, and Christian Burkhard with whom I discussed some of the Austrian and German stories from this book.
- Judith Scaliger, Erica Rasputin, Darya Serebryakova, Alexandre Grenkow, and Ronni Wocnerg, all of whom helped me with Velonotte Romeo, scientifically, artistically, and musically.
- Elisa Andreoli, Gianmario Andreoli, and Patrizia Quirini who hosted me in Garda and were so kind to show me around the lake. Daria Danilishina for inspiration.
- Michele Poceddu for driving me through marshy lands of Bassa Veronese. And all of his family for their hospitality.
- Historians Maria Vittoria Capitanucci and Alessandro DeMagistris, for the Milanese and Turinese points of view.

- Luca Brentaro, Erica Buson, Ronni Wocnerg, Nikki Simionel, Nicoletta Potorac, the administration of Lombardy and Trentino and Alto Adige, as well as the site *www.gardalombardia.com* for supplying the images for the book.
- My friend and travel companion Julia Zinkevich for pushing me through.
- My friends Manu Merlo and Petr Kovalev, with whom I made countless art trips in Eurasia and discussed our experiences in Verona.
- Valentin Dyakonov and Olga Shirokostup who took the first critical look at the manuscript.
- This book was written during the spring 2020 COVID-19 quarantine in the beautiful dacha of Olga Levitskaya, Vladimir, and Gosha Polkov.
- Alexander and Irina Nikitin, my parents, who listened to many of the stories included in the guidebook.
- The book owes a lot to Roberto Bianconi, who helped me organise a visit to the Valpolicella area and who was also kind enough to take some missing pictures during the COVID-19 days.
- Pier Paolo Brugnoli and Loredana Olivato, researchers from Verona University, without whom I couldn't have written this book.
- I am grateful for the participation of historians Gian Maria Varanini (Verona University), Franco Cardini (École des Hautes Études en Sciences Sociales; Harvard University), T. C. W. Blanning (Cambridge University), and the late archaeologist Peter Hudson.

Author

Luca Brentaro

Sergey Nikitin-Rimsky

PhD., musician, historian of cities and architecture, specialised in the twentieth century. He's been teaching history of architecture in the universities of Moscow, was a visiting professor at the University of Verona and Politecnico of Milan. He is senior researcher at the Museum of Moscow. Current projects: courtyard studies, industrial heritage.

Nikitin-Rimsky is a founder of *VeloNotte* – a series of 26 thematic nocturnal architecture bike rides in Rome, London, Istanbul, Berlin, Moscow, St. Petersburg, Irkutsk, New York, Ivanovo, Kazan, Florence, and Verona.

Instagram @nikitin_rimsky
www.velonotte.com

The *Deutsche Nationalbibliothek* lists
this publication in the Deutsche
Nationalbibliographie; detailed
bibliographic data is available at
http://dnb.d-nb.de.

ISBN 978-3-86922-090-1

Copy-editing
Martina Filippi

Proofreading
Sandie Kestell

Design
Cristina Montellano López

Maps
Katrin Soschinski

QR-Codes
Lupe Bezzina

Printing
Bilnet Matbaacılık ve Yayıncılık A. Ş.,
Istanbul
www.bilnet.net.tr